User-Centered Translation

Translators want to take their readers into account, but traditional translation theory does not offer much advice on how to do that. User-Centered Translation (UCT) offers practical tools and methods with which end users can be taken into consideration systematically and effectively.

UCT emphasizes the central role of the user in the translation process by gathering information about users throughout the translation process with a variety of methods. This information is then used to create a usable translation. The UCT model is based on tested usability research methods, also taking into consideration the aspects of user experience and cultural usability. This text offers a wide range of tools, from creating mental models such as personas to testing translations with usability testing methods to carrying out reception research. The book contains assignments, case studies and real-life scenarios ranging from the translation of user instructions and EU texts to literary and audiovisual translation.

UCT empowers translators to act for their readers, provides a source of innovation for the translation industry and is essential reading for students, translators and researchers.

Tytti Suojanen is Senior Lecturer and Head of Technical Communications Programme, University of Tampere, Finland.

Kaisa Koskinen is Professor of Translation Studies, University of Eastern Finland, Finland.

Tiina Tuominen is Acting Professor of Translation Studies, University of Tampere, Finland.

Translation Practices Explained

Translation Practices Explained is a series of coursebooks designed to help self-learners and teachers of translation. Each volume focuses on a specific aspect of professional translation practice, in many cases corresponding to actual courses available in translator-training institutions. Special volumes are devoted to well-consolidated professional areas, such as legal translation or European Union texts; to areas where labour-market demands are currently undergoing considerable growth, such as screen translation in its different forms; and to specific aspects of professional practices on which little teaching and learning material is available: the case of editing and reviewing or electronic tools. The authors are practicing translators or translator trainers in the fields concerned. Although specialists, they explain their professional insights in a manner accessible to the wider learning public.

These books start from the recognition that professional translation practices require something more than elaborate abstraction or fixed methodologies. They are located close to work on authentic texts, and encourage learners to proceed inductively, solving problems as they arise from examples and case studies.

Each volume includes activities and exercises designed to help self-learners consolidate their knowledge; teachers may also find these useful for direct application in class, or alternatively as the basis for the design and preparation of their own material. Updated reading lists and website addresses will also help individual learners gain further insight into the realities of professional practice.

Sharon O'Brien
Kelly Washbourne
Series Editors

User-Centered Translation

Tytti Suojanen, Kaisa Koskinen and Tiina Tuominen

Routledge
Taylor & Francis Group

LONDON AND NEW YORK

First published 2015
by Routledge
2 Park Square, Milton Park, Abingdon, Oxon OX14 4RN

and by Routledge
711 Third Avenue, New York, NY 10017

Routledge is an imprint of the Taylor & Francis Group, an informa business

© 2015 Tytti Suojanen, Kaisa Koskinen and Tiina Tuominen

British Library Cataloguing-in-Publication Data
A catalogue record for this book is available from the British Library

Library of Congress Cataloging-in-Publication Data
Suojanen, Tytti, 1969– author.
  User-centered translation/Tytti Suojanen, Kaisa Koskinen and
Tiina Tuominen.
  pages cm. – (Translation practices explained)
  Includes bibliographical references and index.
  1. Translating and interpreting – Study and teaching. 2. Translating and
interpreting – Problems, exercises, etc. 3. Translating and interpreting –
Self-instruction. I. Koskinen, Kaisa, author. II. Tuominen, Tiina, author.
III. Title.
  P306.5.S86 2015
  418'.02071 – dc23
  2014024144

ISBN: 978-1-138-79549-5 (hbk)
ISBN: 978-1-138-79550-1 (pbk)
ISBN: 978-1-315-75350-8 (ebk)

Typeset in Times New Roman
by Florence Production Ltd, Stoodleigh, Devon, UK

Contents

Illustrations

Figures

Tables

Acknowledgments

We would like to express our warmest thanks to the editors of this series, Sharon O'Brien and Kelly Washbourne. With their extensive knowledge and their sharp eye for details, they made our writing process a true journey of learning, pushing us continuously to widen our horizons and to improve our text. Any remaining shortcomings are, needless to say, the responsibility of us authors.

Our students have given us the impetus and motivation for *User-Centered Translation*, and their enthusiastic reception of our ideas in and outside the classroom has also produced some concrete case studies, which are presented in this book. We are grateful to Anni Otava, who conducted several case studies for us as a part of her Master's thesis for the University of Tampere (2013). Her input gave us valuable information about the usefulness of UCT in practice, and we want to thank her for allowing us to present the cases here. We also thank Anni for allowing us to use her drawing of the UCT model in our Introduction. Furthermore, a group of students at the University of Eastern Finland gave us pioneering input on conducting usability tests on translations and provided us with yet another case study to be used here, as well as a user test for the usability of the Finnish-language textbook. We wish to thank them all, particularly Juho Suokas who was instrumental in designing the usability tests.

We are also grateful for all the support, encouragement and insight we have received from numerous colleagues in the academia and in the translation industry. In addition to a big collective thank you, we wish to personally thank Tiina Leivo and Pia von Essen for their contributions and support. Our thanks also go to Elli Oravainen for bringing the readership of this book to life with her drawings of the three reader personas we created.

We would also like to express our gratitude to the School of Language, Translation and Literary Studies at the University of Tampere, Finland, for providing financial support for this book project, and for allowing us to use our Finnish book *Käyttäjäkeskeinen kääntäminen* as a basis for this extended and reworked version of UCT. We also thank Elsevier for granting us the permission to reproduce Figure 2.1.

Finally, we as authors would like to thank each other: the writing process has been a mutually enriching learning experience, but also a journey of friendship, perseverance and joy.

1 Introduction

A proposal for a user-centered model of translation

It is almost a truism to say that translators always think about their future readers. Nevertheless, it bears repeating that most translators would like to prioritize the target readers and their needs when they make translational decisions. However, the ways in which this taking into account is actually accomplished have remained rather implicit and unratified in practice and under-theorized in research. Since the 1980s, functionalist translation theory has been one main trend in translation studies, focusing on the purpose of the translation and arguing that the translator needs to adapt the text according to the needs of the future readers. However, moving from abstract theorizing about audiences to actual practice has not always been smooth. In her recent overview of the current state and future of functionalist theory, Christiane Nord (2012: 32) laments the difficulties of bridging this gap between theory and practice:

> Audience orientation has been a particularly sensitive aspect of functionalist theory and applications from the start. Critics have been asking how translators know what the audience expects of a translation. Indeed, it is easy to talk about the audience's expectations but much more difficult to obtain empirical proof of what audiences (for certain genres or in certain nonlinguistic fields) really expect.

In this book we offer practical tools and methods for making reader-orientedness an explicit part of the translation process. **User-Centered Translation (UCT)** is, in other words, closely related to functional translation theories, and we consider the UCT tools as a means to operationalize the ideas of translation as a purposeful and skopos-oriented action (see also Section 3.5). User-centered translation is a neologism, coined to emphasize the central role of the user, or reader, in the translation process. UCT means that we gather as much information about our future users as we can through various methods during the entire translation process, and that we design and revise the translation based on this information. Utilizing various practical tools and methods described in this book, translators can improve their skills at taking the needs of the target audience into consideration and enhance the usability of their translations.

The methods described in this book allow translators to obtain empirical proof of actual readers and their needs and preferences. As a textbook, this book also helps fill in another gap: Nord (2012: 32) emphasizes the affinities of functionalist theories with translator training but she argues that "the development of functionalist teaching material is still in its infancy". Furthermore, although the textbook format indicates academic readerships, we also hope that this book finds readers within the field of practical translation.

The translation industry has recently been characterized by a highly competitive market situation, as companies have tried to secure customers, and, for lack of other suitable criteria, calls for tenders have been won by the lowest bidder. To step beyond this game, translators and translation companies need to become more versatile and more innovative, offering translation-related services that are clearly identifiable and bring added value to the customers. User-centered translation offers one model for such diversification that allows translation companies to escape the blood-red oceans of rivals fighting over a shrinking pool of profits and to sail to the less contested blue oceans by creating new value to customers and by redefining the products and services offered (Kim and Mauborgne 2005). UCT is a comprehensive framework that can be aligned with the client's overall information management process and designed individually for each project to ensure a maximum fit between the translated text and its users.

To empower translators and to widen the palette of services that they can offer, we have turned our attention to interfaces between **usability research** and translation (studies). The tools and methods described in this book have been selected from among those regularly in use in usability research and design. This book is practical in its aim: we want to offer translators and translation students new tools and new ways of thinking, with which they might be able to bring a more user-centered approach to their work. We look for links between usability and translation studies, and introduce concepts and findings from usability research into the practice of translation. Translation students and teachers will find, however, that the step from translation studies to usability research is not always very long, and that many methods – such as think-aloud protocols, eyetracking, or focus groups – are familiar to them from translation research, although they are not regularly employed into translation practice. In addition to translation practice, these interfaces between usability research and translation studies will also offer new angles into translation teaching and research.

The two important concepts behind user-centered translation are **usability** and **user experience**. Usability refers to the ease with which users can use a product to achieve their goals; they should be able to achieve their goals according to their expectations and without obstacles or hindrances. When software is designed and texts are produced in a user-centered way, the aim is to create products and texts that are as usable as possible. To the user, high usability means having to take less time to learn new things, and being able to get a grip of the task at hand more quickly. Improving usability also promotes memorability and allows us to work more efficiently. The users make fewer errors, and they feel that they are enjoying the task (Ovaska *et al.* 2005: 14). The notion of enjoyability emphasizes the role of user experience: while usability focuses on products being learnable or memorable, user experience is a holistic concept encompassing issues such as aesthetics, fun and pleasure.

The concept of usability is not widely used in translation studies as of yet, and studies that do take advantage of usability are limited to some areas of translation, predominantly in the technical field. In his work *Technical Translation: Usability Strategies for Translating Technical Documentation*, Jody Byrne (2010) focuses on usability in technical texts, considering how translators can improve the usability of user instructions during the translation process. At the end of his book, Byrne (2010: 255–256) raises the question whether usability has any role outside technical translation. Our answer is yes, and this book continues where Byrne leaves off: we will investigate usability in a wide context, taking into consideration different areas of translation; to us, the world of usability does not only pertain to technical and instructive texts, although the idea of using a text and usability is more easily applied in some genres than in others.

One of the pathways through which usability issues are gradually making their way to translation studies is technical communication, where usability has been an important consideration for a long time. Technical documentation, such as user instructions, is being produced as an inherent part of the interface, device or system that is being documented; consequently, the usability considerations associated with the interfaces, devices or systems extend to various forms of user assistance, too. Because of this background, this book takes advantage of elements from technical communication where appropriate. The connection between translation studies and technical communication is, in fact, quite logical, as many technical communicators who design and write technical documentation were originally trained as translators and they produce texts that often end up being translated (Suojanen 2010; Risku 2004).

Usability research and translation studies are both fields that have a strong practical orientation. The juxtaposition of theory and practice can occasionally lead to some conceptual dilemmas: Do we talk about *translation* or *translation studies* when we refer to the topic of this book? Is user-centered translation a theory or a practical model, or can it be both? We do not think that theory and practice must be separated from each other: while our position for offering this model is academic, we see it as a framework for practice, something that we as researchers feel we can offer for practising translators. Thus, *translation* and *translation studies* go hand in hand in this book. The same can be said for *usability* and *usability research*, where it can be difficult to decide which term is most suitable for which context. One of the overarching objectives of this book is therefore to transcend these divides and to encourage interaction between translators and researchers, and between usability experts and translation professionals and scholars.

1.1 The UCT process

The title of this book, *User-Centered Translation (UCT)*, is a coinage parallel to *User-Centered Design (UCD)* familiar from usability research. During the

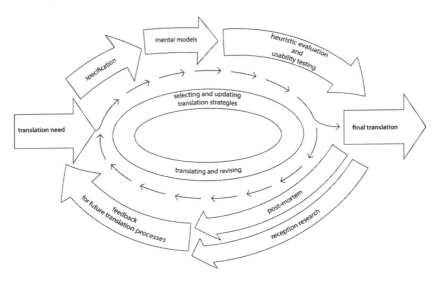

Figure 1.1 The user-centered translation process © Anni Otava

user-centered *design* process, the emphasis is on methods that are used to gather information about users and ways in which this information is brought to software development. Correspondingly, we define user-centered *translation* as follows:

> In user-centered translation, information about users is gathered iteratively throughout the process and through different methods, and this information is used to create a usable translation.

In this definition, **iterativity** refers to a cyclical mode of operation, where users are analyzed and usability evaluated via recursive usability research methods. In a user-centered translation process, translation, revision and quality assessment are also done iteratively rather than in a linear fashion. Figure 1.1 demonstrates our model of user-centered translation and indicates the areas covered in this book.

Figure 1.1 contains the following elements:

- **Inner circle: translation strategies, translating and revising**
  UCT concerns translation, and it is thus logical that translation itself lies at the heart of the model. The translation process contains a number of iterative evaluation phases, and these shape the translator's work. Translation strategies and solutions are continuously re-evaluated according to accumulating knowledge produced during the project and acquired from previous projects with the help of the tools and methods visualized as the outer circle of Figure 1.1.

- **Translation need**
  A fundamental assumption behind UCT is that there is a communicative need for the translation (or, as is often the case, several translations into different languages simultaneously), and thus also a necessity to define and describe

the users and to try to make sure that the translation matches their needs and expectations. In the case of websites in particular, the involvement of end users may begin here, before the actual translation even begins. The interactive nature of the medium allows for feedback systems where users can make requests for particular pages to be translated, which provides an opportunity to assess the real need for a particular language version.

- **Specification**
  A detailed written specification is drafted to ensure mutual understanding of the goals of the translation between the stakeholders. The stakeholders also determine the expected usability level of the translation and decide which UCT methods are going to be employed, how and when. This may require negotiations and alignment of views: the specification is not simply a client's wish list, but is to be drafted in dialogue and in mutual respect of the other party's expertise. In cases where some usability measures have already been employed for the drafting of the source text, some information may already be available, and these are to be listed in the specification. In addition, the desired quality level and the agreed measurements to assess it need to be recorded. At the end of the process, the translation is then assessed, not against some ephemeral ideal of a perfect match, but against the specifications and against whether or not the translation's agreed *usability* goals have been reached.

- **Mental models**
  Once all existing knowledge of the intended users has been made available at the specification phase, the translator can build a clearer picture of who the users are with the help of various mental models. The methods for mental models include analysis of intratextual reader positions, audience design and the development of personas.

- **Heuristic evaluation and usability testing**
  As the translation progresses, its usability is repeatedly assessed, and if necessary, the translation strategies are revised and then re-evaluated by heuristic evaluation and usability testing. Heuristic evaluation is performed by an expert or a group of experts with the help of heuristics – that is, usability guidelines. In usability testing, the behavior of people belonging to the translation's real target group is observed while they use it to perform predefined tasks. The aim is to get information about the usability of the text during the translation process. Both heuristic evaluation and usability testing can also be employed after the translation process has been concluded, but in UCT we emphasize the usefulness of an iterative process that helps to redirect the course of the translation process at an early stage, if necessary.

- **Post-mortem**
  Once the entire translation cycle has been completed, the project team members reflect on their performance – namely, they produce a post-mortem analysis of the project. This analysis covers not only the finished text but

also, and in particular, the process behind it from the negotiation phase to the accuracy of mental models, reliability of usability evaluation, and so on. A documented post-mortem provides systematic **feedback** for redefining and fine-tuning the tools and methods for the next project cycle.

• **Reception research**
   The UCT process does not end at the point where the translation is finished and delivered to the client. The finished translation can also be assessed with different reception research methods. The purpose of reception studies in general is to find out how readers understand translated texts or what kinds of translation strategies are most useful and acceptable from the readers' perspective. The findings of the reception studies also give feedback into new UCT processes. Reception research can be employed strategically: feedback from particular user segments can be solicited directly, online or offline, but it is equally important to appreciate unsolicited feedback from the client representatives and end users alike.

The benefits of user-centered translation are especially high in large, cyclical translation processes, because the model is based on iteration: profiling and evaluation tasks are repeated during the process, and after each iteration, user profiles and user needs become more and more detailed. This, in turn, helps the translator to employ the appropriate translation strategies to benefit the user.

Translation strategies themselves are not discussed in this book. It would actually defeat our purpose if we advocated particular strategies or translation styles, labeling some of them user-centered and others less so. The strategies best suited for a particular case always need to be assessed locally, and all major decisions made during the translation process stem from the user, who is always unique and has to be profiled again and again. We also assume that our readers have learned translation skills through other means, and this book offers practical tools to add to their translation competencies, as a way of enhancing their skill set. This focus also leaves out detailed discussions of translation technology, such as machine translation and translation memories. A user-centered translation process may, however, involve many variations of computer-assisted or machine translation, and decisions related to technological choices can be informed by the user-centered thinking we advocate. For example, the decision on whether or not to use machine translation and on how to ensure its usability can be made within the context of the UCT process.

In addition to machine translation, another contemporary trend is to crowd-source the production of a translation. Consequently, user-centered translation might raise connotations of **User-Generated Translation (UGT),** which refers to ways of harnessing Web 2.0 services and tools to create online content in different languages with the help of volunteer translators (e.g. Perrino 2009; Drugan 2013). We bring up user-generated translation very briefly in Chapter 3 in discussing whether a translation can be considered a product of its own and how the roles of producers and consumers have become increasingly mixed. It is, however, necessary to emphasize that user-centered translation is not equal to *user-generated* translation. While the initial user research phase of UCT may sometimes reveal such enthusiasm and skills-base among prospective users that it may prove sensible to engage them directly in translating, this is not the assumed or expected state of affairs in UCT. Regardless of whether translation is assigned to volunteers or produced with the help of machine translation, in UCT the professional translators are always in the driver's seat, deciding on what is most advantageous and making sure that agreed usability goals are achieved. In other words, it could be argued that UGT is UCT in its most extreme application.

1.2 Conceptual solutions

In the course of this book, we rely on a number of concepts. We have written this book with translation students, their teachers as well as professional translators in mind. We thus assume that concepts originating from the field of usability research may be new to many of our readers, while concepts from translation studies are more familiar. All central concepts will be defined and explained as they appear in the text, and no previous knowledge of usability research is expected.

The term **user** has particular significance in this book. While translation studies have referred to *target audience*, *reader* or *recipient*, the term *user* has not been a part of the active vocabulary until only recently (e.g. Byrne 2010; Pym 2010). Are we dealing with an entirely new way of thinking, or is *user* only a new designation for something we already know? Do we *use* translations in the same way we might use electronic devices, for example? In this book we suggest that if translation, and translations, can be seen as a means to an end, reading translations can be seen as using. We encourage the *users* of this book to consider for themselves whether and in what contexts they feel the readers of translations can be referred to as users. Because we believe that usability is a beneficial consideration in translation, we argue that *user* can, indeed, be fruitfully employed in many contexts, and that is why we use it interchangeably with other, more conventional terms, such as *audience* and *reader*. However, the use of the different terms in either singular or plural presents a problem. For example, each *user* has unique characteristics, thus making it difficult to profile each user type. Despite this uniqueness, however, in practice users have to be grouped together in one way or another so that designing products and texts is at all possible, and we are therefore also using the plural form. A textual element is also relevant when opting for the plural form: using *they* instead of *he/she* makes the text more fluent and has thus been favored, but at the same time we realize that the singular would sometimes be more appropriate.

1.3 Target groups

In writing this book, we have had three different target groups in mind. To describe these groups, we have used one of the tools presented in this book –

namely, **personas** (see Section 5.3). Personas are imaginary characters who represent real user groups. They are fictive archetypes of users, representing the needs and characteristics of real users. Personas are used as an aid in designing different kinds of products and services. We have created three personas for this book: Leo, Emma and Julia, who are introduced below (pictures © Elli Oravalnen). After the basic characteristics of each persona, we explain how they came across *User-Centered Translation*, what their interest in the book is, and what we, as authors, hope the book will offer the persona.

LEO: student

Age:	22 years old
Family:	No siblings
Neighborhood:	From a small town
Education:	MA student in a translator training program. Leo wanted to study translation because he had a keen interest in languages and cultures. He was originally interested in literary and audiovisual translation, but has become unsure about employment prospects in those fields. Still, he wants to be a translator and has an open mind about alternative opportunities.
Hobbies:	Leo loves reading science fiction in the original language. He is an avid tweeter and keeps a literature blog. He watches a lot of indie films and is a geocacher. Leo works as a volunteer translator for Amnesty International.
Personality:	Leo is a quiet type.
Social groups:	Leo has a small circle of like-minded friends, who meet regularly to play games, etc.

Leo and UCT:

- Leo came across the UCT book through his studies. It was a set book in a technical translation course, which he took to expand his employment opportunities.
- Leo is familiar with the basic concepts of translation studies and has taken some practical translation courses.
- The UCT book gives Leo the tools he needs in order to become an advocate for the users of translations and helps him find his place in the professional field of translation.

EMMA: teacher

Age:	33 years old
Profession:	Teacher of translation
Education:	Ph.D. in translation studies. Emma recently defended her Ph.D. thesis on crowd-sourced translation. She has also completed ten ECTS of pedagogical studies.
Family:	Married with two daughters age 5 and 3. Her husband has a one-man IT company and works from the home office (part-time).
Hobbies:	Yoga and pilates.
Work experience:	Emma has four years' experience in teaching translation courses. Occasionally she works as a freelance translator translating a wide variety of commercial texts.
Personality:	Emma leads a busy life, but she is good at multitasking. Emma has a positive outlook on life. She is not tenured, but she is ambitious as a teacher and wants her courses to prepare students well for working life. Emma is also looking to widen the scope of her research.

Emma and UCT:

- Emma is in the middle of a curriculum design process, looking for new course books. She saw the UCT book in a Routledge newsletter.

- The UCT book offers Emma a ready-made package with reading material and assignments for a full UCT course, fresh ideas for research and potential pathways towards usability research as a whole, and avenues for professional diversification, which she can introduce in the translation classroom.

JULIA: translation professional

Age:	44 years old
Profession:	CEO of a small translation agency, which she started ten years ago; it has three in-house translators, two coordinators and a large number of freelancers.
Education:	MA from a translator training program in 1995, specializing in technical texts, and a minor in business management.

Family:	Divorced, teenage daughter.
Hobbies:	Horseback riding.
Personality:	The hectic business world has made Julia slightly cynical, but she is fighting against it by trying to stay open to new ideas. She is also curious of present-day translation studies and university offerings, which have changed since her time as a student.
Social groups:	Julia is an active alumna of her home university. She also visits a nearby university and gives occasional lectures to translation students on professional skills.

Julia and UCT:

- Julia's company is doing well, but the market is competitive and she is thinking of new ways of profiling. Julia wants to be able to produce high-quality products for clients, but she has had trouble finding a reliable assessment system. She wants to cater to good, large customers and build a long relationship with them. She also wants to offer her translators new, meaningful projects. Julia has heard about user-centeredness from customers, and she found out about the UCT book through a Facebook translation group.

- The UCT book brings transparency to the translation process, highlighting what is needed for user-friendly translations; it offers Julia ideas for different kinds of translation products and a different palette of services with added value for clients; and gives new tools to the company translators, motivating them to add to their skill set.

To meet the needs of these personas, we have made the following types of solutions in the book. First, as the personas are familiar with central concepts in translation studies, the main focus is on introducing usability research and its various methods. This focus is manifested in the definition and explanation of central usability-related terms, for example. Second, links are drawn between usability (research) and translation (studies), bringing up fresh ideas and forming the basis for the whole UCT model. Third, in building and arguing for the UCT model, a practical orientation has been a priority: examples are given to illustrate a point, and the assignments encourage the personas to test the ideas and methods presented in the book. Fourth, the book is textually designed so that elements that are especially relevant for each persona are brought up. However, some of the chapters are more relevant to one persona than another.

1.4 Pedagogy

We have designed the structure of the book so that it allows for different types of uses: the book can be used as a traditional textbook which structures a full UCT module; its chapters can be integrated into practical translation classes or translation theory classes; and it can be used as required reading for a book examination or as material for independent study. At the beginning of each chapter we have compiled a checklist of the key points of that chapter. Central concepts in the text are emboldened for emphasis, and words that are emphasized or used meta-linguistically, as well as the titles of publications, are italicized. Each chapter ends with a list of assignments related to the themes of the chapter in question. The assignments can be used either in class after the chapter has been discussed, or the teacher can just as easily pick assignments mid-chapter to demonstrate and practice a certain theme. In addition, the assignments can be used to support independent study. The assignments vary in terms of type and workload: some are more theoretical and demand extra reading, while others are very practical but at the same time might require more leg work from the student.

We first introduced the UCT model in a Finnish textbook (Suojanen *et al.* 2012). We have therefore had a chance to experiment with UCT. We have taught full modules on user-centered translation with the help of the Finnish-language book and used it as a set book for a book examination. Both we and our colleagues have also used individual tools and assignments introduced in the book in other classes, including practical translation courses. This experience has shown us what a useful model UCT can be, and our experiences have informed the writing of this current book. We want to emphasize that this current book is not a translation of the Finnish book: it is an expanded and updated volume. The sections on user experience and cultural usability, for example, are new, and many other sections have undergone significant changes as our own thinking has advanced, and as feedback and experiences from teaching have guided us to make revisions.

In fact, our process of writing about UCT can be seen as a genuinely user-centered undertaking: the Finnish book was conceived as a part of a pre-existing course on user-centered thinking in translation (studies), and draft chapters were tested by students and teachers – the book's intended users – while the book was being written. Then, feedback on the Finnish book and our experiences of using it in class affected our choices when writing the English version, and during the writing of the English version we have received constructive expert feedback from our editors. Thus, the project has been truly iterative, and we hope that the publication of the current book is not the end of this process. Therefore, we invite feedback from the users of this book. We look forward to continuously fine-tuning our model, reviewing the methods it contains, and designing even more usable and appropriate tools on the basis of actual users' experiences.

1.5 Structure

The first four chapters of this book are designed to provide the theoretical background into user-centered translation, and in Chapters 5–9 we examine the practical applications of user-centered translation. The current Introduction outlines the whole book and describes the main idea and characteristics of user-centered translation. Chapter 2 defines usability and user experience, the two key concepts in the book. While Chapter 2 mainly relies on usability research, Chapter 3 starts to explore more thoroughly the concept of the user and what it means to use texts in the context of translation studies. Chapter 4 presents the textual elements of usability – namely, legibility, readability, understandability and accessibility.

The core of UCT is the user, and it differs from many other reader-oriented approaches to translation in its concrete tools and methods for taking the user into account in translation. We begin the empirical application of UCT ideas with introducing mental models in Chapter 5: the chapter brings up intratextual reader positions, audience design and personas as methods in profiling the translation's future users. Chapter 6 presents the idea of usability heuristics, which is similar to practices presently used in the translation industry, as translation agencies often employ somewhat similar evaluation approaches. In addition to presenting heuristics from the field of usability research, we also develop specific usability heuristics for user-centered translation. Chapter 7 is devoted to usability testing, focusing on the involvement of real users in reviewing and testing texts: special attention is paid to some key usability testing methods. Chapter 8 offers an overview of reception studies in translation studies, and we discuss how these research methods can also be employed in the translation industry. Chapter 9 discusses the connections between user-centered translation and the contemporary translation industry, particularly the relationships between usability and quality assessment. This chapter also puts user-centered translation to the test: it presents several case studies that investigate the possibilities and restrictions of our model when used in the translation industry. Chapter 10 concludes the book, returning to the beginning and reflecting on the potential utility and usability of the UCT model.

2   Usability and user experience

Key points in this chapter:

- **Usability** is the ease of use of a product in a specified context of use; users are able to use a product effectively, efficiently and to their satisfaction.

- Usability is culture-bound and dependent on the user and the context; **cultural usability** tackles the cultural diversity of users.

- **User experience** is a holistic concept, which includes all the user's emotions, beliefs, preferences, perceptions, physical and psychological responses, behaviors and accomplishments.

- Translators are the user's representatives, and as members of design teams, translators can help to create a full user experience.

In this chapter we will introduce the concept of usability and consider how it can be applied to translation. First, we introduce some usability definitions. Second, we describe the development of usability discussions from an engineering approach to user-centered design and to the latest wave of user experience. Third, we address the idea of cultural usability and the ways in which it links to the practice of translation. We conclude this chapter with a discussion of user experience.

2.1 Usability

Usability brings to the fore the user of machines and devices – namely, the **human factor**. Usability is one key area of the **Human–Computer Interaction (HCI)** discipline. Initially, it was known as **Usability Engineering** (Nielsen 1993), but is now also called **Usability Research**, expanding from engineering into other user-centered research designs as well as to the development of suitable usability methods. With a growing interest towards users' motivation, attitudes and values, the term **User Experience Research** is also increasingly used (on the many names in this field, see Anderson 2011).

Traditionally, **usability** has concentrated on human–computer interaction, and studies have targeted various computerized interfaces (cell phones, e-commerce applications, computerized industrial processes, etc.), but almost any human activity can be studied from the point of view of usability. In addition to concrete tools and products, recent applications of usability include more abstract areas such as service design. Usability has been defined in an ISO standard (ISO 9241–11: 1998, cited in Ovaska *et al.* 2005: 4). According to the standard, usability is: "the extent to which a product can be used by specified users to achieve specified goals with effectiveness, efficiency and satisfaction, in a specified context of use."

We may tend to think that usability is a product characteristic, that tools and programs are more or less usable as such. It is, however, noteworthy that usability is ultimately about the *user's* relative experience of the success of use. Usability is thus, in essence, user- and context-dependent (Ovaska *et al.* 2005: 4). The standard also repeatedly points to the specificity of particular users and their contexts of use. The phrase "specified users" in the standard, however, has been criticized: many theorists (e.g. Ehn and Löwgren 1997: 299; Bannon 1991: 26–27) think that the concept of the user itself is problematic, because all individuals have their own unique characteristics and it is thus impossible to profile each user type according to the criteria in the standard (see more on the concept of the user in Chapter 3). Consequently, more emphasis has been placed on the importance of the situation of use (Byrne 2010: 98). In other words, a product is considered usable if users can typically use it in a satisfactory manner in the context for which it was intended, but this does not guarantee that every single user in the target group will be able to use it to their full satisfaction.

It is indeed central to consider the **context of use**, which consists of several elements: user characteristics, the quality of the task, the equipment and the environment. If usability is ultimately the user's subjective experience that the use has been successful, it is also relevant to gather information about **user experience**, not just about the problems that the user experiences when using the product (Ovaska *et al.* 2005: 4). Since the turn of the twenty-first century, the feelings and emotions of the user and various affective factors, such as motivation, state of mind and attitudes, have become increasingly important, and since Web services have become more common and widely used, demands for good user experience are on the rise. These experiences are affected by elements such as the service itself, the situation of use, users' earlier experiences and their opinions about the usefulness of the service (Sinkkonen *et al.* 2009a: 18–23). We will return to the discussion on user experience in Section 2.5.

A much-used usability definition is that of a well-known usability consultant, Jakob Nielsen. According to Nielsen (1993: 26), the main attributes of usability are:

1   *Learnability*: the system should be easy to learn.
2   *Efficiency*: once learned, the system should be efficient to use, increasing the user's productivity.

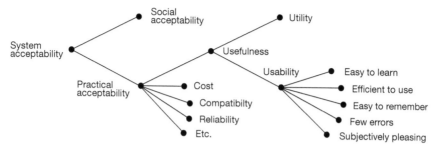

Figure 2.1 Model of the attributes of system acceptability (Nielsen 1993: 25)

3   *Memorability*: when users return to the system after a period of time, they should not have to learn everything again.
4   *Errors*: there should be few errors in using the system, and if users do make errors, it should be easy to recover from them.
5   *Satisfaction*: the users should be subjectively satisfied with using the system.

These attributes can be observed by employing various usability engineering methods to improve the usability of the user interface. What is problematic is that these attributes are often mutually conflicting when user interfaces are designed. For example, a user interface that is easy to learn might contain too many steps and instructions to be efficient. Thus, at the beginning of a project it is advisable to define what type of usability is strived for and which attributes are prioritized, such as whether learnability is more important than user satisfaction (Nielsen 1993: 41–42; Ovaska *et al.* 2005: 3).

Usability is part of Nielsen's wider model of system acceptability. Figure 2.1 demonstrates that usability is one element of **acceptability**: a system has to be good enough to satisfy the needs and requirements of different stakeholders, most importantly users and managers. Acceptability has two parts: **practical** and **social acceptability**. For example, a system may work in practice, but it might be socially questionable due to the gathering of delicate personal information. **Usefulness** is concerned with whether a system can be used to achieve the intended goal.

Usefulness, in turn, is divided into two parts: **utility** and **usability**. Utility signifies whether a system provides the right kind of functionality so that the user is able to perform relevant tasks, while usability is concerned with how well users can use the functionality. For example, an education program has utility if it helps a student to learn, and an entertainment application has utility if using it is fun (Nielsen 1993: 24–26; also Ovaska *et al.* 2005: 3). Usability itself is a web of intricate elements, some of which, such as social acceptability, are communal, and others, such as intuitiveness and affective factors, are personal. However, they share one important feature, which in the end is very down-to-earth, as Jeffrey Rubin and Dana Chisnell (2008: 4) state: "when a product or service is truly usable, the user can do what he or she wants to do the way he or she expects to be able to do it, without hindrance, hesitation, or questions."

For a reader familiar with translation studies, Nielsen's figure elicits some connotations: **acceptability** is familiar from Gideon Toury's (1995) well-known concept pair, where the other concept is **adequacy**. In Toury's concept system, adequacy refers to equivalence to the source text, whereas acceptability refers to adherence to target culture norms and is thus close to Nielsen's concept of social acceptability. Issues linked to Toury's notion of adequacy can also be identified from Nielsen's model. For example, compatibility and reliability are not very far from the idea of source text equivalence. Acceptability, utility and usability, in turn, are close to the ideas in functional translation studies and skopos theory (see Section 3.5).

Thus, if it were drawn from the viewpoint of translation studies, Figure 2.1 might just look a little different, because traditionally translation studies has emphasized the effect of target culture norms on the reception process (see in particular Toury 1995). While in Nielsen's classical figure, social acceptability is located far from the centre of usability, in translation the examination of social acceptability has been considered particularly relevant because of the intercultural elements inherent in translation. Even if a product is highly usable, it may lose its utility completely in a target culture if its use is not socially acceptable. In translation studies, social acceptability has not been widely discussed in the framework of usability, but related issues such as norms, ideologies and censorship have traditionally been important research topics. Power relationships between cultures and different social groups and how those relationships are visible in texts have given rise to entire trends in translation studies, such as postcolonial translation theory (see, e.g. Robinson 1997) and feminist translation (see, e.g. Simon 1999).

In connection with usability and user interfaces, another concept that is often raised is that of **intuition**: our familiarity with something in light of our earlier world of experience with it. If a device that we encounter reminds us of devices we already know, it is intuitive to us and we are able to use it (Kuutti, W. 2003: 13). Intuitiveness, like usability, is relative and individual: what is intuitive for one might be utterly unintuitive for someone else (ibid.). Intuitiveness is also linked to cultural usability (see Section 2.3): we perceive culturally familiar systems and interfaces as intuitive and thus usable, and culturally alien ones as defective and counterintuitive. Some aspects of intuitiveness are related to worldviews, content knowledge and exposure to technology (for example, today's teens, who are used to searching for information online, may find printed dictionaries unexpectedly difficult to navigate); others are linked to more deep-seated cultural differences such as reading direction (left to right, or right to left; vertical or horizontal). In translation, conventions that support intuitiveness are highly important – for example, in subtitles, which we will discuss more in Chapter 8.

2.2 Historical developments in usability research

To describe some historical developments in usability research, we can take advantage of technical communication literature, as mentioned in the Introduction.

The development of the concept of usability is obviously linked to the history of technology: problems involved in the human use of technology have been reported since ancient times, but the early twentieth century and the influence of Taylorism and Fordism brought along the important criterion of **efficiency**. In the decades that followed, the use of technology became more widely spread, and so did problems with the use of technology, which led to the addition of another criterion: **accuracy**. Efficiency, together with accuracy, gave rise to new methods of measuring human behavior and actions in fields such as ergonomics (Johnson *et al.* 2007: 321–322).

World War II was a significant turning point in the history of usability for a number of reasons. First, it was a period of rapid technological development, and to operate new appliances safely and efficiently, the users needed usable interfaces. Industrial psychologists were employed to observe and research users' behavior to improve their performance. Second, World War II brought forth a new awareness of usability issues also in the context of texts: soldiers who were drafted into the military were trained to operate dangerous machinery such as artillery, but the training was textbook-based and took place in traditional classroom settings. The soldiers then tried to apply their knowledge in the field and the outcomes were often disastrous, leading to injury and death. As a result, new efforts were made to understand how people read texts and then apply what they have learned in the use of technology. This opened a window for technical communicators to influence the use of technology and the transfer of knowledge about technology, thus also opening up new roads for usability (Johnson *et al.* 2007: 321–322).

Johnson *et al.* (2007: 322–328) take advantage of Charles Percy Snow's (1993) famous division into two cultures – namely, culture and science – through which they address the issue of usability. Traditionally, usability had been seen as a scientific activity, but the incursion of technical communication changed this setting: usability is also a rhetorical art – that is, applicable to texts. Thus, usability can be seen to exist at the nexus of epistemologies. The time between World War II and the personal computer revolution can be called an era of bridge-building: engineers and rhetoricians bridged the two cultures, those of culture and science, and usability, along with user-centered design, was the bridge. Edmond Weiss (1985: 10–11) aptly states that as usability became more central in technical communication, user instructions also started to be seen as types of devices (cited in Byrne 2010: 69). Technical communication is epistemologically adjacent to translation (and these two professions have significant overlaps). It thus makes sense, we think, to approach questions concerning the usability of translations from the perspective of technical communication, where usability issues have been prominent for a long time.

A central impetus in the development of usability that we described above has been Patricia Sullivan's article "Beyond a Narrow Conception of Usability Testing" (1989), where she criticizes the so-called **end-of-the-line problem** in usability testing. Sullivan was one of the first to acknowledge that the potential of usability testing cannot be exploited in full when it is only applied to all-but-finished documentation. This way of working does not allow user input, which could be highly beneficial during the product design cycle. If we compare this setting to that in the translation field, we find the exact same problem: translations are usually assessed and revised only at the end of the actual translation process and users of the translation are rarely involved in the process at all. In fact, although Sullivan limits the problem to usability *testing* (see Chapter 7), it is an apt idea in characterizing design, writing and translation processes in more general terms (see, e.g. Drugan 2013: 18).

According to Sullivan (1989: 256), technical communicators are central to making users a more prominent part of the development process. Technical communicators are the user's advocates in the organization, and they have knowledge about the user group based on various user- and task-analysis methods (see also Johnson *et al.* 2007: 320; Hart-Davidson 2001). The more experience they have and the more feedback they get from the field, the better they are able to understand users and their information needs. We argue that the position of translators is similar: the translator acts as the advocate of the target readers, and translators have specialized knowledge of these readers. With the help of various usability methods they can solidify and concretize this intercultural knowledge, and they will gain a more detailed understanding of particular user groups in specific contexts of use.

The history of usability research is not yet long, but it has had several distinctive phases. Above we have focused on technical communication and the role of rhetoric in usability discussions. On a more global view, it can be argued that usability research has actually developed in three waves (Kamppuri 2011: Section 2.1): the first wave was characterized by performance-oriented usability engineering that relied on ergonomics, cognitive psychology and cognitive science as well as on an experimental approach to research. This was followed by a second, user-centered design wave. The development of personal computers in the late 1980s and the perceived shortcomings of earlier individualistic laboratory testing led to new approaches focusing on teamwork and contexts of use, backed up by theories of situated learning and distributed cognition. This by now traditional UCD is nowadays often complemented by an increased focus on designing for user experience, and in this emerging third wave, designers are increasingly attempting to integrate participatory technologies with the more designer-led approaches to user-centered design.

Again, one can see parallels in technological developments and usability approaches: the development of new interaction devices and increased interactiveness of digital media have made user experience a buzzword in the world of digital technology (Kamppuri 2011: 21). Our model of user-centered translation is a combination of these three waves; as explained in the Introduction, we have obvious affinities with the second wave, with its emphasis on user-centered design, but in the following sections we will include both traditional testing strategies and some discussions linked to user experience.

2.3 Cultural usability

In translation, cultural issues are always to the forefront. Above, we have discussed usability without much consideration for this crucial element. In fact, as Andy Smith and Fahri Yetim (2004: 1) note, cultural issues were ignored in HCI for a long time. Similarly, Minna Kamppuri (2011: 23) argues that during the first two waves of usability research, cultural issues did not play a significant part. The first special edition on cultural issues for the journal *Interacting with Computers* was in 1998 (vols 9: 3 and 9: 4; ibid.: 1–2). In his editorial, Daniel Day (1998: 270) described well the inherent problems of usability studies:

> What these firms have recognised is that ALL factors measured in usability studies to date have been dependent at some level upon the cultural context in which users apply software products and that the vastly different contexts at overseas locations may call into question some of the special case findings of Western-dominated HCI research.

Since the special issue, **cultural usability** has been explored more widely – for example, with the support of sociology, social psychology and anthropology. However, culture is a difficult object of study because of the complexity of human behavior. A further challenge in studying cultural usability is that it should address both the product and the process of information systems development: in terms of products, cultural differences in meanings, norms or values, for example, raise various research issues, and in terms of process, cultural differences have an effect on the ways in which users can participate in the design of products and be a part of evaluation studies (Smith and Yetim 2004: 1–2).

There is a rich tradition of research that is based on the assumption that cultures are fundamentally different from one another in a number of ways. Research on these **cultural dimensions** is often based on Geert Hofstede's (1980) classic model of cultural values. Having conducted extensive interviews of IBM employees in 53 countries, Hofstede concluded that cultures vary along five fundamental dimensions: power distance, collectivism vs. individualism, femininity vs. masculinity, uncertainty avoidance, and long- vs. short-term orientation. These dimensions have been studied in numerous case studies across disciplines (for an overview, see Taras *et al.* 2009). For example, Aaron Marcus and Emilie West Gould (2000) have applied Hofstede's theory to Web-user interfaces by suggesting how each cultural dimension such as power distance may influence different aspects of user interface and Web design. Gabrielle Ford and Paula Kotze (2005) also give support to the use of cultural models and to Hofstede's cultural model in particular. Although more evidence is needed, their experiment, in which an interface was tested by a multicultural group of students in a usability test, interestingly suggests that the specific sides of Hofstede's dimensions – namely, high power distance, high uncertainty avoidance, masculinity and short-term orientation – "would provide a more usable interface to all users than one that is designed to accommodate the opposing sides of these dimensions" (ibid.: 723–724).

Hofstede has been highly influential in cultural analysis, both in and outside academia, but his model has also been severely criticized for its focus on national cultures, its essential nature and its sweeping overgeneralizations (Piller 2011: 77–83). Later work in intercultural communication has indeed focused more on professional cultures in multinational contexts and on individuals whose cultural belongings are much more diverse – or even super diverse – than homogenizing national models allow for (ibid.: 83–94). The need for a similar movement has been identified in cultural usability studies. To tackle the cultural diversity of users in an increasingly global world, different solutions have been suggested. Torkil Clemmensen (2011: 635) gives examples of the different paradigms that have been put forward on culture-specific HCI: **cultural computing** (Rauterberg 2006), **culturally sensitive information technology** (Zakaria *et al.* 2003), **intercultural usability engineering** (Beu *et al.* 2000), **culturability** (Choi *et al.* 2006) and **cultural usability** (Barber and Badre 1998; Hertzum 2010). Still, as Clemmensen *et al.* note (2009: 212), much of research into usability evaluation methods assumes that cultural issues do not have an effect, for example, on task scenario or interface heuristics – namely, rules or guidelines that are used to evaluate products.

Above, we discussed the three waves of HCI and usability research. Kamppuri (2011: 25–34) assesses the role of culture in each of these. The first wave of usability engineering inspired two kinds of approaches: studying culture through cross-cultural experiments and using statistical cultural models of cultural dimensions. In these experiments culture was seen as a variable between groups of participants, and the findings were often generalized to entire populations in a particular country. For example, a study by Olaf Frandsen-Thorlacius *et al.* (2009: 1) showed that usability is not understood similarly by users in different cultures. Their 412 users from China and Denmark differed in how they understood and prioritized different usability aspects: the Chinese were more concerned with visual appearance, satisfaction and fun than Danish users, who rated effectiveness, efficiency and lack of frustration higher than the Chinese. These kinds of generalizations are seen as problematic because of their essentialist view of culture and their easy conflation of nationality and culture. Obviously, researchers are aware of the dangers of simplification. For example, Hertzum *et al.* (2011) discuss the problem of culture at length. However, their solution to avoid the pitfalls by abandoning culture for nationality – which they consider more neutral – does not fix the underlying problem of essentialism. Nationalities, similar to cultural affiliations, are not stable and fixed for all participants, and national culture is only one cultural affiliation among many, as we are also affected by our regional, ethnic, generational, gender-based and professional cultures, and many others.

During the second wave of usability research, with its focus on users and contexts of use, cultural issues were logically included in the context of use – that is, rather than seeing cultural aspects as a personal trait, they were seen as a contextual factor that affects the person's perceptions, values and manners of work. In the third wave, as usability methods began to migrate towards more qualitative orientations, from interviews in in-situ observations to fully fledged ethnographies, cultural elements also became more readily observable. Kamppuri is not too explicit about this third wave of research and, according to her (2011: 31), approaches linked to the first wave such as Hofstede's model, have been more prominent in studying the effects of culture in design. The first wave approaches are, however, nowadays viewed with renewed reflexivity and criticism, not only for the risk of essentialist bias in national cultures but also for more deep-seated cultural biases. This interrogation of the basic tenets of usability research and the increasing number of critical voices towards assumed shared understandings are, according to Kamppuri (ibid.: 33), implications of the emergent third wave of HCI. Another central feature of the third wave is the concept of user experience and its cultural implications (see Section 2.5).

Obviously, culture is not only an observable factor to be studied in usability research but also an underlying factor affecting the research design itself. Clemmensen *et al.* (2009) found several cultural differences between "Westerners" and "Easterners" (people from China and from other countries who have been heavily influenced by Chinese culture) – for example, in the overall relationship between the evaluator and the user. In another study, Clemmensen (2011: 665) found that there is agreement across countries as to what usability professionals consider to be part of a usability test: as a result, he created cross-cultural templates for usability testing where some parts are constant and other parts vary depending on the context. What is clear is that the cultural dimension is present in usability testing itself – for example, differences in cultural background between the observer and the user might affect the test results and thus possibly also distort both the design and the localization process for which the tests are performed (see, e.g. Sun and Shi 2007; see also Hall *et al.* 2004). In fact, research has shown that there is, overall, great variety in the practice of usability testing across organizations, let alone cultures (Clemmensen 2011: 636).

Another meta-level issue concerns usability itself: our cultural background may well affect what we understand to be usable and why. There may be contexts where participants have a different concept of usability, not only differing viewpoints as to what it entails. This internalized concept of usability was explored in the above mentioned comparative interview study of the personal usability constructs of Chinese, Indian and Danish users, and the researchers found out that some elements considered central in usability literature (they mention ease of use in particular) may be assigned a widely different value in different cultural settings (Hertzum *et al.* 2011). However, the same researchers found much more funda- mental differences between developers and users. Users were more similar to each other than to developers and vice versa, even though both groups comprised Chinese, Danish and Indian participants (ibid.: 754). The users, who were not familiar with dominant usability definitions, brought forth interesting new aspects such as usefulness, security or fun. This finding of differences between stakeholders rather than nationalities emphasizes the role of professional cultures, and it is a useful reminder of cultural differences not always coinciding with national cultures.

Although the link between a national culture and a national language may well be the prototype most commonly used in both translation studies and in intercultural communication, it is a core principle of user-centered translation to look for other distinctions as well. One common translation task involves a move from professionals to lay people, or from experts to ordinary readers. Typical examples of cultural divides include the medical professions versus patients, or the technology-savvy engineers to lay users of devices. These users' aptitudes and attitudes may vary significantly, and different user groups differ not only in what they know or do not know but also in how they approach a situation of use: for some, complex technology is a miracle they do not even wish to understand, while others may be fearful and alienated (Mitra 2010: 46, 96).

It is also interesting to consider the role of language in usability test situations, which, according to Clemmensen (2011: 639), has not been studied much. Some evidence suggests that the language used in the evaluation may prime some users' mode of thinking (Clemmensen *et al.* 2009: 217). This problem of **equivalence** in multilingual test materials has received substantial attention in disciplines such as health sciences or marketing research, which are heavily involved in cross-cultural comparative surveys (e.g. Malhotra *et al.* 1996: 19–21): how can the researcher make sure that the scales, stimuli and formulations used in the survey material measure the same aspects and have the same force in all cultural contexts? Translation is a core element of these research designs. Traditionally, its validity has been tested by back-translation, a method not considered very reliable in translation studies. Recently, more usability-oriented methods have been promoted, and researchers are encouraged to employ pretests and pilot studies for trans- lated surveys in a manner similar to the testing of the original survey, and to use methods such as focus groups to assess the translations in an iterative manner (Harkness 2013).

2.4 Cultural usability and translation/localization

Leo Lentz and Jacqueline Hulst (2000: 313) have studied the process of document design in a multilingual setting and note that studying usability in such contexts requires a more sophisticated approach than when one is dealing with a linguistic- ally homogeneous group of native speakers. They call for a more integrated approach to the evaluation of multilingual texts: to be able to evaluate multilingual documents, expertise in technical communication, usability studies, translation theory and linguistics is required (ibid.: 321). However, in the usability research literature reviewed for this book, the role of the translator in terms of cultural usability seems almost nonexistent.

Based on the above discussion, the understanding of cultural usability could be one area where translation research could contribute productive perspectives, as culture penetrates usability in many respects: in definitions of usability, in the design of products and in methods that are used to evaluate usability in different contexts. One overlapping area of interest for both HCI and translation studies is localization. Localization is where usability factors of the interface and the usability elements involved in written and visual communication interact to the fullest; it is also a prime example of the inherent existence of culture in the usability of translations. Localization has traditionally been defined as translation and adaptation of computer software into another language and culture (Salmi 2008: 55). Nowadays, in addition to software, localization covers a number of different areas such as websites, video games, mobile appliances and multimedia. These areas share many characteristics: the text is digital by its nature, information is presented on screen, the texts are interactive, and the projects consist of cooperation between the translators, localization engineers and developers (Jiménez-Crespo 2011: 4).

The creation of different text versions for different cultures implies that the organization is prepared to consider the needs of consumers from different backgrounds (de Bortoli *et al.* 2003: 3). The ethos is thus similar to user-centered design, where the user's needs come first. However, one of the most common problems in a localization project is designers' inadequate understanding of other cultures and settling for a superficial localization, which does not consider cultural differences in a profound way (de Bortoli *et al.* 2003: 4–5; for similar critiques, see also Sun 2006: 457; Kamppuri 2011: 23–25). Localization is also known to suffer from the end-of-the-line problem mentioned above, which is familiar from many translation projects and also known in usability research; the experts in these fields are finding it difficult to push their contribution upstream in the design process to the phases where they can still contribute to the more fundamental decisions.

Huatong Sun (2006: 457), in fact, notes that the vision of localization practices has been static and narrow. He has found that usability problems are related to a lack of understanding of language and cultural issues during localization (ibid.: 457; see also Agboka 2013: 29). Sun also connects the end-of-the-line problem to a wider cultural context and to localization; companies do not have a vision of localization strategies in product design and they settle for **developer localization** – that is, "localization only occurs at the developer's site, and it ends when the product ships" (Sun 2006: 460). As an answer to this problem, Sun (ibid.: 459) proposes **user localization**, which has potential in expanding "the scope of cultural IT product design for localization studies". User localization shifts the focus into designing IT products for local audiences in terms of their culture, which also means evaluating IT products at the user's site. Sun (ibid.: 458) argues that users themselves are the best experts of their local culture and contexts, so localization work belongs both to designers and users: "users work with designers and producers as actors/constructors to co-construct the whole practice" (ibid.: 477). Thus, localization becomes an open-ended process, reaching beyond the design stage to the use and consumption stage (ibid.: 476). Because of the "dialogic interaction" (Salvo 2001: 288) between developer and user localization, developers can respond to user needs quickly and improve localization performance (Sun 2006: 476).

With regard to culture and usability, Sun's suggestion proposes certain standpoints. First, instead of applying general cultural conventions (e.g. Hofstede's dimension of power distance) to localization, local technology should be designed with a deep understanding of use activities in context (Sun 2006: 459, 474). Second,

Sun (ibid.: 466) views usability as a diffusing feature (Spinuzzi 2001) that covers interactions in entire networks; usability becomes a mediation process: "It is both (a) material interaction with the artifact and its contexts and (b) an interpretation process of this activity." Clay Spinuzzi (2001: 16) himself uses the term **distributed usability** to refer to this process; instead of testing how individual users employ isolated products in controlled settings, usability should be seen "as distributed across the genres, practices, uses, and goals of a given activity"; it becomes distributed across an entire activity network (ibid.: 21).

As we mentioned above, the cultural awareness inherent in translation and localization could be a source of meaningful contributions to usability. It has long been acknowledged that successful translation requires an awareness of not only linguistic equivalences but also, and significantly, of the cultural contexts of both the source and the target texts. In expositions of translators' competences, this area has traditionally been labelled as *cultural competence*, and it has been a widely held understanding that translator training needs to include advanced knowledge of the foreign or B language culture in particular (although training programs may also offer courses on the A culture, they are less common). One could argue that translator training and translation tends to suffer from a national culture bias similar to the first wave of cultural usability research and early intercultural communication research. Often the implicit starting point is based on an essentialized view of national cultures, proceeding from generalizations about entire linguistic or cultural areas. This conflation of nation-states, cultures and target groups leads to sweeping statements such as: "One does not need to explain this or that to the French"; "American readers do not know culture-specific item X"; or "Foreigners are not familiar with details of Finnish history". From the point of view of user-centered translation and adaptation, a readership this wide is too heterogeneous and easily remains approximate: "It is often impossible for the translators to know the exact knowledge base of their recipients. Adaptations are thus based on an estimated 'average knowledge'" (Vehmas-Lehto 1999: 112 (trans. the authors)). Only too often, the translators may also end up using themselves as a measure for adaptation needs, basing their translation on an (erroneous) assumption that the target readers are familiar with anything that the translator is familiar with, and that one needs to explain to the target readers everything the translator was unfamiliar with in the text (Vermeer 1989: 180).

More recently, a notion of a particular intercultural competence has been brought forward (PICT 2013). Similar to traditional notions of cultural competence, *inter*cultural competence presupposes a knowledge and understanding of cultures that are perceived as distinct, but the emphasis is on how to deal with differences and how to alleviate and preferably avoid potential conflicts, and it also allows for recognizing more individual cultural affiliations. For translators, the emphasis on avoiding conflicts is quite recognizable; in practical translation situations it is not enough to identify cultural differences, but the translator also needs to decide whether something needs to be done to reduce the **culture bumps** (Leppihalme 1997) in the translation or whether it is actually advisable to allow the reader of the translation to encounter a cultural difference. From a usability perspective, however, a culture bump is always a usability problem. Translation strategies developed for avoiding culture bumps (see also Section 4.3) can be fruitfully adopted to nontranslated text production as well.

2.5 User experience

One crucial element of intercultural competence is **empathy** – that is, the ability to put oneself in others' position and to understand their emotions and reactions. That same skill is also at the core of understanding **User Experience (UX),** which is the current third wave of HCI. If the buzzwords in the 1980s and 1990s were *functionality, usability, usability engineering* and *user-centered design,* in the 2000s *user experience* has taken the floor; the focus has shifted from product usability, such as ease of learning or satisfaction, to encompass issues such as aesthetics, fun and pleasure that define users' emotions and affects rather than qualities of the product (Wilson 2005: 6). In fact, the term *user experience* covers all the interaction that the end user has with a company, its services and its products (Nielsen and Norman n.d.: n.p.).

In user experience, the focus is on all sensations and feelings during interaction, not only on cognitive aspects. Some researchers argue that designers should go even further: usability or user experience are not the ultimate goals but only the means to an end, and that end goal is **worth,** or, the creation of value (Kamppuri 2011: 33). There is a strong ethical dimension in this shift; it is more important to think what we *should* achieve with technology, rather than what we *can* achieve.

Similar to usability, user experience has been defined in an ISO standard (ISO 9241–210: 2010). User experience is typically associated with perceptual and emotional aspects, and the standard defines UX as follows (cited in "User Experience Definitions" n.d.: n.p.): "[User experience is] a person's perceptions and responses that result from the use or anticipated use of a product, system or service." User experience thus includes all the user's emotions, beliefs, preferences, perceptions, physical and psychological responses, behaviors and accomplishments. User experience is affected not only by the user, but by the system and the context of use.

In addition to the ISO definition, user experience has been defined in many other ways (see, e.g. "User Experience Definitions" n.d.: n.p.), just like usability. Pabini Gabriel-Petit (2013: n.p.) defines user experience as follows:

> [It] comprehends all aspects of digital products and services that *users* experience directly—and perceive, learn, and use—including products' form, behavior, and content, but also encompassing users' broader brand experience and the response that experience evokes in them.

Gabriel-Petit (ibid.) continues: "Key factors contributing to the quality of users' experience of products are learnability, usability, usefulness, and aesthetic appeal." In other words, the discussion goes full circle but returns to traditional product-oriented definitions of usability. This is understandable, as designers do not have any other tools to affect user experience than the product, but it might lead to a narrow conception of user experience. Another potentially problematic issue in an excessive focus on user experience is that it emphasizes individuals at the expense of shared views and interactive co-construction of experiences, and it is thus prone to create a hedonistic design culture (Battarbee and Koskinen, I. 2005).

Katja Battarbee and Ilpo Koskinen (2005: 6–7) distinguish three different approaches to user experience: measuring, emphatic and pragmatist. The measuring approach continues the laboratory tradition of usability research, claiming that experience can be measured from bodily reactions. The emphatic approach, then, is linked to qualitative research traditions and aims to understand the desires and motivations of the users. The emotions of the designer are considered equally important as those of the users, and the aim is to get on the same wavelength to achieve **design empathy**. Finally, the authors see the pragmatist approach as more holistic than the other two. But they argue that it, too, lacks an understanding of a fundamental feature: the social nature of the human condition. According to them (ibid.: 8):

> Of user experience approaches, only the pragmatist perspective really accounts for the situated unity of action, emotion and thought in the individual in a theoretical way. The pragmatist perspective is broader than the others in its scope; in fact, other models can be seen as its special cases. However, all these approaches are individualistic, thus missing a crucially important aspect of human experience. People as individuals depend on others for all that makes them truly human.

All of these approaches are relevant to bear in mind when designing for user experience. User experience is a holistic concept, and this holistic nature leads to some fuzziness in what it means to design for user experience. This is why definitions for **User Experience Design** or **Research** tend to be open-ended. For example, User Experience Design has been said to refer to

> the judicious application of certain user-centered design practices, a highly contextual design mentality, and use of certain methods and techniques that are applied through process management to produce cohesive, predictable, and desirable effects in a specific person, or persona (archetype comprised of target audience habits and characteristics). All so that the affects produced meet the user's own goals and measures of success and enjoyment, as well as the objectives of the providing organization.
>
> (Cummings 2010: n.p.)

What is central here is that user experience design is contextual in nature and encompasses the entire design process. Although user experience design aims to create desired effects on specific users, this definition interestingly also considers organizational perspectives.

Jessie James Garrett (2002: 21–24) has done seminal work on user experience and has produced a much-cited model on the elements of user experience in web design. Garrett divides user experience into five component elements, which he calls planes. The first plane at the bottom is the **strategy plane** where everything begins: what do both developers and users want to get out of a website? Above strategy is the **scope plane**, which defines which features will be included in the site, such as whether users will be able to save previously used addresses for future need. The third plane is the **structure plane**: it defines how the pieces of the site fit together – for example, the way in which navigational items are arranged. Above the structure plane is the **skeleton plane**: it is the arrangement of buttons, tabs, photos and text blocks on the website. Finally, the top plane is the **surface plane**, which embodies the user experience as it contains the text and the images. During the development process, decisions become more and more specific and detailed plane by plane.

Garrett's diagram models the website development process from the point of view of the designer. Another interesting conception of user experience design has been produced by Michael Cummings (2010), who looks at the process from the user's point of view. His model has more or less the same ingredients as Garrett's, but their order of priority is turned upside down. The levels are: written language, graphic design, sound, motion, information design, interface design, interaction design and programming. While both Garrett and Cummings recognize the role of text and language, in Cummings's model written language is the *entry* level; it is the first interface that the user encounters, and if it is in any way problematic, that will result in decreased user experience. While interface designers focus on system functionalities, they tend to consider language as a secondary, surface-level feature. However, the actual users will never be able to appreciate the elegant system design, if the textual level is not accessible to them.

Translation studies scholars have recently expressed growing interest in the affective aspects of translating and translations, but direct links to user experience design are still few. To our knowledge, the most advanced direct engagement with UX thus far is the field of game localization where it is, logically, renamed as **Player Experience (PX)**. Minako O'Hagan and Carmen Mangiron (2013: 312–318) lament the lack of empirical user tests in the localization industry and argue for user-focused empirical research. Digitalized games are particularly susceptible to an affective and emotional focus because they are entertainment products, and player satisfaction, fun and pleasure are to the forefront. Game localization might thus function as a bridge between translation and UX research, and adjacent fields such as audiovisual translation will benefit directly from findings made in PX.

In this chapter, we have introduced the core concept of user-centered translation: usability. We also discussed two related issues that are central to our model: cultural usability and user experience. We argue that to achieve optimal usability for translated materials it is essential to take into account cultural differences, often demonstrated linguistically, and not to take for granted that users in different contexts experience things in similar ways. In practical terms, a good cultural fit can be achieved by employing translators upstream in the design process, not only at the very end. Translators should be members of design teams and participate in all design phases, as they are the user's representatives and can contribute to creating a full user experience. This is what user-centered translation aims to achieve.

Assignments

1   Apply Nielsen's acceptability model (Figure 2.1) to the practice of translation. Draw a similar picture of the elements of translation in a user-centered translation process and discuss your drawing. For example, system acceptability can be thought of as the acceptability of a translation, which is divided into social and practical acceptability.

2   Choose a language and culture pair that is familiar to you and discuss how the cultural norms of these two languages/cultures differ from each other. What kinds of usability problems can these differences cause in translations?

3   Figure 2.1 divides acceptability into two parts: practical and social acceptability. How might social acceptability affect the usability of translated magazines, and what methods can a translator use to solve these problems? Alternatively, you can choose to reflect on the acceptability of translated websites. Selecting a particular example – a local version of the *Cosmopolitan* magazine, for example, or a localized website of a multinational firm – will help pinpoint potential acceptability issues.

4   Visit a website that has been translated to your own A language. Reflect on your own user experience: What kinds of emotions or reactions did you have? Did you notice culturally unexpected elements, and how did they affect your user experience?

5   Section 2.5 introduces Garrett's model of the elements of user experience. Garrett originally developed the model in the context of website design. Do you think this model also applies to more traditional software products or even other kinds of user interfaces such as household appliances or printed books? Why or why not?

3   Users and using texts

Key points in this chapter:

- The idea of usability is based on the assumption that there is a product and this product has a user. In the case of texts, we must stop to think whether these conditions are met: Is text a product, and is the reader or recipient a **user** of a text?

- Users can be categorized in many different ways, e.g. according to their level of expertise.

- Usability not only applies to user interfaces; our entire living environment can be evaluated from the viewpoint of usability.

- **Functional translation theories** emphasize the aim, the **skopos,** of the translation, and the recipients of the translation are one focus within these theories.

- Eugene A. Nida can be seen as a pioneer of user-centeredness in translation studies. His concept of **dynamic equivalence** focuses on the needs of the end user of the translation. In Nida's books, one can also find numerous early examples of usability testing.

In the Introduction, we raised the question of whether the **user** is just another designation for an old concept or whether it opens up an entirely new way of thinking. Do the concepts of the user and of usability bring some added value to the practice of translation and translation research? In this chapter, we will consider the development of these concepts and, in particular, the relationship between the *user* and the *reader*, which is a more familiar concept in translation studies. In this examination we will take advantage of technical communication, as it has much to offer to the discussion about users and, similar to translation, it has a text-based approach to usability. In Section 3.5 we will then chart the tradition of translation studies, identifying points of contact with usability thinking in functional translation theories in general and in Eugene A. Nida's pioneering work in particular.

3.1 Know thy users

If we as consumers could choose, some of us might not like to be called *users*. The term is vague and it can have negative connotations of an addiction related to another kind of "use". The term *user* also conjures a simplified picture of us, if we think about computer use, for example. After all, with the computer, we do a variety of things: we work, we keep in touch with friends or play games. Still, the starting point of usability engineering is a phrase from the 1970s, "Know thy users!" (Ovaska *et al.* 2005: 2; also Kuutti, K. 2001). Since then, the concept of the user has also been defined in more detail: "The user is a person who installs, uses, adjusts, cleans, repairs, transports or destroys a product" (Danska *et al.* 1996: 5 (trans. the authors)). So the user does not exist in a vacuum, but rather, in direct interaction with a device or system. Byrne (2010: 99) confirms this by saying that users and usability are essentially about the interaction between the user and a product or system.

In the above definition of the user, *product* most likely refers not to text but to a concrete technical device or system produced as a result of a product development process. However, the definition could also be interpreted differently: could a text, such as user instructions, be a product? This interpretation can be supported by a number of arguments. First, although the definition does not actually mention the user instructions, it comes from a publication that discusses user instructions. Second, it has been said that user instructions are an integral part of the delivery of the product (ISO/IEC GUIDE 37: 1995). Third, legislation in many countries stipulates that all products on the market must include user instructions. Fourth, the field of technical communication employs the concepts of **information products** and **communication products**, which specifically refer to technical documentation such as user instructions. Finally, technical documents are, in essence, **utility texts** or **necessary texts** (Cook 1995: 15; Pilto and Rapakko 1995: 37–39). They are not read for entertainment or sophistication, but for a certain purpose – for example, to solve a problem with a device or system. Thus, interaction extends beyond an individual and a machine to interaction with text; the user instructions act as a bridge when an individual and a machine interact.

In fact, in Timo Jokela's (2010: 15) guide to usability-led interaction design, user instructions are defined as **interaction media** (Jokela's term). Interaction media include all the means with which the user communicates with an application. It is a particularly apt term because of the dependence between usability and interaction, as was just discussed. In addition to user instructions, the concept includes the sales package and related materials, support and training materials, and even marketing materials. Thus, interaction media is an alternative designation for **user assistance**, a concept commonly used within the localization industry. All interaction media have an effect on the users' experience of the application, and consequently, all of them need to be taken into consideration in the design process. User-centered translation extends this idea to the translation process of interaction media, too.

The prerequisites for the interaction between a product and the user run surprisingly deep. Sociological technology studies utilize the concept of **inscription**: in designing devices, engineers work from the basis of both conscious and unconscious assumptions about their users and inscribe their views into the design[1] (Kotro 2006). Madeleine Akrich (2000: 208) describes this inscription by saying that "[d]esigners thus define actors with specific tastes, competences, motives, aspirations, political prejudices, and the rest, and they assume that morality, technology, science, and economy will evolve in particular ways". So technical devices contain user configurations that guide the future use of the device. Despite this inscription, a company might not always have a clear idea or methods to take advantage of all the tacit information it has about its users (Kotro 2006). The difficulty in inscription is that users and designers have different conceptual models and ways of understanding systems. The designer must make sure that the system describes a conceptual model appropriate to the user (Preece *et al.* 1994: 134–138; see also Oudshoorn and Pinch 2005: 7–8). In that way, devices themselves already contain an idea of the user, and naturally, textual information should support this idea.

As mentioned above, when we consider the idea of the user from a textual point of view, technical communication offers a fruitful starting point. The idea of the reader as user started to spread in the field of technical communication along with the introduction of the personal computer. As early as the 1990s, technical communication researcher Mary Coney (1992) presented a taxonomy of readers, which charted different reader roles inscribed in texts. There are five roles in Coney's taxonomy: 1) reader as receiver of information; 2) reader as user; 3) reader as decoder; 4) reader as professional colleague; and 5) reader as maker of meaning (see Section 5.1.2 for a more detailed discussion of Coney's taxonomy).

The role of the reader as user is so dominant in the field of technical communication that it is often extended to define all of the roles readers assume when confronting technical discourse. This type of reader is goal-driven and only interested in information that can be applied to predetermined tasks quickly and with minimum effort. A text is only a tool through which the device is being used. David Dobrin (1983: 242–243; see also Coney 1992: 59) aptly describes this type of mindset:

> Technical writing is writing that accommodates technology to the user. [. . .] "User" is appropriate rather than "reader", because technology is meant to be used; moreover, "user" reflects the fact that technical writing exists within a system which measures actions, people, and things by the criterion of use. "Technology" is more than an array of tools or procedures. It extends to the way human beings deploy themselves in the use and production of material goods and services.

When the reader is seen as a user, documents become only the means to an end: explanatory information is only provided in as much as it is important from the viewpoint of usability, and text volume and rhetorical devices are kept to a minimum. Sentences are short and simple, verbs are heavily imperative, and the tone is informal. Furthermore, these types of documents are usually rich in graphics, which supports users in completing their tasks (Coney 1992: 59–60). The above definition of technical communication by Dobrin has also been criticized; it has been said that the term *user* belittles the significance of text in relation to the device or system which it explains. The term also, in this view, reduces the significance of the writer: the writer's intention is not to express oneself, but to make technology useful for others and to bend to the will of the user-reader (Couture 1992: 28).

Coney's (1992: 61) notion of the development of the user role is relevant here; it was not until technical communication evolved and documentation was being tested more that the role of the user – unknown until then – started to develop. In fact, since the 1990s the term *user* has often been synonymous with *reader*. Although Coney criticizes the dominant position of the user role and suggests that readers can be engaged in many other ways, too, we cannot escape the fact that technical documents are utility texts, as we argued above. Thus, it would seem that the operational role of technical communication has an effect on its idea of text, and consequently, on the way in which it sees reader relationships.

The relationship between reader and user is intriguing, as we can perceive *user* in two different ways. On one hand, in Coney's taxonomy it is a role in which a reader operates or which has been inscribed in a text, but on the other hand, it is also a given position into which people enter when they interact with a device and its instructions: in order to get something done, a person has to use a device and thus becomes a user, but textually users can also adopt other rhetorical roles. This setting also raises another interesting question: which position is primary – the position of the reader or the user? It would seem that the reading act of a technical document is an instrumental activity for the reaching of a goal and that goal can only be achieved through use. Furthermore, if we consider that reading is often selective browsing and instructions are used as a reference (e.g. Schriver 1997: 213–214), a person reading a utility text is primarily a user.

Another issue is the willingness of users to read instructions overall. For example, Karen Schriver (1997: 213–214) reports on a case study where 201 users were asked whether they read the instructions of home electronics (e.g. video, stereo): 15 percent reported to read cover to cover, 46 percent reported to browse, 35 percent reported to use as reference and 4 percent reported not to read at all. When asked in what situation the users had read the instructions of the most recently purchased device, 23 percent had read them before trying out a new function, 42 percent had read while trying out a new function, 17 percent had used the instructions only when they had a problem and 19 percent said they had not used instructions. The results of this case study raise two interesting points: first, the percentages for those not reading instructions is not very high compared to the common assumption that people do not read instructions, and second, the spectrum of technical documentation is so wide that the general question "Do you read user instructions?" is actually a difficult one, because the willingness to read is affected by many factors such as the type of the product (e.g. medicine, mobile phone), price, difficulty, familiarity, etc. The various reading strategies also indicate that reading or not reading is one element of the context of use, and that reading and using are closely intertwined in a case of written utility texts.

3.2 User interfaces and product variety

As we saw in Chapter 2, usability is traditionally connected specifically with user interfaces (Kuutti, W. 2003: 15).[2] However, it does not only belong to computer applications (Kuutti, W. 2003: 13). Our whole living environment can be evaluated from the viewpoint of usability, and thus, we can all be perceived as users. Routio (2007: n.p.) divides products into three classes according to the user's level of activity:

1   **Passive product, active user.** This class contains consumable goods (e.g. food, water, electricity), semi-finished products (e.g. yarn, fabrics, electrical accessories), and casings and containers, the purpose of which is to keep and protect the contents (e.g. buildings, clothes, furniture). This final subclass also includes containers for nonphysical content, such as catalogues, dictionaries, handbooks and databases.

2   **An interactive product** can function only if the user has full control of it, and the class includes products and services "the content of which is negotiated or which are targeted at changing users themselves, such as teaching packages and health and beauty care" (Routio 2007: n.p. (trans. the authors)).

3   **Active product, passive user.** This class contains products that, once installed, function without the user either continuously or by starting and stopping. These products include automatic devices such as heaters, fans and lifts, and services with predefined content (public transport, post office). Furthermore, regarding this class, Routio (2007: n.p.) adds: "If we can talk about the 'use' or 'consumption' of art, this class can also include music and TV entertainment, for the 'use' of which the audience only has to be there" (trans. the authors).

Just being there leads to the idea that the audience is passive, which is problematic. For example, TV audience research has emphasized the activity of the audience and started to dismantle the myth of the passivizing influence of television. Moreover, audience research has increasingly started to study audiences as interactive users of media: the active viewer has become the interactive user, as the audience has more choices and the audience's own role as producer of content has become stronger. In fact, media studies address the media as text on one hand, and as object on the other, and correspondingly, people are seen as interpreters of media texts on one hand, and as users of media objects on the other (Nikunen 2008: 235–237; Livingstone 2004: 83–85). Overall, research on uses and gratifications[3] carried out within mass communication has found that people have several reasons for using mass media (Kunelius 2003: 113–120), and thus, the third class described above paints a slightly limited portrait of the audience's role. A similar shift has occurred in technology studies: passive users have come to be seen as active adapters of technology (Oudshoorn and Pinch 2005: 5).

If we consider the above product classification, a translation can also be a product of its own. Routio's classification can be analyzed through Katharina Reiss's (1971: 24–53) text type typology: the first class could be seen as the informative text type, which includes genres such as encyclopaedias, reports and travel brochures. In these genres, the user is traditionally the recipient of the text and the genres serve the interests of the user. The second class could be seen as the operative text type, which includes genres such as advertisements, propaganda texts and sermons. In these genres, it is more the writers who use texts to advance their interests. The third class could be seen as the expressive text type, which includes plays and poems, for example. Reiss categorizes user instructions as informative text types, as does Byrne (2010: 11), who characterizes technical translation as a communicative service. However, user instructions can also be considered a combination of the informative and the operative functions.

The inclusion of encyclopaedias in Reiss's examples of the informative text type produced for passive recipients is to a present-day user outdated, if we consider Wikipedia, for example. The innovations of Web 2.0 have led to many new modes of activity, where the roles of producers and consumers are mixed. In translation, this has manifested itself in what Saverio Perrino (2009: 62–63) calls **User-Generated Translation (UGT)**. The term implies collaboration between users, whether amateurs or experts; it suggests ways of harnessing Web 2.0 services and tools to create online content in different languages. According to Perrino (ibid.), user-generated translation includes professional translation networks, translation wikis, user-generated dictionaries, online subtitling practices and volunteer website localization. Within the model of user-*centered* translation introduced in this book, however, the focus is on providing professional translators with tools to enhance usability and user experience. This is not to say that those tools could not be applied to user-generated translation, but a full discussion of UGT would require a book of its own.

3.3 The idea of use in the context of literary translation

It is easy to recognize that usability and the user are useful concepts when investigating instructive technical texts whose purpose is to indicate to the reader how to act. The usability of user instructions can, of course, be studied whether the instructions are translated or not: both the original text and the translation have a user who attempts to perform tasks with the help of the text. In that sense usability is an equally productive concept in translation studies and in technical communication. A more significant question, however, is whether the usefulness of these concepts is limited to instructive texts. Byrne (2010), for example, limits his book with these criteria: the usability perspective is only applied to technical translation.

Is this exclusion of other genres justified? How about audiovisual translation? Do we *use* subtitles as a facilitator of the viewing of a foreign-language program?

A similar question could also be posed with respect to administrative texts: we might not automatically consider their reader a user, either by role or by fundamental position, but many administrative texts, such as benefit-claim forms or letters from official institutions, are a means of using public services (cf. Alanen 2008, where the hospital as a whole is thought of as a user interface). Perhaps, then, we should approach this question through the medium. Is the reader of a website always a user, regardless of the content of the website? This question is easy to answer in the affirmative, as usability research is linked especially with human–computer interaction. On the other hand, the medium cannot be the only deciding factor, because it is possible to test the usability of user instructions even if they are printed on paper. In this case, the genre is the deciding factor.

Usability thinking originates in the world of technology, in an atmosphere emphasizing efficiency, productivity and experiences of using machines and appliances. In translation studies, on the other hand, most prominent attention has been given to literary translation, which appears to represent an entirely different world. It is therefore worthwhile to give some thought to what – if anything – usability and user-centered thinking might contribute to literary translation in particular. Do we *use* literary works and their translations? Can an aesthetic experience be thought of as a user experience (see Section 2.5)? If we want to, we can certainly take the following approach. The theater uses translated plays as one part of its entire drama product, whose purpose is to offer experiences and entertainment for viewers and produce financial profits for the theater. A teacher may use (translated or original) literature to expand the students' worldview, to bring variety to the lesson or to enhance the students' knowledge of their mother tongue and of literature. Parents may read children's books (which are often translated) aloud to their children to calm them to sleep and to enhance their language learning (for more on translating children's literature, see Oittinen 2000). In all these cases, even a literary text can be thought to exist within a specified context of use. As such, it has instrumental value, and the usability characteristics of this instrument can therefore be investigated within this context.

All of these somewhat arbitrarily chosen examples take a form where the purposeful *user* of literary texts is not the recipient but a mediating actor (the theater institution, the teacher/school, parents). In the translation process, this kind of an actor could be defined as a **patron** (Lefevere 1992): an actor who enables translation by supporting it through donating either cultural capital or financial resources. It is, however, possible to imagine situations where it is the reader who uses a literary text in an instrumental manner, such as in order to enjoy beautiful verbal expressions, in order to experience suspense or to relax. A literary translation can also be seen as an instrument of understanding a story which would have been inaccessible in the original language. Furthermore, the current commercial publishing business supports the portrayal of literary works and their translations as products (see, e.g. Gouadec 2010: 378).

However, it must also be immediately emphasized that from the point of view of literary experts and scholars, this kind of instrumental thinking is controversial, to put the matter mildly. Similarly, translation studies would question the view of a literary translation as an instrumental, supportive text without artistic value in itself. On the other hand, if we look at the usability of literature and the aesthetic experiences related to literature, we can find ways to emphasize the psychological dimensions of usability, the perspective of user motivation and the significance of emotional reactions (on affectivity, see Koskinen, K. 2012). In that sense, looking at usability and literary translation can help us advance our understanding of user experience and translation. According to Jokela (2010: 19), the ISO standard for usability, which we introduced in Chapter 2, has been criticized for its rather narrow perspective which focuses on the benefits gained from use. Because of this limitation, it is difficult to apply the standard to the usability of, for example, entertainment applications. Therefore, Jokela proposes that the definition should be expanded by including the dimension of **enjoyability**. In Nielsen's well-known classification (see Figure 2.1 in Chapter 2), a similar role is occupied by **satisfaction**. One of the ways to tackle the problems related to the standard is to use the concept of user experience that was discussed in Section 2.5.

To summarize the thinking in this section, we can say that it is worthwhile to consider use and usability even in genres that, at the outset, do not seem to fit the framework of usability. As we saw above, the idea of use can be applied quite successfully to different genres, even literature, but the extent and nature of the application varies. Thus, we can think of the use of genres as a continuum.

3.4 Categorizing users

Different genres have different links to the concept of usability. Similarly, the users of texts can be classified into different categories according to their characteristics and interests. Furthermore, just as different genres are treated differently in translation, reaching different user categories requires different translation strategies and approaches. User-centered translation puts particular emphasis on accounting for the differences between user categories and making decisions about the translation accordingly. Several practical tools can be used as an aid in producing information about real users, and we will introduce them in detail later in the book (Chapters 7 and 8). In this section, however, we will discuss some ways of categorizing users and making sense of the different types of users a translation might have. Technical communication, again, provides useful models, which can be applied to user-centered translation.

JoAnn Hackos's (2002) categorization of user levels is one useful example of understanding different types of users. In Hackos's (2002: 271) model, users of information are divided into what she calls "four stages of use": **novice, advanced beginner, competent performer** and **expert performer**. Each stage requires different amounts of information and different styles of presenting it. In Hackos's categorization (ibid.: 272), **novices** are those users who "are completely focused on solving their problems" and "want to get started quickly and focus on performing tasks and finding answers to their questions". In other words, novices are not familiar with the subject matter and want the documentation to help them perform their tasks as easily as possible. **Advanced beginners,** on the other hand, "have gotten over the fear of using a new product or making a new decision", but "still don't want to spend time learning". According to Hackos (ibid.: 272), most users never advance beyond the level of advanced beginner. In terms of translation, this could mean that "average" readers of translations correspond to the level of novice or advanced beginner and expect a text that is easy to read and feels familiar. The third stage, **competent performer**, describes users who "are far enough along in their task-based doing that they begin to get curious about how the product really works" and "are willing to spend more time learning, but only for those products that are important to them" (ibid.: 272). Adapted to the context of translation, this could mean users who are somewhat familiar with the genre or the source culture and are therefore, for example, comfortable with foreignizing translation strategies or expect some specialized terminology. Finally, **expert performers** "are willing to invest considerable time and energy learning all there is to know about a product or subject" and "want all the connections to all the information that is available" (ibid.: 272). Thus, expert performers in the case of translations are the most specialized and learned users of a text, or perhaps those who are deeply interested in the source culture and who are therefore willing to put effort into understanding all details and nuances of the text, even if those details and nuances might have a considerably foreignizing effect.

In the context of translations, Hackos's user levels can be understood in two distinct ways: either with regard to the users' linguistic, cultural and textual competence (e.g. their knowledge of and interest in the source culture), or as describing the users' knowledge of the subject matter. Both are important considerations in user-centered translation. For example, in subtitling it can be relevant to discover whether viewers understand the source language that is available alongside the translation, usually through a different channel, namely the auditory channel. Viewers who understand at least some of the source language can be considered either competent or expert performers in a linguistic sense, and they will benefit from subtitling strategies which remain as close as reasonably possible to the original message, because discrepancies between the two messages might cause confusion or suspicion. In the case of technical or legislative documents, on the other hand, the translator must consider the expected readers' knowledge of the topic at hand.

Hackos (2002: 273) also suggests that on a website, for example, users can be provided with different kinds of content of which the users themselves can select what they feel is appropriate for their own level. Expert users can choose to click through to more advanced explanations, while novices might settle for the basics. Here we come to an emerging paradigm in computer science – namely, **content personalization**: users are classified and content is targeted according to the classifications (Padilla 2006: n.p.). Ideally, users are able to make more decisions about content that they want to access regularly (Hackos 2002: 280), but although personalization sounds promising, defining relevant user characteristics and targeting content to meet their specific needs is far from simple (Padilla 2006: n.p.).

Considering this from the viewpoint of translation, websites should, of course, also enable users to select the language that they want (Hackos 2002: 280), and we can go even further: it might be possible to offer additional background information on the source text for those who are interested, or to produce both an abridged version for novice readers and a full translation for interested experts. In fact, it is easy to find examples of translations, and literary translations in particular, where something similar has occurred, even if the alternative versions have not been produced simultaneously. For example, the difference between academic and literary translations of classic texts has received continuous attention. Maria Tymoczko (1999: 122) discusses these two traditions of translating early Irish literature into English, stating that literary translations are "eminently readable [. . .] but departing radically from the textual material, formal properties, and linguistic structures of the Irish sources", whereas scholarly translations "are close textual transpositions verging on nearly unreadable gloss translations". In other words, literary translations could be seen as translations aimed at a novice or advanced beginner audience who read the texts for pleasure, and scholarly translations are meant for professional use by expert performers in the field. The different types of translations thus serve different purposes of use and are directed at a different audience segment.

Another framework from the field of technical communication which is useful in the context of translation is Thomas N. Huckin's and Leslie A. Olsen's audience categorization. Huckin and Olsen (1991: 59) describe the variety inherent in real-world audiences in a way that is very fitting for user-centered translation, stating that

> these audiences are likely to consist of *a variety of readers;* instead of a single audience for a single communication, you may well have *multiple audiences* for that one communication. These readers will probably know less about the subject than you do, which means you'll have to *explain* things to them. They may differ in background knowledge, in needs and purposes, and in reading conditions. Thus, they may differ in their *reading strategies*, some reading only one part of the document, others skipping from section to section, still others studying every word.
>
> (Italics in the original)

The same is often true for translation. Texts are typically translated for a large and varied audience, which consists of individuals with differing background knowledge, differing linguistic abilities, and differing ways of reading texts and using them for their own purposes. Therefore, user categorization is needed to navigate these multiple audiences and it serves as a reminder of the audiences' inherent multiplicity.

Huckin and Olsen's (1991: 60–66) framework offers suggestions on writing strategies for different target groups: **managerial audiences, nonspecialist audiences, peer audiences, international audiences** and **mixed audiences**. According to Huckin and Olsen (ibid.: 60–61), individuals in a **managerial** position are an important audience in technical communication, but they have little time for reading and reflection. Therefore, information must be made easily and quickly accessible for this audience. **Nonspecialist audiences** (ibid.: 61–62), on the other hand, require a great deal of explanation, as well as simplification of technical terms, conventional ways of presenting information, and other means of making a message accessible to those who are not experts in the subject matter. In contrast to nonspecialists, **peer audiences** (ibid.: 62–63) know the subject matter as well as the writer, which means that the writer can use specialist vocabulary and does not have to explain commonly known concepts. Each of these three audience types can be relevant in a translation project: the readers can be in a position where they only want the main gist of a text to be provided, they may be unfamiliar with the subject matter, or they may be the writer's or translator's peers.

Huckin and Olsen's (1991: 63–64) fourth audience type, **international audience**, is, of course, also very relevant in translation, which is largely an international activity. For international audiences, Huckin and Olsen recommend that the text should not be structurally very complicated and that idiomatic vocabulary should be avoided. In essence, this recommendation advocates for the use of an international language variant such as International English. For example, in technical communication, guidelines have been produced for writing English-language technical documentation for an international audience (see www.tekom.de/upload/alg/INTECOM_Guidelines.pdf). Translations can also be directed at an international audience where some readers are not native speakers of the language of the translation, such as English, and in those cases using an international version of English can be a useful strategy. In addition, it is helpful in any kind of translation to keep in mind the fact that source-language idioms and culture-bound elements are not necessarily accessible to target-language audiences and might therefore need some modification in translation. In that sense, all translation audiences are international audiences and the international aspect is a fundamental factor all translators must work with.

Although all of Huckin and Olsen's categories can be usefully applied to user-centered translation, what is particularly interesting is their final category of **mixed audiences** (Huckin and Olsen 1991: 64), which is an audience consisting of representatives from all or some of the previous categories. Huckin and Olsen (ibid.: 65) suggest that a mixed audience is best served by layering a document "so that different sections are aimed at different audiences" or democratizing the writing "so that all audiences can understand all parts of it". They (ibid.: 65) explain that, to democratize a document, "[y]ou aim each part of the document at its most important audience, but you add little touches that make the parts accessible to other audiences as well". This is good advice in translation, as the audiences of translations can easily be mixed simply due to the cultural differences which the foreign origin of a text invites into the communicative situation. For example, even though a text might be aimed exclusively at nonspecialists, the nonspecialist group might still be heterogeneous, because it could include both those nonspecialists who do not know either the source culture or the topic very well, and those who are familiar with the source culture but not with the subject matter of the text. In such cases, democratizing and layering which take the differences in cultural knowledge into account may be useful translation strategies. Furthermore, the same text might appear in a number of different contexts (e.g. website and printed material) or be later adapted for a different use, and strategies which democratize and layer the text would make this kind of reuse easier.

3.5 Users and usability in translation studies

User-centered translation is a new term, but the idea of taking users and readers into account is not a novelty in translation studies. Rather, one can argue that reader-orientedness is one of the recurrent themes, or memes, in discussions about translation. In the following sections we will examine some well-known translation theories from the point of view of user-centeredness.

3.5.1 Functional approaches versus usability

Many theories are based on the idea that translation is first and foremost a communicative act: the source language writer or speaker has a message to deliver, and he or she needs the translator's or interpreter's help in transmitting it to a target language audience (see, e.g. Hatim and Mason 1997). In this model, the translator decodes the message and transcodes it into language B, thus becoming the sender of this recoded message (see, e.g. Nida 1964: 146). These kinds of communication models date from the 1960s, and they reflect the thinking of the time (e.g. the influence of Shannon and Weaver 1949), but similar lines of thought can be found repeatedly in translation theories. In these models translators function as mediators who have two tasks: to clarify what the message consists of, and who the recipients are and how they should be approached. In other words, the translator's communicative function includes aspects of user-centeredness. In practice, however, many communication-oriented translation theorists such as Basil Hatim and Ian Mason (1997) mainly emphasize the need to recognize and to convey the explicit and implicit meanings of the source text, and the focus is on the translator's discursive skills both as a recipient and a sender (see also Hatim and Mason 1990). Less attention, in practical terms, is paid to the potential independent communicative functions of the translation, or to getting to know the actual recipients of the translated message. In other words, although communicative theories raise important points regarding reception, concrete discussions of how to analyze or categorize the recipients are fairly rare in them (for an exception, see the discussion of audience design in Section 5.2).

As we stated in the Introduction, the concept of user, although not unknown, is not commonly used in translation studies literature. In contrast, Hatim and Mason (1997) use this concept extensively. In their usage, the term *users* refers to both the producer of the text (who uses it for a particular purpose), the translators (whose ways of using the translations are not discussed) and the recipients (who use the text for their own purposes). Rather than the end user, Hatim and Mason focus on the producer. Their approach, in other words, is diagonally opposed to the one we adopt in this book. Still, Hatim and Mason's viewpoint is a useful reminder that usability research in fields such as technical communication was first introduced because the producers needed to achieve their own goals (financial or otherwise) with the help of maximally usable products and texts. It would be naive to assume that user-centeredness and usability originate from the users themselves; users rarely sit in the driver's seat in designing and launching new products.

Communication aspects are also brought to the forefront in functional translation theories, where the focus shifts from the source text to the purpose of the translation. In functional theories, the guiding principle of the translator's work is the *function* and *task* of the translation, known by its Greek name, *skopos*[4] (Vermeer 1996). In addition to the two tasks described in the above section – mediating the message and finding out who the target readers are – the translator's third, and most important, task is to determine the *goal* of the translation. Both the analysis of the source text and the analysis of the target audience are subordinate to this overarching aim; the core question is what the task of the translation is, what it is going to be *used* for. **Skopos theory** is indeed a theory of *action*, and the translation is seen as one potential outcome of **translatorial action** (parallel to, e.g. paraphrase, summary or an entirely new text, or even nontranslation) (Vermeer 1989). Recipients, target audience or readers are thus part of the goal of the action. Hans J. Vermeer (1996: 6) summarizes this as follows:

> Functional approach means: whenever someone – the so-called "commissioner" (*Auftraggeber*) – "commissions" or "orders" (*in Auftrag geben*) a translation, he wants it for a particular purpose. The translation is meant to serve its intended purpose in the target-culture as well as possible, including, naturally, the intended recipients ("addressees"). What will be considered the best possible translation is determined by the circumstances actually prevailing at the moment of translating.

More than reception, skopos theory emphasizes **specification**. The specification ideally informs translators of the intended skopos and thus allows them to base their decisions accordingly (Vermeer 1989: 182–187; cf. p. 180). Target recipients are also part of the specification, but although they are acknowledged, they are not centrally involved; it is more a shared task of the translator and the client to work out the purpose of the translation and decide how it is best served (Vermeer 1996: 7). Still, functional translation theories provide support for user-centeredness as they give translators explicit permission, or even a requirement, to deviate from the source text contents and form if necessary (e.g. Reiss and Vermeer 1986: 65).

The question of deviation is closely related to a longstanding dispute in translation practice and theory: should translations be fluent, natural-sounding and easily understandable, or should they rather bend and stretch the resources of the target language and introduce readers to foreign elements? This binary discussion is widely known as the debate over **domesticating** and **foreignizing** translation strategies. A domesticating translation strategy immediately appears very user-oriented; it is based on using familiar structures, avoiding foreign elements and avoiding the pitfalls of culture bumps. The foreignizing strategy, in contrast, seems diametrically opposed to user-orientation. According to a well-known adage that originates in Friedrich Schleiermacher's famous essay (1813/1977), it is not the task of the translator to move the author to the reader but to take the reader to the author. In other words, the reader needs to make the effort; it is not for the translator to make the translation easy to read or to digest.[5]

The best-known proponent of foreignizing translation in modern translation studies has been Lawrence Venuti (see, e.g. 1998), who has criticized the dominant fluent translation strategy in Anglo-American literary translations. According to Venuti, this strategy is tantamount to arrogant and ethnocentric violence, and he has urged translators to oppose this trend by choosing more challenging texts to be translated and by translating these in ways that force the readers to confront their foreignness. However, it would be a simplification to interpret Venuti's position as diagonally opposed to user-friendliness or as oriented towards the source text and culture. One can argue that his approach – one applied mainly to literary translation – rather focuses on the target readers. He states that "to translate is to invent for the source text new readers" and that the domesticating effect fundamental to all translation effectively decontextualizes the translation (Venuti 2013: 25, 35). Thus, to best serve these new readerships, the translation needs to acknowledge and to set to motion its domestic inscriptions and its target-culture remainders (ibid.: 13–16).

Fluent translation strategies are, according to Venuti, deceptively easy, but they deprive the reader of a possibility of fully comprehending the foreign text. In other words, Venuti (2013: 74) argues that easy readability obstructs deeper comprehensibility (cf. Section 4.3), and he wants to "turn the reader into a translator" by cultivating plurilingual strategies that alert the reader to the incommensurability of languages. Relating this approach to learnability (see Chapter 2), we notice that there are different layers to learnability. While in case of instructive texts, it may be most relevant to learn to operate on the basis of the contents of the text, Venuti has more global political and ideological aspirations in his translations. The reader is to learn new ways of thinking and the translation is to open up new interpretative avenues: "The translation that sets going an event introduces a linguistic and cultural difference in the institution, initiating new ways of thinking inspired by an interpretation of the source text" (Venuti 2013: 4, 157).

3.5.2 *Eugene A. Nida: pioneer of user-centeredness*

Venuti's (2013: 113) fundamental point is that the translation can never produce a reading experience similar to the one produced by the source text. It is interesting to contrast his views with those of Eugene A. Nida, Bible translator and pioneer of modern translation studies, whose concept of **dynamic equivalence** (that is, using various adaptive strategies to produce the same experience) is among the first topics to come to mind in thinking about the connections between usability and translation. Read through the lenses of recent usability research,

Nida's key books from the 1960s, *Toward a Science of Translating* (1964) in particular, turn out to even far richer than just the idea of dynamic equivalence. Nida's early thoughts and pragmatic advice for translators correlate with usability discussions to an amazingly large extent. In his books, one can find seeds of usability testing and translators' heuristics (see Section 6.3) as well as of researching the cognitive and psychological aspects of user-centeredness. A core element of Nida's work, and the notion underlying the idea of dynamic equivalence, is the culture-bound nature of reception. This is directly linked to more recent discussions of cultural awareness in usability (see Section 2.3). It is thus only appropriate that we devote ample space for a discussion of Nida's theoretical ideas and, in particular, of the contact point between them and thinking on usability.

Above, we discussed some communicative translation theories. Similarly, Nida's (1964: 43) translation philosophy is based on communication and its intentionality. In line with prevalent communication theories of that time, Nida (1964: 51, 147) emphasizes that communication is always tied to its cultural and social context. That context also includes aspects such as the participants' relation to the code (such as the language of the message, and in the case of translation, the change of that language) as well as to one another and to the community where the communication is taking place. Language is essentially a functional code that is used for a particular purpose (cf. skopos theory, above), and it thus needs to be observed primarily from a dynamic point of view. According to Nida (ibid.: 120), this is particularly important for translators, since the production of equivalent messages is not merely a process of matching the parts of utterances but also of reproducing the total dynamic character of communication. Nida emphasizes that in a communicative situation the message binds together the sender and the receiver, and they are both active participants in that situation. In contrast to some other communicative translation theories, in Nida's model (ibid.: 145) translators are also accorded an active role in this dynamic process.

From the viewpoint of user-centered translation, where **iterativity** is considered a crucially important element, it is interesting to find that **feedback** is an essential element of Nida's interactive communication model. On one hand, feedback refers to the immediate monitoring of responses produced by speakers/writers themselves during the communication process; on the other hand, feedback is provided by the recipient both during the communicative situation (facial expressions, gestures, nodding, etc.) and afterwards (Nida 1964: 120). Another useful concept is **noise**. Nida (ibid.: 121–122) states that communication situations are always hampered by noise – that is, unwanted disturbances affecting understandability. Noise can be caused by the communication channel (e.g. stains on the print), or the environment (e.g. several competing sources of information). Of particular interest to translation is **semantic noise**. For example, errors in punctuation or grammar, difficult vocabulary, or sloppy structuring can function as noise, obstructing the message. Noise can also be psychological: fatigue, pain or negative attitudes can be a source of noise for the sender and the receiver alike (on cognitive aspects of usability see, e.g. Preece *et al.* 1994).

A particularly interesting aspect of Nida's model concerns **feedforward**, a kind of anticipatory and preventive feedback in which the sender anticipates certain objections and makes adjustments in advance to avoid criticism. Nida (1964: 121) emphasizes that all good speakers and writers make these adjustments to meet the needs of their audience, and describes such "two-directional feedback" as "continuous, reciprocal, and mutually re-enforcing". Anticipatory feedback is also linked to the necessity of adjusting the message according to the estimated decoding abilities of the receivers. Noise levels need to be controlled; complex structures, opaque expressions and illogical or confusing terminology may hamper communication. On the other hand, too dense a style with no redundancy may also be difficult to digest.

When linguistic and cultural boundaries are crossed, adjustments often need to be more extensive. If the target audience's existing knowledge on the subject matter is less than that of the source audience, or if there is reason to believe that they lack the implicit cultural presuppositions encoded in the source text, one can describe their channel for receiving the message as narrower than that of the source audience. Without alterations, the message cannot pass through it and the translator needs to adjust the message so that it fits in the receivers' channel (Nida 1964: 131). (Another option, of course, is to widen the receivers' channel via education and training, but translators rarely have that option.) On the other hand, too extensive explanations and over-zealous simplification may also be risky, because the receiver may find the result boring; a slim but extremely long message is not an optimal solution either, and the entire message is then in danger of turning into noise (ibid.: 142). In principle, we are dealing, in other words, with the same premise that we discussed earlier in this chapter: the designer needs to make sure that the conceptual model that is being used matches that of its users.

The dynamic nature of communication presupposes that the active role of the recipients is taken into account. That is why formal equivalence, focusing on preserving the form and content of the message, is rarely a sufficient translation strategy. Instead of formal correspondences between the source and target text, Nida (1964: 159) argues for "equivalent effect"; the aim is to reproduce a dynamic relation between the target readers and target text that is similar to the one between the source readers and source text. This is what dynamic equivalence is about.

Most translations are located somewhere between extreme formal equivalence and extreme dynamic equivalence. Nida himself does not deny the usefulness of formal equivalence in some translation contexts, but he makes it clear which strategy he favours. Nida (1964: 166) describes dynamic equivalence as "the closest natural equivalent to the source-language message". The three words – *closest*, *natural* and *equivalent* – delimit and define the agency of the translator in producing the target text. *Equivalent* makes it clear that we are dealing with translations, not a writing process in the target language, and the translation needs to reflect the aims and purposes of the source text (ibid.: 166). The requirement of *naturalness* shifts the balance away from the source and towards the target language, target culture and the target readers. A natural translation suits both the target language and target culture in general and the particular communicative situation, and it is perceived as natural by the target audience (ibid.: 167). Natural-ness covers linguistic structures and vocabulary as well as genre features and cultural conventions. It is thus a central component of the definition of dynamic equivalence. Naturalness and fluency are, however, delimited by the third keyword, *closest*. The aim is to keep as close to the linguistic expression and semantic content of the source text as possible, as long as naturalness does not suffer too badly. Dynamic equivalence is also controlled by cultural expectations of fidelity as well as the weight of tradition, which is particularly felt in Bible translation (ibid.: 176, 179). The translator is also constrained by the view that a dynamically equivalent translation can make aspects that remain implicit in the source text explicit in the translation, but entirely new explanatory material is not encouraged (Nida and Taber 1974: 111).

Nida's approach has often been considered to be an extremely domesticating one, and it has been thought that dynamic equivalence presupposes that lambs are to be translated as seal pups in an Inuit version of the Bible, and that palm tree sprigs need to be transformed into fir branches in a Finnish version (cf. Nida and Taber 1974: 111). However, Nida (1964: 168) actually emphasizes that all foreignness cannot and need not be removed, and that conveying foreign cultural elements is often much less problematic than is commonly assumed; people do understand that other cultures may have customs that are different from their own. Instead, the impression of naturalness is challenged by those features that are considered disgusting or offensive, or those that arouse emotions that are entirely different from the ones that are sought after (ibid.: 168–169). In other words, we return to the concepts of cultural usability, social acceptability and user experience (see Chapter 2). Nida (ibid.: 42–43) also emphasizes the bodily "intraorganismic" aspects of meaning. According to him (ibid.: 171), these are the ones that often suffer most in the process of translation because their emotive connotations are often difficult to convey in another language and culture. Nida's thinking is nicely aligned with the current emphasis on user experience and the understanding that psychological issues are elemental to usability and that *enjoyability* should be seen as a factor of usability.

Dynamic equivalence aims at a translation that is easy to understand (in the intended manner) for the recipient. According to Nida (1964: 175), this is equal to a "high degree of decodability". Efficiency of translation, its success, is judged by "maximal reception for the minimum effort of decoding" (ibid.: 182). But how can this success be measured? Nida (ibid.: 182) lists a set of criteria. First, decoding work is reduced by redundancy, and redundancy is thus a sign of a successful translation. However, too much redundancy carries the risk of noise, but because of the cultural and linguistic barriers, translations are more likely to contain too little redundancy than too much. Elsewhere, Nida and Taber (1974: 99) point out that translators may find it difficult to put themselves in the readers' position and that they have a tendency to translate above their readers' heads. In other words, translators' expertise may turn into a disadvantage.

The second criterion is comprehension of the original intent. The judgment needs to be based on whether the translation follows formal equivalence or dynamic equivalence. In the case of a dynamically equivalent translation, it is not relevant to measure its similarity to the source text but the extent to which the intent can be interpreted and understood in the target context (Nida 1964: 182). This is linked to the third criterion: equivalence of response (ibid.: 183). The reader of a formally equivalent translation is expected to understand the reactions of the source text reader; the dynamically equivalent translation is supposed to incur similar reactions in the target readers.

In addition to assessing a finished translation, and in more detail, Nida introduces a number of methods to measure the success of the translation during the translation process (1964: 140–141; Nida and Taber 1974: 168–173). Quantitative methods for analyzing the frequencies of particular linguistic features were already available at that time, but Nida is rather cautious about their usability. Instead, he proposes a number of pragmatic methods that the translators themselves can utilize. One such method is the **cloze test**: every fifth or tenth word of a text is removed, and the readers are asked to fill these slots with words they consider most appropriate (Nida 1964: 140). This test, and the relative ease of completion by the participants can be seen to signal comprehensibility, predictability and coherence (see also Puurtinen 1995).

Nida (1964: 140–141) is concerned with the risk of communicative overload, and he discusses reading out loud as a method for assessing this. It is less objective than a cloze test, but it is often easier to organize. Hesitations, corrections and mistakes made by the test readers can reveal areas of excessive cognitive load. One can also ask the test readers to read the text or listen to someone else read the text and then repeat what it was about. If repetition repeatedly proves inadequate, it may well be that the cognitive load is too high for the target audience. It is also possible to ask for readers' comments of different translation variants before making the final decision (Nida and Taber 1974: 171). In lengthy translation projects (and Bible translations often are lengthy) the best method of eliciting feedback may well be to publish parts of the text and subject them to public criticism (ibid. 1974: 172). For contemporary translators, social media offers new opportunities for subjecting text sections and translation solutions to reader evaluation before making final decisions.

Usability research is based on a solid culture of testing that may at first glance appear as foreign to mainstream translation studies. However, Nida's classic book from the 1960s contains inspiration for both computerized analysis of texts and usability research methods. Some of these methods are actually quite similar to those used in reception studies within translation studies (see Chapter 8). Nida worked on Bible translation throughout his extensive career. However, he repeatedly emphasizes that although he takes his examples from the field of Bible translation, his pragmatic ideas are meant to be applicable to all text genres. Nida's approach to Bible translation also urges a reconsideration of the role of usability in literary translation. If we can conceive of sacred texts as *utility texts* that have some particular modes of use (such as reading out loud) that affect their translation strategies, and particular purposes (such as converting, awakening spirituality) that also have a bearing on the translator's solutions, one can ask whether we should exclude any genres entirely from usability viewpoints (cf. Byrne 2010). Many of today's client relationships and translation projects are extensive, multilingual and lengthy, and the models proposed by Nida (see, e.g. 1964: 246, 249), as well as his emphasis on teamwork (ibid.: 239) seem quite relevant. The last chapter of *Toward a Science of Translating* deals with machine translation, but it is self-evident that in 1964 Nida could not foresee the contemporary setting of translation memory tools, digital information mining or the role of social media in translating and revising. However, these recent developments are in no way contradictory to Nida's basic ideas. The heritage of Eugene A. Nida, as well as of various other translation theories, provide a solid foundation for our explorations of usability research and a rich soil in which to plant our ideas of user-centered translation.

In this chapter, we have suggested the possibility of using the term *user* to refer to the reader of a translation. We have also discussed different genres and the ways in which the idea of use might apply to them, and we introduced some ways of categorizing users themselves into different groups, and of using this categorization as an aid in user-centered translation. It should be a routine part of a user-centered translation process to outline the different use expectations concerning different genres, and especially to analyze the expected users of translated texts. The basic elements for categorizing users introduced above are a first step towards a user-centered understanding of a translation's users. We will offer more detailed, practical methods for user profiling in Chapters 5–7.

At the end of this chapter we also revisited some central theories of translation to identify points of contact between usability thinking and the history of translation studies. We found skopos-theoretical approaches particularly relevant for UCT. Different functional approaches place a different emphasis on the recipient, but they all share a view that the translation, when needed, will be adapted according to the interpretative context of the recipient. Still, it is quite remarkable how few concrete and pragmatic methods for identifying and concretizing the recipients or target audience these theories offer. We paid particular attention to Eugene A. Nida, who we perceive as an early pioneer of user-centeredness in translation theory and practice. His extremely target-oriented translation method allows translators to focus on their future readers not only mentally but also through various empirical methods similar to the ones that will be discussed in Chapters 5–9 of this book.

Assignments

1   Give examples of some genres you encounter and/or texts you have translated: is it meaningful to see the recipient of these genres as a user? Why/why not?

2   Find a product that contains some kind of translated material. Discuss the use of this product from the perspective of activity and passivity.

3   Technical communication could be criticized for having been too keen to see the reader merely in the role of the user, without considering the possibility that the relationship between the writer and the user-reader could be interactive and dialogic. What kind of a user are you and what kind of a user would you like to be?

4   Choose a website to be translated and localized. Use Huckin and Olsen's audience framework to analyze the target audience of the translation.

5   Choose a translation studies-related book or article. Consider how the text relates to the ideas of usability. Write a short report based on your findings. (See, for example, our discussion of Nida in Section 3.5.2.)

6   Use a machine translation system to translate a Wikipedia article into your A language. Analyze the results from the point of view of noise: what kinds of noise can one observe in the text and how could this be reduced by editing the translation? (When available, you can also compare the machine translation to the existing entry in the same language. Does it contain noise, and if yes, is it similar or different from the noise detected in the MT version?)

Notes

1   This way of thinking is similar to the concept of the implied reader familiar from literary studies (see Section 5.1.1).

2   For a more detailed discussion on the definition of a user interface, see Byrne 2010: 151–152. He notes, for example, that user instructions can be considered an extension of the traditional human–machine interface.

3   Uses and gratifications research can be defined as "A functionalist approach to the mass media framed in terms of people's motivations and needs – concerned, in other words, with why people use the media rather than with media effects on people" (Chandler and Munday 2011: s.v. uses and gratifications).

4   Vermeer (1996: 4) gives the following English translations: *purpose, aim, goal, finality, objective, intention.* They all seem to indicate a focus on the sender/author/commissioner of the translation rather than on its end user.

5   It is common to see foreignizing and domesticating translation strategies as two mutually exclusive categories but in reality, translations fall rarely, if ever, squarely into one category or the other. They are rather located somewhere along a line of more or less domesticated or foreignized strategies. Further, they may exhibit foreignizing tendencies in one aspect but domesticating aspirations in another (see Paloposki 2011).

4 Textual elements of usability

Key points in this chapter:

- **Legibility, readability, comprehensibility** and **accessibility** are fundamental concepts defining the usability of texts.

- The **legibility** of a text means that the text is visible, and that the characters, words and lines are discernible and the text decipherable.

- The **readability** of a text is affected by stylistic factors such as word choice, argumentation structure, the rhythm of the text, smooth transitions between text parts, active versus passive voice and reader-orientation.

- **Comprehensibility** refers to how well a text fulfils its communicative function – that is, how well readers understand the text.

- Explicitation and other pragmatic adaptations are translation strategies that can be used to increase comprehensibility.

- **Accessibility** refers to efforts making products and services available to all people, regardless of their individual abilities or backgrounds.

As we learned in the previous chapter, it is not necessary to make a clear-cut division between readers and users. Rather, these two aspects are emphasized differently in different genres and contexts. However, when we are dealing with the usability of products that are text-based, the user is obviously always also a reader. And it follows that concepts such as readability or comprehensibility are closely related to the usability of texts.

In this chapter we will look briefly at some central concepts to do with the reading process: 1) legibility, 2) readability, and 3) comprehensibility (or under-standability). These terms are sometimes used interchangeably and definitions for all of them vary. Here we present a tripartite classification that aims to avoid conflating the different dimensions of text characteristics and ease of reading. We start by defining the technical and visual aspects of reading as **legibility**. Moving on to aspects of textual organization such as sentence length and paragraph division we discuss various possibilities of measuring the **readability** of a text. Readability, defined in this manner, is thus a quality of the text, and many aspects of it are measurable and quantifiable. **Comprehensibility** and **understandability**, which we take to be synonyms, are more directly linked to the reader, as they depend not only on the organization of content and the provision of enough scaffolding for the reader but also, and significantly, on the reader's willingness and ability to follow the text. This third dimension can also be considered the highest, as both legibility and readability aim to support comprehensibility. These three dimensions are intertwined in the reading process: we may lose our motivation if the text is too difficult to decipher, and a nicely structured text makes previously unfamiliar content easier to understand. Finally, we end this chapter with a discussion of how texts and translations can support **accessibility**, which is an overarching concept encompassing all efforts towards making texts available to all readers.

4.1 Legibility

A minimum requirement for any written text to be readable is that it should be visually legible – that is, that it can be seen, and that the characters, words and lines be discernible and the text decipherable. Legibility concerns typographic issues such as font styles and sizes, line height and length, and the overall page design, as well as more technical aspects such as document formats, paper size and color, surface structures and ink qualities. It is linked to physiological and cognitive skills, as well as aesthetic preferences. These physiological aspects of reading have recently received a lot of interest in process studies, and fascinating insights into how we read have been revealed (see, e.g. Göpferich *et al.* 2008). These types of studies will help researchers to re-evaluate the optimal technical properties of texts (e.g. the timing of subtitles; see Perego 2012).

The visual and technical qualities of texts are sometimes considered to be beyond the control and responsibility of the translator. This line of thinking makes sense. Typography, graphic design and information design constitute professional fields of their own, and they require expert knowledge that translators rarely have and are rarely paid for. On the other hand, typography, for example, has a direct bearing on the products of translation, and translators can only benefit from having some understanding of its basic principles. Jürgen Schopp (2005) argues that since translations normally have a typographic format (i.e. they exist in text form), this visual form has to be taken into account, and the translator needs to have the professional skills to cooperate with other professionals in the team. Schopp's argument is that translators often lack the ability to assess and appreciate the visual nature of texts, and that translator training should include basic skills in typography and visual design. They are all the more important when producing translations in a source-culture setting rather than in the context of the target culture, because in these situations translators may often be better placed than other team members in assessing whether the layout and other visual elements include intercultural aspects that may affect legibility or text acceptability in unexpected ways. For example, Schopp (2005: 137–147) discusses the cultural associations linked with particular typefaces. He puts particular emphasis on the meanings of Fraktur for different users; outside Germany, it tends to be associated with general Germanness, but within Germany it is linked to extreme right-wing ideology. In translation, the use of typefaces that have a strong national connotation may need to be reconsidered (for more on typography see, e.g. Bringhurst 2002).

In an article on paratranslation – textual activities around and adjacent to actual translation – in children's literature, José Yuste Frías (2012: 120; see also Oittinen 2000: 102–107) discusses orthotypography as one example of paratranslational activity, emphasizing the need for translators to enhance their visual literacy: in children's picture books, for example, "the slightest typographical detail becomes a paratextual element that translators must read, interpret and paratranslate". This imperative does not only apply to picture books. We live in an increasingly visual world, and an understanding of fields such as information graphics and visual design can greatly help translators. On the other hand, texts have always had a material existence. In written text, the verbal cannot exist without the visual.

4.2 Readability

Whereas legibility can be defined as the visual and technical design of texts, readability can be summarized as the style of writing. Word choice, sentence length, argumentation structure, the rhythm of the text, smooth transitions between text parts, active versus passive voice, and reader-orientation all affect the readability of a text. Moreover, readability is conventionalized: we expect certain familiar text features and find them easy to read. Therefore, readability is also culturally determined, as particular conventions have developed in their distinctive ways in different cultural contexts. For example, the style expected and appreciated in administrative texts, newspaper articles, legal documents or academic texts has not traditionally been universal. However, in today's world, where English as a language dominates, its stylistic conventions are also becoming more and more contagious (Bennett 2013).

Readability issues are a wide area of study, and a number of both general and language-specific criteria and measurement systems for evaluating the readability of texts have been developed since the 1920s. Most of the traditional readability indexes are based on measuring sentence and/or word length. Other quantifiable elements include lexical density (the type/token ratio of words),[1] frequency of words and the number of propositional phrases (see Al-Khalifa and Al-Ajlan 2010). One widely known and frequently used method of readability assessment is the Flesch–Kincaid readability formula, which calculates the supposed readability of a text on the basis of its sentence and word length. The result of the formula is a grade level (of the American educational system), indicating to what level of education the difficulty of the text would correspond (Si and Callan 2001: 574). This allows simple pronouncements such as stating that newspaper articles, official documents, user instructions or any number of other texts are written at a certain grade level or "for" students on that grade. In addition to the Flesch–Kincaid formula, other similar calculations include the Fry Readability Formula, FORCAST and SMOG (Simple Measure of Gobbledygook).

The automated readability tests have a wide range of everyday, practical applications. The Microsoft Office software, for example, offers its users the possibility of testing readability with a simple automatic function based on the Flesch–Kincaid formula. In addition, readability formulas are used as an easy-to-understand definition of the difficulty level of a text in contexts such as education (see, e.g. http://elibrary.sd71.bc.ca/subject_resources/socials/ancient_egypt.htm) and healthcare (e.g. www.exitcare.com/easy-to-read-documents.html), where the aim is to inform the general public of readability. Readability formulas are thus an easy way of conceptualizing textual characteristics, allowing users to assess the difficulty levels of particular texts.

Obviously, mechanical calculations are just one way of measuring the readability of texts, and these indexes need to be used with caution. A favorable grading is no direct guarantee of readability, and even incoherent nonsense can be assessed as readable as long as it consists of short sentences and words with few syllables. A text consisting of short, simple sentences may be assessed as easy to read, but it can also be judged annoyingly monotonous and poor in cohesive linkages – that is, not very readable. Therefore, it would be a mistake to assume that a text that is highly readable according to these criteria would also automatically be extremely usable. As we discussed in Chapter 2, usability consists of many more complex factors, and several aspects of readability lend themselves less effortlessly to automated analysis. Cohesion, logical flow of text, termino-logical consistency versus variation and the use of metaphors are examples of text features of a more qualitative nature.

Readability indexes are to be handled with particular care when applied outside the language for which they have been originally designed. For example, Finnish is an agglutinative language with long words (one-syllable words are rather rare, and those with three to four syllables are quite common) and a tendency to create compound words. Syllable counts in Finnish thus need to be interpreted differently from those in English. Most of the best-known readability formulas have been developed for English and are therefore of limited usefulness in other languages. One example of a readability index developed for another language is the LIX index, which is based on Swedish. The LIX calculation is also based on sentence and word length ("LIX räknare" n.d.: n.p.).

Thus, these methods cannot be taken at face value, and they have been criticized for a product orientation that overlooks the role of the readers; mechanical calculations alone do not produce an exhaustive picture of the reading process. As Sharon O'Brien (2010: 144) states, readability formulas "tell us little about how much cognitive effort is involved in reading [texts], understanding them, and translating them". In order to understand how readers operate when reading texts, and to determine which elements attract their attention, experimental methods are also needed. One such method is **eyetracking**, or measuring and recording the reader's eye movements (see Section 7.3). Eyetracking studies on reading have provided information on how the eyes move, how pupils dilate and where eyes fixate during reading, thus explaining how reading happens physiologically. Eyetracking provides information on cognitive effort, as it can be presumed that longer fixation times and higher numbers of fixations on certain parts of text reflect more difficulty in processing those parts (ibid.: 146–147). Thus, eyetracking data can point out potential obstacles for readability.

Similar to readability tests, eyetracking data on reading is to some extent language-specific, and all findings cannot be applied across linguistic boundaries. Languages with different orthographies are particularly likely to result in different findings in eyetracking studies, and the information density of a language appears to affect the speed and concentration of eye movements (Schotter and Rayner 2012: 93–96). Therefore, to be reliable, each language would need its own readability studies, but even studies in other languages can provide some general impressions of how the reading process works, and this information can then be used to improve readability. Eyetracking data can offer a useful complement to the mechanical readability formulas and help in fine-tuning the readability aspects of texts.

Ultimately, what matters is not only the text's readability characteristics but also the readers' ability and willingness to read: technical reading skills, age, presuppositions, pre-existing knowledge and motivation. Readability is a function of text–human interaction,[2] and optimal readability is achieved by matching the text to its prospective readers. To tackle this interactive and complex nature of reading, various readability tests have also been designed to measure readability in terms of suitability to a particular audience. Reading out loud, cloze tests and text comprehension tests aim to match the text characteristics with those of a particular group of readers. Automated data-driven techniques have, however, some significant benefits over these more reader-oriented methods: there is no need for recruiting test users; a number of tests are freely available online (e.g. www.online-utility.org/english/readability_test_and_improve.jsp); the results are computed in a split second; and the results are given in unambiguous figures that allow for classification and comparison of texts. These benefits, together with an increased worry over accessibility and inclusion, are driving their use in various domains such as education, governance and healthcare, particularly in English-speaking countries (Al-Khalifa and Al-Ajlan 2010: 105). In spite of the inherent shortcomings of these techniques, they also have a place in the toolkit of user-centered translation because of their easy availability and applicability.

4.3 Comprehensibility

Readability is a textual matter, but ease of reading is also crucially related to the content and context of the text. We thus need to introduce yet another concept, comprehensibility (also, understandability), to assess how well a text fulfills its communicative function. While one can argue that legibility and readability are, at least mainly, qualities of the text, comprehensibility is situational and interpersonal: what is fully comprehensible for one can be entirely beyond the grasp of another. The greater the distance between the author and the recipient gets – culturally, historically or mentally – the more challenging comprehensibility becomes. In everyday conversations we have all experienced this. For example, generation gaps between teens and their parents can create some barriers to understanding; on the other hand, there may also be aspects of family life that only require a particular code word for mutual understanding.

Comprehensibility is an extensive area of research, which often concentrates on learners' skills and abilities. Reading is a cognitive process, and the amount of effort needed is affected by the legibility and readability of the text, as well as by the individual's personal cognitive traits. There is a limit to how far the writer can control comprehension, but by enhancing legibility and readability, and by taking into account cultural usability factors, one is able to support comprehensibility and thus to produce a better user experience.

Reducing cognitive effort relates to **cognitive ergonomics**. The term **ergonomics** is most typically associated with the physical aspects of work, reading or other activities. However, the concept of cognitive ergonomics extends ergonomical considerations to mental processes. The International Ergonomics Association (2014: n.p.) defines cognitive ergonomics in the following way:

> Cognitive ergonomics is concerned with mental processes, such as perception, memory, reasoning, and motor response, as they affect interactions among humans and other elements of a system. The relevant topics include mental workload, decision-making, skilled performance, human–computer interaction, human reliability, work stress and training as these may relate to human–system design.

In other words, cognitive ergonomics is a crucial aspect of the usability of texts, and the focus is on, among other things, learnability, intuitiveness and memorability, or the means with which the user's cognitive load can be lightened and the user's motivation and satisfaction increased. While physical ergonomics is a familiar concept to most, cognitive ergonomics is still often forgotten in everyday life and work. Therefore, many knowledge workers face the daily risk of overextending their brain and memory capacity. Another matter which has not received much attention so far is the fact that, in a world flooded with texts, the comprehensibility, clarity and easy usability of texts would enhance cognitive ergonomics significantly (Byrne 2010: 153). However, despite this general lack of attention, enhancing the comprehensibility and readability of some texts, such as administrative texts and legislative language, has been discussed actively in recent years (see, e.g. Clarity n.d.: n.p.). In intergovernmental organizations and in our increasingly multilingual countries and municipalities, questions of the quality and functionality of administrative language are very often also questions of the quality and functionality of translations and interpreting.

For assessing the comprehensibility of translations, Susanne Göpferich (2009) has developed the *Karlsruhe Comprehensibility Model*. In addition to structural aspects, her model consists of *concision, correctness* and *motivation* – that is, the text's ability to awaken and sustain the interest of the reader. Motivation is also linked to the subject matter and its relevance to the reader as well as to the reader's emotional attachments to the topic, the text and the author. Concision, correctness and motivation are close to usability factors, but Göpferich warns against automatically equating comprehensibility with usability. In addition to comprehensibility, legibility and readability, she emphasizes that a usable text needs to be complete and correct, and to conform to legal requirements with regard to form and content, and it needs to fulfill its intended function.

The link between motivation and comprehensibility is particularly interesting. In translation, it is related to the intricate balance between old and new information, and familiarity and newness that we briefly discussed in Section 3.5 in terms of domestication and foreignization. To allow for enough scaffolding for the target readers, translators often need to consider deviating from the source text content in different ways. Of particular interest for user-centered translation is the extensive literature on **explicitation**. In these discussions, the role of the recipient attracts special attention, and researchers approach the subject from two opposing directions, either excluding the recipients and translators' intentionality alike in favor of explanations of explicitation as a universal of translation, or emphasizing the reader-orientedness of translators' conscious choices.

In short, explicitation means that grammatical, semantic or pragmatic aspects that are implicit or presupposed in the source text are made explicit in the translation. Explicitation has received renewed interest in translation research as it has been considered one of the most promising candidates for a translation universal – that is, a universal characteristic of all translations, regardless of the language and culture pair, individual translator or other contextual variables. Many findings from large digitalized corpora have supported this hypothesis (see, e.g. Olohan and Baker 2000), but in recent research critical voices have become more audible (see Becher 2010). These researchers do not challenge the greater likelihood of explicitation in translated texts as such, but new explanations as to its prominence have recently been put forward. For example, relying on relevance theory and the concept of **audience design** (see Section 5.2), Gabriela Saldanha (2008: 32) maintains that explicitation is, in fact, a translation strategy that translators use to meet the assumed cognitive context of the readers of the translation. Frequent explicitation can be seen to improve readability and comprehensibility, and it thus makes the reader's interpretation task easier. In other words, it is not the translation process in itself that would unavoidably lead to explicitation, but many translators' intentional attempts to support their readers, and this increase is then visible in large corpora.

In addition to explicitation, many other pragmatic adaptation strategies are important in taking the target audience into account. Pragmatic adaptations can be used to fit the target text into its new communicative context and its new readership (Vehmas-Lehto 1999: 99 (trans. the authors)). These adaptations include:

- *additions* (the aforementioned explicitation, but also other kinds of explanatory or supplementary additions);
- *omissions* e.g. omitting taboo elements);[3]
- *replacements* (e.g. replacing a foreign allusion with a more familiar one); and
- *textual rearrangements* (e.g. changing the theme-rheme structure or fronting).

Pragmatic adaptations are needed when the translation is drafted in a different time, different place, for a different purpose or otherwise under normative constraints different from the source text. They are also necessary in bridging differences in background knowledge between different sub-audiences and in leveling out culture bumps caused by cultural differences (Leppihalme 1997) and in smoothing differences between genre conventions and expectations. An extreme example of pragmatic adaptations is **thick translation,** a translation strategy developed on the basis of anthropological thick description (see Geertz 1973) that aims to increase the comprehensibility of the cultural *Other* in the target culture (Appiah 1993/2000). While it may well be that research may prove some sort of explicitation to be a universal feature of translation, it is equally true that explicitation can be used as a conscious tool to improve the comprehensibility of the translation.

To summarize, comprehensibility can be seen as a combination of subject matter, context of use and the personality and state of mind of the reader. Bearing in mind the elements of user experience introduced in Section 2.5, comprehensibility could be seen as a crucial pathway into a positive user experience. Moreover, as legibility and readability are elements of comprehensibility, it follows that user experience also encompasses legibility and readability, because it includes the user's perception as well as physical and psychological responses. In user-centered translation, legibility, readability as well as comprehensibility need to be taken into account. Out of these three, comprehensibility in particular is difficult to control because of its individualistic nature. The tools offered by user-centered translation help translators assess the target audiences and their ways of comprehending more specifically, and translators are thus better placed to make the necessary translation strategy adjustments according to the needs of the users.

4.4 Accessibility

Beyond the textual and situational characteristics determining ease of reading, which we discussed above, the usability of a text can be approached even more holistically by evaluating the **accessibility** of texts. Accessibility, then, is one further significant topic to be considered in the context of textual usability, and particularly the usability of translated texts. According to Jan Gulliksen *et al.* (2004: 1), an ISO standard (ISO 9241–171: 2008) defines accessibility as: "The usability of a product, service, environment or facility by people with the widest range of capabilities." As we can see from this definition, accessibility is an all-encompassing concept which does not explicitly refer to any particular user group, although it is often associated with assisting groups with special needs, such as the visually or auditorily impaired.

Accessibility can be seen as an element of usability, but the two concepts should not be confused with each other. Mauro Mosconi and Marco Porta (2012: 106) distinguish the two in the context of website use by stating that "[t]he aim of accessibility is to enable *all* users to access any service and content offered by the web, while the purpose of usability is to enable them to do so as intuitively and efficiently as possible". Gulliksen *et al.* (2004: 3) emphasize that addressing the context of use is vital for both usability and accessibility, and that usability goals need to be considered separately for each situation and each special group.

While textual usability as such is the responsibility of the text producer and can either be ignored or embraced, accessibility is regulated by a number of laws, in recognition of all citizens' equal right to access, regardless of their abilities. Therefore, the creation of accessible products and services, including texts, is not a fully independent choice of their creators but, in part, a regulated necessity.[4] This necessity means that there are also a number of both official and unofficial guidelines for accessibility services. In the context of texts and communication, accessibility services include intralingual subtitles for the hard of hearing, Braille translations, simplified texts and the use of plain language for those with cognitive challenges or limited language skills, and so on.

One interest group working to achieve full accessibility of Web content is the World Wide Web Consortium (W3C), whose guiding principle is stated as "Web for all, Web on everything" (W3C 2012: n.p.). One of W3C's projects is a *Web Accessibility Initiative*, which makes the case for accessible Web content and offers accessibility guidelines as well as standards for evaluating Web accessibility (see Mosconi and Porta 2012). W3C is thus a rich resource for accessibility design and an example of how accessibility has become a significant consideration in the current technological landscape.

One aspect of accessibility mentioned by W3C, as well as many others, is language: "The Web is fundamentally designed to work for all people, whatever their hardware, software, language, culture, location, or physical or mental ability" (W3C 2013: n.p.). This statement serves as a reminder of the fact that translation itself is often an accessibility service, allowing readers access to a text which they might not have been otherwise able to understand. Offering translated user instructions, governmental documents and other crucial information ensures that the information is available and understandable for as many users as possible. Accessibility is therefore a crucial consideration in the context of translation, particularly user-centered translation where the central purpose is to direct texts to their specified user groups and the needs of these groups. Some translation strategies, such as pragmatic adaptations, can be seen as efforts to enhance accessibility, while a significantly foreignizing translation full of source-culture jargon might not be easily accessible to all target-language readers. It depends on the context and on the intended use of the text how closely the principles of accessibility should be followed in translation.

Accessibility is often mentioned in connection with administrative communication, where various different recipient groups should be taken into account, as all people have an equal right to access public information, but accessibility has also been discussed actively in the area of audiovisual translation. As we mentioned above, intralingual subtitles are one established accessibility service, and other similar services in the area of audiovisual communication include theater surtitles; audio description of films, pictures and other visual media for the visually impaired; and sign language interpreting of audiovisual content (Miquel-Iriarte *et al.* 2012: 260). This is an area where both research and practical applications are rapidly expanding to make use of technological innovations to increase accessibility. For example, portable mobile devices are being tested as a new medium for providing accessibility services for the hard of hearing and the visually impaired to allow access to live events, including educational contexts (Miquel-Iriarte *et al.* 2012: 260–261). Thus, advances in technology are allowing more and more accessibility to events which have previously been unavailable to some populations with special needs, and generating more work opportunities for those creating these accessible texts. However, many of these services are still being developed, and research is needed to determine the best way of serving these specific populations. One key consideration in enhancing accessibility services is usability, and providing accessibility is thus certainly an area where user-centered thinking is needed.

In this chapter, we have discussed important elements that contribute to the usability of text-based products – namely, legibility, readability, comprehensibility and accessibility. Out of these four, comprehensibility is most crucial in the creation of a positive user experience. It is also the most difficult one because it combines numerous elements and is, to a great extent, dependent on individual users. UCT helps translators assess users' comprehension of texts and adjust their translations accordingly.

Assignments

1   Select a short text (approximately one page) in one language and translate it into a language of your choice. Then familiarize yourself with a freely available readability test (see, e.g. www.online-utility.org/english/readability_test_and_improve.jsp or www.ideosity.com/ourblog/post/ideosphere-blog/2010/01/14/readability-tests-and-formulas). Write a summary of what language the test has been based on, what it measures (and what it does not), and contemplate on how well its measuring system might reflect readability issues in the two languages you selected for the translation assignment. Then test both the source text and your translation and compare the results.

2   Find additional information about performing a cloze test (e.g. www.nngroup.com/articles/cloze-test-reading-comprehension/), and choose

a translated text or texts whose readability you want to test. Then, design a test for evaluating the readability of this text. Explain how the test would be performed and what kinds of test groups would be selected. If you have the time and resources, you can implement a pilot experiment within your course group, for example.

3   Think about typographical conventions and publishing environments – either online or in print – in cultures you are familiar with. Are there type fonts that carry special connotations, either positive or negative (for example, those linked to cultural heritage or affiliated with a particular phase in history)? Research the history of one such type. Pay particular attention to any potential pitfalls on using that font in translation.

4   Choose a website that has been translated into one or more languages. Compare the accessibility of two language versions. For the comparison, take advantage of the W3C accessibility checklist (www. w3.org/WAI/eval/preliminary.html). Can you think of some other, translation-related accessibility issues that are not covered by the checklist?

5   Choose a text in a specialist field (for example, medicine, law or economics) and translate it into English in plain language for a target audience of your choice. For guidelines on plain language, see, e.g. www.plainlanguagenetwork.org/About_Plain_Language/aboutplain language.html.

Notes

1   If a text has 500 words, it has 500 "tokens". However, many of these words will be repeated and there may be only 200 different words in the text. "Types" are thus the different words. In other words, type/token ratio is the relationship of these two elements.

2   Controlled languages, computerized authoring and digital readers are now changing this human-oriented perception, but our discussion of usability and readability here is restricted to cases of human users of texts. Usability issues would take on an entirely different meaning in environments where writing, translating and reading processes are entirely automatized (see, e.g. Doherty 2012; Hartley *et al.* 2012).

3   Omissions include deletion or implicitation of material considered unnecessary or self-evident. Corpus research indicates that omissions are typically less common in translating than additions – that is, translators are more prone to explain things than to expect various items to be superfluous for their readers. On the other hand, in some genres omission and summarizing are central translation strategies – for example, due to space limitations (e.g. subtitles, comics, localized computer programs).

4   For example, the EU has an accessibility act: see www.epc.eu/documents/uploads/pub_ 3393_the_accessibility_act.pdf.

5   Mental models
of the user

Key points in this chapter:

- In user-centered translation, before translation itself begins, the translator constructs an image, or a number of images, of the future users of the translation. As real users always constitute a more or less heterogeneous group, it is advantageous to include various methods of categorizing and classifying users in the planning phase.

- The construction of **mental models** is the basis for a number of methods which can be used in profiling users and targeting a translation. These methods include **intratextual reader positions, audience design** and the development of **personas**. Both the intratextual reader positions and audience design are already somewhat familiar in translation studies, whereas personas have long been used in the field of usability.

- **Intratextual reader positions**, such as the concept of an **implied reader**, are reader positions built into texts.

- **Audience design** refers to recipient-oriented shaping of messages, which is based on five audience categories.

- **Personas** are fictive archetypes of users.

Identifying the user of a text is a crucial issue in translators' work, because it is key to making appropriate decisions that support the functionality and usability of a text. In this chapter, we will introduce the idea of constructing **mental models**; they can be used from the early stages of the process onwards to outline the characteristics of future users and to use this information as an aid in translation.

It is the goal of user-centered design to collect as much information as possible about users. Users' behavior must be studied before, during and after a product design process. Before the actual product development starts, the design team will put together descriptions of users. In order to be able to construct these descriptions, the team must decide how to collect information about users and their behavior:

the available options include methods such as observation, journal, logs, interviews and combinations of various methods. Then, users are classified into user groups (see Section 3.4). The classification of various types of users is typically based on the individual's role, needs and experience as a user of the product. In addition, the classification can be based on education, age, ability, and place and context of use. After classification, the design can be oriented towards these groups, or preferably towards **personas** (see Section 5.3) representing each user group. This targeted design allows the design team to become thoroughly familiar with the user's world and the tasks the user will perform (Sinkkonen *et al.* 2009b: 23).

Unlike user-centered design, the translation industry rarely makes use of real users when planning a translation project. However, the use of mental models is intuitively familiar to translators. It is natural for translators to devise some kind of an image of the future readers of their translations, even if they do not use systematic profiling tools. The user-centered model of translation, which we are introducing in this textbook, proceeds according to the principles that are used in user-centered design. Therefore, before the actual translation work begins, user-centered translation requires the translator, the translation team or some other project participant to collect appropriate data and then to construct a description of the translation's future users. This description is called a mental model, and it can be created by using a number of different methods. We have chosen to introduce three tools which can be used in the construction of mental models: **intratextual reader positions, audience design** and **personas**. Both the intratextual reader positions and audience design are already somewhat familiar in translation studies. They have been adopted into translation studies from literary studies and sociolinguistics respectively. Personas, on the other hand, have long been used in usability engineering.

5.1 Intratextual reader positions

We begin the introduction of mental models by discussing those reader images which can be discovered in the text itself. We call these images **intratextual reader positions. The implied reader** is a rather well-known instance of these in translation studies, while in technical communication we also find the concept of **reader as a rhetorical participant**.

5.1.1 The implied reader

In the past few decades, a great variety of studies on translation have explicitly mentioned reception and investigated translation from the recipients' point of view. However, even though the titles of the studies might mention readers or reception, this does not always mean that the study concentrates on concrete experiences that real people have had with translations. Instead, questions of reception and readership are often approached from a more text-oriented perspective. Many different terms have been used in translation studies to describe intratextual reader positions, including *implied reader*, *addressee* and *intended reader.*[1] We will use the term *implied reader* as the overall term referring to intratextual reader positions, but we will also introduce a few studies which have used different terminology.

While actual readers are the concrete, flesh-and-blood people who read texts in real life, the implied reader is a term that refers to reader positions built into texts themselves; implied readers are hypothetical readers to whom writers target their texts or whom a researcher can construct from the text through textual analysis. The difference between actual readers and the implied reader is also visible in the way we refer to these two concepts: when we talk of actual readers, we usually use the plural to indicate the multiplicity and heterogeneity of this group of people, while the singular implied reader is an abstract representation of the text's entire readership, a collection of characteristics which do not apply to every single reader but which are thought to be representative of general tendencies within the readership. According to Peter Hühn *et al.* (2009: 170), the implied reader can mean two different things: either "an assumed addressee to whom the work is directed and whose linguistic codes, ideological norms, and aesthetic ideas must be taken account of if the work is to be understood", or "an image of the ideal recipient who understands the work in a way that optimally matches its structure and who adopts the interpretive position and aesthetic standpoint put forward by the work". In this book, we use the term to refer to the former definition: a theoretical construct which tells us what the text expects of its readers in terms of presuppositions and pre-existing knowledge, for example. In other words, the writer's decisions, such as whether to explain technical terms or not, what register to use, and what kinds of cultural references to include, are all indicative of the text's implied reader. From the perspective of user-centered translation, the implied reader is significant as a tool for analyzing the source text and planning the target text, and for uncovering the ways in which the reader becomes evident in texts.

One practical example of the use of an intratextual reader construct as a tool in analysis is a study by Christiane Nord (2000: 195), in which she attempts to find ways for translators to understand their target audiences and the audiences' expectations in specific situations. One tool which she suggests for this purpose is the idea of a reader built into the text, which she calls the **addressee**. The addressee is the intended recipient of a translation, and Nord (2000: 196) describes the concept in the following way:

> The addressee (or target audience) of any text or translation is not a real person but a concept, an abstraction gained from the sum total of our communicative experience, that is, from the vast number of characteristics of receivers we have observed in previous communicative [occurrences] that bear some analogy with the one we are confronted with in a particular situation.

Thus, the addressee is a reflection of either the translator's or the researcher's experiences which determine the kinds of readers to whom the translation is targeted. Nord (2000: 203) suggests that the audience images of an individual translator or researcher could be supported by putting together text type-specific parallel text corpora, which would allow the translator or researcher to see what methods are usually used in taking the readers into account in a specific genre. Thus, the corpora would allow translators and researchers to investigate the kinds of implied readers that texts usually contain. This is, indeed, a useful suggestion: as empirical reception research is not always a viable option, searching for established reader images from previous texts could be a helpful tool for the user-centered targeting of translations. For example, a translator could use a corpus of commercial texts to examine **you-attitude**, which is one of the principles of effective business communication: you-attitude means that the reader is seen as a genuine participant in a communicative situation and that a text shows sensitivity to the reader's perspective (Rodman 2001: 11). You-attitude can be examined, for example, by studying the use of pronouns, the passive or active voice, or linguistic politeness strategies used in the text (ibid. 2001: 12–17). Such a practical text analytical approach shows how the concept of the implied reader can help translators distinguish those features of a text which are central to adjusting the text for its users, and it can offer suggestions on which translation strategies to use in particular contexts.

However, the use of parallel texts is not very common when discussing the implied reader. Most often the reader construct is based on the translator's or researcher's personal analysis of the source text and the translation context. Such an analysis is represented by, for example, Cristina Sousa, who studies the translation of children's literature and compares the differences in cultural background knowledge between the intended audiences of the source text and the translation. According to Sousa (2002: 21), both the author and the translator should evaluate the reader's cultural knowledge, because it is a significant factor in how the reader relates to the text. The author's and the translator's evaluations are then reflected in the text they produce. Because the readers of a translation are typically more distant from the source text's cultural background than the readers of the source text, the translator might consider it necessary to adapt the text so that it will correspond with the readers' perceived level of receptivity (ibid.: 22).[2] Thus, Sousa states that the translation and the source text will have different implied readers with different levels of receptivity.

The implied reader constructed into the translation is influenced by the translator's evaluations of the target audience as well as of the differences between the target audience and the implied reader of the source text. In fact, this concept of implied reader is similar to the idea of inscribing assumptions about users into technical devices, as was discussed in Chapter 3. However, one visible difference between Sousa's suggestion and our user-centered model is the fact that Sousa talks of a single "TL reader", implying that even the real target-language readership constitutes a homogeneous whole, while user-centered translation attempts to understand the varied users of translations through categorization and profiling. Thus, Sousa's text is also an example of a rather prevalent tendency in translation studies to see the readership of translations as a single entity, which has led to a shortage of tools for targeting texts more specifically to their users. This is what user-centered translation attempts to address, and it is the reason why technical communication and usability research, where user profiling has long traditions, can offer significant contributions to user-centered translation.

A third example of how an intratextual reader position has been applied in translation research is Brian Mossop's study, in which he refers to this reader construct as an **intended reader**, a concept very similar to the addressee. Mossop's study concentrates on discussing reader reactions to different translation solutions by evaluating the supposed reactions of intended readers:

> Reader reaction to translation can be considered from two points of view: from the point of view of reception, there is the actual reaction of the reader; from the point of view of production, there is the reaction imagined in the mind of the translator. It is the imagined reaction which will be of concern here.
>
> (Mossop 2007: 203)

Mossop also presents an approach that looks at reception from the perspective of the text's producer and the text itself. In his article, Mossop (2007: 202–203) introduces different translation strategies for French Canadian proper names, such as leaving the name in its original form, using the conventional English equivalent, or replacing a proper name with an explanation. He evaluates what kinds of reader reactions could result from different strategies and how the consideration of reader reactions might influence a translator's decisions. He lists three possible reader reactions which the translator might want to take into account: experience of readability, potential for misunderstanding and "a sense that the text emanates from another culture" (ibid.: 203.) Each of these is affected by the translator's solutions, and they are therefore useful categories to consider when analyzing intratextual reader positions.

Both Sousa and Mossop evaluate the expectations and interpretations of the intended reader on the basis of the translator's or the researcher's personal consideration. This is one of the fundamental challenges of intratextual reader constructs: when personal experiences and textually oriented analysis are the most important tools, any conclusions drawn on the text's readers are necessarily somewhat tentative. Therefore, Mossop (2007: 210) concludes that it would also be interesting to collect empirical data on the effects of translations. The intended or implied reader alone is not enough, and, particularly in the context of user-centered translation, the construct should be built on data collected about actual readers. Nevertheless, this kind of textual analysis, where the text is considered on the basis of its interaction with its readers, is necessary in user-centered translation, as it helps the translator keep the users' needs in mind throughout the project.

Finally, to distinguish the implied reader from other mental models introduced here, we must keep in mind that it is primarily a textual tool, a way to analyze how readers and their characteristics are visible in texts. Although it is built upon situational factors and impressions of target audiences, the fundamental purpose is to consider how these become evident in texts, both source texts and translations. Thus, in a UCT project, the implied reader could be used as a tool for analyzing the source text and again when evaluating the finished translation. In addition, it is useful to keep the implied reader in mind throughout the translation process as one criterion for decisions and adaptations.

5.1.2   The reader as a rhetorical participant

Intratextual reader positions have also been used in technical communication. Coney (1992: 58–59), whose taxonomy was briefly mentioned in Chapter 3, has investigated the readers of technical documents in particular, and she has advocated for a more extensive understanding of the roles within which readers construct meanings. Consequently, she sees readers as **rhetorical participants** in the communication process rather than mere objects to be analyzed. Coney has created a taxonomy of readers, which is not based on actual readers, but rather on the roles into which readers enter during the reading event. The difference between Coney's taxonomy and the implied reader in translation and literary studies is that in Coney's taxonomy, the reader is thought of as an active selector of the role and not only as a predetermined position constructed into the text or dictated by the situational context. The taxonomy, which we will introduce in the following paragraphs, consists of five roles: 1) reader as receiver of information, 2) reader as user, 3) reader as decoder, 4) reader as professional colleague, and 5) reader as maker of meaning.

The concept of **reader as receiver of information** is rooted in logical positivism, according to which research must be based on observable phenomena and verifiable states of affairs. According to Coney (1992: 59), this is the model of reality which most actors in the field of technical communication use. In it, the reader is a passive consumer of products, and it is the writer's task to decipher the potential reader, including the reader's educational background, level of expertise and the attitudes the reader brings into the reading process. In other words, this needy reader is lacking something and cannot influence the substance or the meaning of the message. All power rests with the writer, who takes responsibility for the message and its reception.

The importance of the **reader as user** role in technical communication was already discussed in Section 3.1. In this role, the text is merely a tool through which equipment is used. On the other hand, from the perspective of translations, the reader's role as a user is not as obvious. This thinking fits in easily with the text types associated with technical communication, whereas the variety of text types associated with translation is wider (see Section 3.3).

The third role introduced by Coney (1992: 60), **reader as decoder**, is a role where the reader is well versed in the topic at hand. Reading is both a source of useful information and a means of maintaining membership in a discipline through one's own skills and identity. When the reader is asked to enter this role, the information is rarely explanatory; rather, it is something of a shorthand: briefly worded, specialized language, cryptic style, acronyms and formulas. The roots of this role lie, first of all, in structuralism, which emphasizes the research of structures and the significance of structures in understanding texts as a whole. The recipient is at the opposite side from the writer, but they are equals: the code and the context are familiar to them both and they are connected to each other by some means of contact (e.g. telephone or a technical report). Roman Jakobson (1978), who has been a leading proponent of structuralism, has stated that this relationship between the coder and the decoder is maintained through the phatic[3] function of language. Second, this role is rooted in information theories, of which Coney mentions Claude Shannon and Warren Weaver's (1949) model. The objective of their model was to improve the accuracy and efficiency of the communication process by measuring the capacity of a given channel, such as the telephone cable. According to Coney (1992: 60), the later version of Shannon and Weaver's model contains an important addition, namely feedback (see Section 3.5.2); in other words, transmission from the receiver to the sender exists unlike in the first role of reader as receiver of information. However, the reader still merely tests the reception, not the meaning, of the message, so dialogic communication is not established. In this sense the decoder and the receiver of information are similar.

In the role of **reader as professional colleague**, the reader is seen as a member of the same intellectual community as the writer. The reader is co-equal or sometimes superior to the author, an expert who represents the standards of the discipline in question. This reader is less interested in practical applications and more focused on more meta-level issues such as argumentation and methodology. This role has many similar characteristics with the previous decoder role, but its roots are in very different, modern sources – that is, in the thoughts of researchers engaged in the New Rhetoric, such as Chaïm Perelman and Lucie Olbrechts-Tyteca (1969) and Kenneth Burke (1969). At the core is the intellectual and social equality between the writer and the audience. The tone of writing is respectful, sincere and honest. Collegial readers do not seek immediate or practical benefit from what they have read. Rather, the creation and maintenance of community is more important than the exchange of information (Coney 1992: 60–61).

Reader as maker of meaning is a role that represents a radical shift in emphasis from the writer's intentions to the reader's interpretation: the reader plays a central role in determining the meaning of a text. Neither the writer nor the text can control or even create the meaning; they only provide the readers with an opportunity for an independent interpretation. This rhetorical equation favors audience interpretation over authorial intention. However, it does not mean that authors should give up, but rather that authors design texts that invite "participation, choice, challenge" (Coney 1992: 61). The reader and the author are in a kind of partnership (ibid.). This role is, indeed, approaching the sphere of literature, which was discussed in Section 3.3.

Coney (1992: 61–62) states that her taxonomy is not exhaustive and that technological development might give rise to new roles. It is notable that the different reader roles are often intertwined: writers may call readers into several different roles, and roles change during reading. In the beginning, the reader may be a naive receiver of information, but as the reading proceeds, the reader's expertise grows. On the other hand, neither readers nor writers are always conscious of their roles, and we often have personal preferences about which roles to adopt. In addition, it is worth remembering that writing and reading can never be fully anticipated, and both sides possess a certain level of freedom in determining the progress of the interaction. The amount of guidance that writers offer readers on how to react varies greatly, as does the readers' willingness to play along. However, readers and writers act differently at different times, and in new contexts, new assessments need to be made.

Even though intratextual reader positions are a text-based tool that has been often used by researchers, they are also easily applicable to user-centered translation practice. For example, it is useful to occasionally pause during the translation project to think about the reader positions assumed by the source text and the positions which are being built into the translation. Similarly, it is useful to critically assess one's own assumptions about the target audience and the effects these assumptions might have on the selection of translation strategies. Whenever necessary, the assumptions should be adjusted on the basis of data acquired from actual readers and real reading contexts.

5.2 Audience design

Whereas intratextual reader positions are a text-based analysis tool, **audience design** focuses on the context of reception. The concept has been borrowed from sociolinguistics and applied to translation studies by Basil Hatim and Ian Mason (Hatim and Mason 1997: 82–84; see also Mason 2000). Audience design (Bell 1984, 2001) could be described as recipient-oriented communication design. Originally created as a method for analyzing the work of radio journalists, audience design is based on the idea that speakers – or similarly writers – regulate their way and style of speaking according to the people they are addressing and the kind of reception their speech is receiving. In Allan Bell's categorization, the recipients of a speech event are divided into five categories (see Mason 2000):

- **Addressees**, to whom the message is directly aimed.
- **Auditors**, who the speaker knows and accepts to be hearing the message but to whom the message is not specifically aimed.
- **Overhearers**, of whom the speaker is aware but who are not taken into account.
- **Eavesdroppers**, who the speaker does not know are hearing the message.
- **Referees**, with whom the speaker identifies or who the speaker particularly respects and whose favor the speaker seeks.

Audience design is associated with all levels of the communicative situation, from macro-level solutions to micro-level details. In the case of translation, even the question of whether to translate something and into what language or languages is a significant factor that limits and defines the readership. Only those who understand the language of the message can be its addressees, or even its eavesdroppers.

As an example, we can apply the idea of audience design into EU translation: the addressees of a translated press release consist of target-language journalists. The translator can attempt to attract their interest by shifting a theme or detail relevant to the country of the target language to the top of the release. The auditors of the release could be all those actively interested in EU-related matters, because the press releases can be subscribed via email as a weekly newsletter. Overhearers, on the other hand, consist of any target-language Internet users, because the press releases are freely accessible online. In such an open communicative situation, it is not easy to distinguish eavesdroppers, but perhaps one type of eavesdropper could be an individual whose knowledge of the target language is not known. Finally, referees are all citizens of the target country, because the fundamental purpose of the EU communications policy is to construct a positive image for the EU. The purpose of the translator in such a context is to create a text that is interesting to the journalists who act as gatekeepers and to motivate them to write a news story, in order to make the message of the translator and the entire institution heard by the referee group (see also Directorate-General for Translation 2009a).

From the translator's point of view, audience design has potential as a tool that clarifies the target audience of the translation.[4] A translation is rarely targeted at just one reader who the translator knows, and the target audience can therefore easily become a murky, faceless entity. The audience design framework can help translators distinguish their primary and intended recipients, and then the translation solutions can be made with the needs of these readers in mind. On the other hand, when the target audience is very large, the auditors (e.g. the client) might even be a more significant audience segment to the translator than the immediate addressee of the message (Hatim and Mason 1997: 83). The referee group, additionally, can consist of colleagues or representatives of award committees, for example.

One illuminating example of how auditors can be a more important audience segment than addressees can be found in literary translation, specifically the translation of children's literature.[5] It has long been a commonplace assertion that children's literature is aimed at a dual audience: both children and adults (see, e.g. Beckett 1999). This idea can be clarified further in practical terms through audience design: in this case, the addressees are, naturally, the children who read a children's book or to whom the book is being read. The adults, who often read the book to a child and are influential in the selection of the book, are auditors. Thus, even though the book is clearly aimed at children, the auditors are a particularly influential segment, because they are the ones who select the books and who therefore have to be convinced to choose a particular book. In addition, the context of reading children's literature could include overhearers, such as a child's older or younger siblings who are not in the book's immediate target audience but could end up either reading or hearing some of the text. Referees could include members of translation award committees, and the group of eavesdroppers could consist of such outsiders as a social services official who is visiting a family and hears children reading to each other while the social worker is interviewing their parents. This example of a rather everyday text shows how audience design can be applied in a variety of different contexts, and how these contexts can dictate the role and significance of each audience segment.

5.3 Personas

The third and final method to be introduced in this chapter is the use of **personas**, imaginary characters who represent real user groups. Personas are used as an aid in designing a variety of products and services. When the design process is conducted with these personas in mind, it is easier to relate to the user's world and put the information gained through user studies to good use for the benefit of the design process (Sinkkonen *et al.* 2009b: 23). Personas are fictive archetypes of users, and they represent the needs and characteristics of real users. Thus, what distinguishes personas from textual constructs such as the implied reader is that the implied reader is fundamentally based on features of the text, whereas personas are based on features of a concrete reader image: the implied reader is sought through the text itself and personas exist outside of it. With the help of a persona, the designer can find a connection to the user: a persona has a name, background, personality and often even a physical appearance (e.g. a photograph). In some situations, it might be necessary to construct several personas for a single project in order to meet the demands of varied audiences (see Section 3.4 for a discussion on profiling users). To see an example of what personas may look like, you can return to the Introduction, where we discuss the target groups we had in mind for this book through three personas, Leo, Emma and Julia.

The invented personas are usually based on empirical information on real users (see Chapter 7 for a discussion on research concerning real users). Personas aim to represent users' needs rather than the designers' conception of who they would like to design for (Calabria 2004). In usability engineering, background information for the construction of personas is collected through interviews or surveys, for example; in translation studies empirical information can also be sought from reception studies (see Chapter 8). In small-scale translation projects, fictional personas can also be constructed simply by using the translator's personal intuition and experiences.

The use of personas, however, also has its challenges, one of which is a mixed audience that requires the creation of multiple, different personas. The usability.gov website advises that while one can develop more than one persona – for one project, they recommend three to four personas – it is best to limit oneself to the main audiences; instead of trying to please everyone, one should focus on the needs of the most important user groups (see www.usability.gov/how-to-and-tools/methods/personas.html). In user interface design, compromises always have to be made, but personas help weigh these compromises and their effects on the users (Sinkkonen *et al.* 2009b: 134). The translator may face a similar situation and has to decide which persona(s) to prioritize and therefore which translation strategies to use. To help make this decision, the specification is a valuable source, as it defines the intended target audience along with the expected usability level of the translation, and audience design may also be used to support prioritizing decisions. In Section 3.4 we also discussed Huckin and Olsen's (1991: 64–65) proposed practical strategies for creating texts for a mixed audience: 1) *layering* the document so that different sections are targeted at different audiences and 2) *democratizing* the text so that all audiences can understand all parts of it. A layered technical report, for example, is aimed at the managerial reader, while the body of the report is aimed at the specialist. In a democratizing document, special information, such as technical terms or brief definitions, is added for each secondary audience. These types of strategies can also be of use to the translator.

Personas are a tool that fits easily within a translator's intuitive work process; it is common for translators to imagine what the readers of their translations are like (in Section 9.2.1 we discuss a real-world example of personas). Personas are also a relatively agile method of integrating end users into each phase of user-centered translation in a concrete way. When a user has been given a name, an appearance and various characteristics, it is easy to keep this prototypical user visible at all times and consider problematic situations and alternative solutions by using the skills and interests of this user as a point of reference. In user-centered design, personas are used for a variety of purposes (see Calabria 2004), many of which can be adopted to user-centered translation. Personas can be used, for example, for the following purposes:

- To recognize what textual features should be emphasized in a translation at both macro and micro levels.
- To determine whether a single translation fulfils the needs of all user segments or whether several different versions would, in fact, be needed.
- To enhance mutual understanding of the intended reader of the translation in projects, that include several translators or multi-professional teams.
- To offer a concrete point of comparison for the translation's quality assessment.

In other words, using personas systematically as a part of the translation project can benefit translators in many ways and help them choose appropriate translation strategies for each situation.

5.4 Using mental models in UCT

Mental models introduced in this chapter can be fruitfully combined in user-centered translation. Different mental models are most useful in different stages of the translation process and they complement one another. In Figure 5.1 we show a visualization of the iterative path from one mental model to the next. Starting from the upper left-hand corner, a user-centered approach to source text analysis can benefit from the notion of the implied reader and Coney's taxonomy. The outcome of this analysis as well as the initial idea of the implied reader of

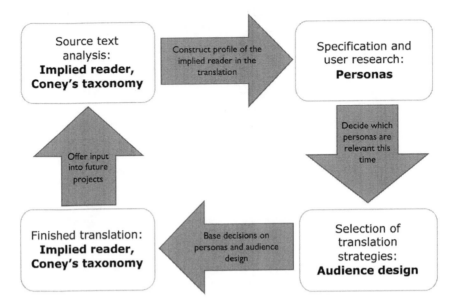

Figure 5.1 Mental models in user-centered translation © Tiina Tuominen

the translation can then be contrasted to the translation specification, thus gaining an understanding of whether changes are needed between the source text and the target text because of a different reader orientation in the two. The specification is used as a basis for audience design and development of personas, and the results of this step support the choice of global and local translation strategies. Finally, the finished translation can also be analyzed from the point of view of its implied readers, and the results can be used both to evaluate the successfulness (and potential revision) of the completed translation and to enhance future translation projects with a similar target audience.

To illustrate how this iterative process can take place in practice, we next discuss a classroom application that we have used in our own teaching. As material we used a site created by the European Union to help and instruct European travelers on their rights and obligations while traveling within the European Union, but basically one can choose any text. The benefit of using EU material is that it exists in many languages, and is thus pedagogically relevant for many student groups.

Step 1, source text analysis, focuses on identifying the reader positions contained in the source text. To arrive at a description one can observe, for example, the following issues:

- Who can access this information (languages, technical skills, accessibility, etc.)?
- What is the user's assumed background knowledge?
- What are the assumed interests of the users?

- What kinds of traveling arrangements are presupposed (for example, long-term or short-term, for business or pleasure, low-budget solutions)?
- Are there requirements for intended readers (such as EU citizenship, adulthood, financial resources)?
- What kind of an ideology can be interpreted?
- What kinds of rhetorical positions does the text offer its readers?

Once a list of reader characteristics has been generated, this list is reviewed from the point of view of translating this website into a new language: are all these identified implied reader characteristics still valid or does the change of language introduce new aspects?

In step 2, the students proceed into creating personas based on the set of characteristics generated in step 1. In other words, intratextual reader positions become the basis for personas. These personas can be produced in groups, with large sheets of paper, scissors, magazines to cut photos from, colorful pens, and so on, depending on the students' and/or the teachers' creativity.[6] At the end, a gallery of personas can be put on display on the classroom walls, each group presenting their persona in gallery walks with their peers. Artistically motivated students may even produce something similar to the persona pictures in Section 1.3 of this book, but simpler visualizations work just as well.

Step 3 introduces audience design as a tool for selecting from among the various personas the ones that could be considered to be the addressees, and would then be used to support the translation process. In the classroom, this can be done by discussing each persona in turn, or for example by voting for the most accurate ones. A follow-up discussion on whether one persona is enough to capture the essential features of users or whether more are needed may also lead to a discussion of whether one translation can meet the needs of all addressees or whether there is need for several versions. (One fruitful line of discussion is the lack of simplified language in EU communication.)

After the source text analysis, the creation of personas and the application of audience design, the work of translation proper can begin. Using a multilingual site such as www.europa.eu for translation assignments naturally arouses the issue of preparing a translation of a text that already has a published translation, but there is also a bonus side as the students can then compare their translations to the official version. In this case, it makes sense to focus the comparison on user-centeredness. In this phase, personas can be used to keep the target audience always in mind and to remain committed to user-centered practices. Therefore, as the persona or personas constantly inform the translation student's work, the personas will eventually become the implied readers and rhetorical participants contained in the translation, and in step 4 these implied readers can be analyzed to see how well the translation matches the persona.

The methods of mental models introduced in this chapter can be helpful for translators in day-to-day translation contexts. As was seen in the case study above, the different methods are not mutually exclusive and they can be combined as is suitable for each particular situation. For example, personas can well be used within an audience design framework. However, one challenge in recipient analysis is the further refinement of information gained through different methods. The study of human–computer interaction has investigated how user needs can be translated into system requirements (Bergvall-Kåreborn and Ståhlbröst 2010). It is equally important for translators to consider what the profiling of recipients means at a grass-roots level, in all the individual translation solutions that are made during a translation project.

Assignments

1   Browse through the website of a representation office of the European Commission in your own language (or any other language you understand), and find the weekly newsletters published on the website. Construct a persona for a reader of the newsletter. This persona must have a name, a photo and at least six characteristics (for more practical guidelines on creating personas, see www.uxmatters.com/mt/archives/2010/10/using-personas-during-design-and-documentation.php). What kind of a translation strategy would you use when translating the newsletter into this language for the persona you created?

2   Find a source text and its translation, and analyze the reader positions they contain (you may want to use a previously completed translation assignment for this purpose). What kind of an implied reader do the characteristics of the texts suggest, and can you identify differences between them? Alternatively, you can select only a translation or only a text to be translated.

3   Find a text that could be translated. Choose at least three reader roles from Coney's taxonomy of readers and discuss how you would translate the text in question for each of these reader groups.

4   Apply the recipient classification presented in the audience design model to a translated text of your own choosing.

Notes

1   In literary theory, the various reader positions are classified in numerous fine-grained ways. However, we have opted here for a simplified and pragmatic approach which suits the purposes of user-centered translation. For an overview of discussions concerning reader positions in literary theory, see, e.g. Herman *et al.* 2005: s.v. Audience; s.v. Reader constructs; s.v. Implied author. Furthermore, in translation studies, some narratological models also include an implied translator (see, e.g. Schiavi 1996; Hermans 1996).

2   Sousa's idea of the different levels of receptivity is reminiscent of Nida's previously discussed theory (see Section 3.5.2), according to which the readers of a translation have a narrower communicative channel than the readers of the source text, which leads to the need to adjust the translated message.

3   Phatic refers to the use of a message for the objective of keeping the communicational channel open between individuals.
4   In translation research, on the other hand, various textual features can help the researcher analyze the translator's target audience retrospectively. Audience design can well be used together with the investigation of interpersonal features, because both are concerned with the relationships between speakers and listeners.
5   We would like to thank Anne Ketola, Karina Kantalinskaja and Tiia Lipsonen for providing us with this example, and Esa Penttilä for completing the example by suggesting the inclusion of a social worker in the eavesdropper role.
6   Exercises with personas are typically well liked by students, and they also offer a rare opportunity for training visual skills.

6 Usability heuristics and translation

> **Key points in this chapter:**
>
> - **Heuristics** are a tool often used in the evaluation of usability. The term *heuristics* refers to a set of rules and principles which can be put together into an easily usable **checklist**.
> - Heuristic evaluation is a good way to uncover **usability problems**, which can then be solved.
> - Quality **checklists** and **style guides** which are used in the translation industry are very similar to usability heuristics.
> - Subtitling is one area where style guides and checklists are commonly used to improve and harmonize subtitle quality and to enhance the viewing experience.
> - Translators can use specific **usability heuristics for user-centered translation** as an iterative tool during the translation process.

Mental models discussed in the previous chapter aim at identifying the user of a text. In this chapter we take a step further, towards identifying and analyzing the usability of translations. For this purpose, we introduce an evaluation method that can be described as agile: **heuristic evaluation** or **expert evaluation**. We discuss several heuristics and conclude the chapter by introducing our own proposal for general translation usability heuristics.

6.1 Heuristic evaluation

Heuristic evaluation is performed by an expert or a group of experts with the help of **heuristics** – namely, rules, guidelines or usability principles; heuristics are basic rules of thumb. Traditionally, heuristic evaluation has been used in iterative product development, where an unfinished product is evaluated repeatedly, its shortcomings are fixed, and the following evaluation rounds are used to confirm that the usability problems have been solved (Kuutti, W. 2003: 47–49). According to Nielsen (1993: 159–160), heuristic evaluation is an efficient and cost-effective method, and it can be used in all phases of product development, for both prototypes and finished products. In fact, the method has been described as a "discount usability engineering" method (Nielsen 1994a: 152; 1994b: n.p.). Its weakness is the absence of the end user from the evaluation. Therefore, Nielsen (1995b: n.p.) recommends that heuristic evaluation be supported by usability testing: first, heuristic evaluation is performed through **iteration**, and then the corrections, made on the basis of the heuristic evaluation, are verified through usability testing.

Heuristics, thus, are a set of rules and guidelines which the user interface in question should follow (Kuutti, W. 2003: 47). Companies and usability experts have created numerous different checklists to evaluate user interfaces in websites and software programs, for example (see, e.g. Nielsen 1994a). The early heuristics were massive collections with hundreds of rules. However, as they have been found too cumbersome to apply in practice, somewhat less detailed heuristics have been more commonly applied to everyday use. The most commonly used heuristic checklist was originally drawn up by Jakob Nielsen and Rolf Molich (1990), and it contains commonly known principles of user-centered design. A number of different versions of the list have been published, but the best-known version is a list of ten heuristics (Korvenranta 2005: 111–114; Kuutti, W. 2003: 47–49). The ten-part list is presented in Table 6.1, and explanations for each item are provided in the right-hand column.

The ten-part list may appear daunting and requires some interpretation before it can be adapted to translation contexts. The original principles of Nielsen and Molich (1990; see also Hartson and Pyla 2013: 493) are much more down-to-earth and more accessible from the perspective of translation:

- use simple and natural dialogue;
- speak the user's language;
- minimize user memory load;
- be consistent;
- provide feedback;
- provide clearly marked exits;
- provide shortcuts;
- design good error messages;
- prevent errors.

Compared to the list in Table 6.1, this list has more references to issues of language and cognitive processing, which can more easily be applied to translation.

In addition to heuristics and checklists, heuristic evaluation can be performed by using companies' own style guides, which provide guidelines for the use of language (e.g. terminology, lexical choices, typographical considerations) in the products of that company. Style guides speed the design process and help the company create uniform and consistently functioning systems. Style guides are

Table 6.1 Nielsen's heuristics

1	Visibility of system status	The system should always keep users informed about what is going on, through appropriate feedback within reasonable time
2	Match between system and the real world	The system should speak the user's language, with words, phrases and concepts familiar to the user, rather than system-oriented terms. Follow real-world conventions, making information appear in a natural and logical order
3	User control and freedom	Users often choose system functions by mistake and will need a clearly marked "emergency exit" to leave the unwanted state without having to go through an extended dialogue. Support undo and redo
4	Consistency and standards	Users should not have to wonder whether different words, situations or actions mean the same thing. Follow platform conventions
5	Error prevention	Even better than good error messages is a careful design which prevents a problem from occurring in the first place. Either eliminate error-prone conditions or check for them and present users with a confirmation option before they commit to the action
6	Recognition rather than recall	Minimize the user's memory load by making objects, actions and options visible. The user should not have to remember information from one part of the dialogue to another. Instructions for use of the system should be visible or easily retrievable whenever appropriate
7	Flexibility and efficiency of use	Accelerators – unseen by the novice user – may often speed up the interaction for the expert user such that the system can cater to both inexperienced and experienced users. Allow users to tailor frequent actions
8	Aesthetic and minimalist design	Dialogues should not contain information which is irrelevant or rarely needed. Every extra unit of information in a dialogue competes with the relevant units of information and diminishes their relative visibility
9	Help users recognize, diagnose and recover from errors	Error messages should be expressed in plain language (no codes), precisely indicate the problem and constructively suggest a solution
10	Help and documentation	Even though it is better if the system can be used without documentation, it may be necessary to provide help and documentation. Any such information should be easy to search, focused on the user's task, list concrete steps to be carried out and not be too large

Source: Nielsen 1994a, 1995a: n.p.

used to ensure consistency throughout the product – that is, to make sure that different components of the same product function in a similar way regardless of who designed them and that the image and appearance of the product is uniform. Therefore, style guides can be used as heuristics to confirm that the guide has been followed and that the product is consistent with the company's other products (Korvenranta 2005: 117). However, we must remember that style guides are not primarily or automatically *usability* heuristics, unless they are specifically designed for that purpose.

In heuristic evaluation, a small number of expert evaluators each take their turn assessing a product, after which they discuss their findings and draw a conclusion. The end result is a list of usability problems and a reference to the heuristic principle which each problem violates. The assessment does not typically make explicit recommendations about how to fix the problems, but the problems can be classified into degrees of severity: each evaluator assesses the severity of the detected problems, after which the evaluators together classify all problems (Kuutti, W. 2003: 48–49; Korvenranta 2005: 114–115). Nielsen (1995c: n.p.) uses a five-point severity rating scale:

0 = I don't agree that this is a usability problem at all.
1 = Cosmetic problem only: need not be fixed unless extra time is available on the project.
2 = Minor usability problem: fixing this should be given low priority.
3 = Major usability problem: important to fix, so should be given high priority.
4 = Usability catastrophe: imperative to fix this before product can be released.

Even when the project allows little time for fixing problems, rating the severity of the problems is worthwhile; in those cases, priority can be given to fixing the most severe problems (Korvenranta 2005: 115).

Even fairly simple heuristics can usually reveal the most prevalent and most severe usability problems (Kuutti, W. 2003: 47). Overall, as Nielsen (1995b: n.p.) notes, both major and minor problems in user interfaces can be found with heuristic evaluation. According to Nielsen (1995b: n.p.), major problems are easier to find than minor problems: in his six case studies the probability that a single evaluator finds usability problems was 42 percent on average for a major usability problem and 32 percent for a minor usability problem. A common recommendation is that the evaluation should be performed by 3–5 evaluators. The evaluators can be usability experts, novices or **dual experts**, who are familiar with both usability and the product which is being evaluated (Korvenranta 2005: 114; Kuutti, W. 2003: 48–49). The evaluators should also keep in mind that even though the main purpose is to find problems, it is a good idea to also list the well-functioning parts and positive features of the product in the report (Korvenranta 2005: 122).

The same heuristics cannot be used for every product and the lists must often be modified, or even a completely new list must be created (Korvenranta 2005: 122). Similarly, different heuristics can be designed for different user groups – for example, by applying the mental models introduced in Chapter 5. Indeed, heuristics have many adaptations: for example, heuristics have been produced for specific audiences, such as the elderly (Smith 2008: 56).

6.2 Heuristics and translation

To our knowledge, the translation industry does not employ general translation usability heuristics,[1] although, as mentioned earlier in this chapter, quality checklists and style guides can be seen to function as kinds of heuristics. However, checklists and style guides are generally designed for the specific needs of companies or other organizations, and they tend to be based on the client's preferences rather than on certain language norms.[2] In the following, we will offer examples of heuristics that we will use – in addition to Nielsen's list – as reference for developing our own translation usability heuristics.

In the search for general translation usability heuristics, it makes sense first to consider specific types of translation for which heuristics or checklists have already been produced. Also, it is natural to integrate usability perspectives into those areas of translation where the text mass is considerable or where translations are embedded into digital products, which is becoming more and more common (e.g. in websites, online forms, localized games and software products). In this chapter, we first discuss the translation of technical documentation and, more specifically, user instructions, because of their natural links to usability. We then focus on subtitling and audiovisual translation, as audiovisual translation research has traditionally been greatly interested in the audience (see Section 6.2.2 and Chapter 8) and the step to questions of usability is therefore a rather small one. Finally, we return to translation usability heuristics and offer a tentative set of usability heuristics for user-centered translation.

Even though the focus of this chapter is on the large-volume translation industry, we must again emphasize that applying the principles of user-centered translation does not require large companies or massive translation volumes. If a translation project does not allow time or resources for wide-ranging usability tests, even small investments can still improve the usability of a product; a translation that is made with the end user's interests in mind is not necessarily more expensive or time consuming than any other translation. Heuristics are one excellent example of a tool with which user-centered translation can be applied to small-scale translation projects.

6.2.1 Translating user instructions

Usability issues are closely related to technical documentation overall, and user instructions represent a genre that is often translated. As was mentioned in the Introduction, Byrne's (2010) book on technical translation and usability also focuses on the translation of user instructions. Heuristic evaluation has proved a useful tool in evaluating the usability of technical documentation. For example, based on Nielsen's list, Vesa Purho (2000) has created the following heuristics:

- *Match between documentation and the real world*: use words and phrases which are familiar to the users and arrange the information logically.
- *Match between documentation and the product*: use the same terms both in the documentation and the product or interface.
- *Purposeful documentation*: if the users are provided with several documents (e.g. installation manual and user guide), make sure that the purpose of each document is obvious, and publish the documentation via an appropriate medium.
- *Support for different users* support users with different levels of knowledge.
- *Effective information design*: make the information easy to find and understand. Address the user directly by using the imperative form and active sentences.
- *Support for various information searching methods*: design the structure, organization and layout of the documentation text in a way that accommodates different users' individual ways of searching for information.
- *Task orientation*: structure the documentation around the users' tasks, not around product characteristics.
- *Troubleshooting*: offer users guidance to help them in case they encounter problems.
- *Consistency and standards*: make sure that the documentation is consistent and follows standards (e.g. terminology is consistent throughout the documentation).
- *Help on using documentation*: provide the users with instructions on how to use the documentation, especially if the documentation is extensive.

Purho's heuristics have not been designed for translation purposes, but they have been successfully applied to translated documentation by Anna Harju (2008). She studied translators' opportunities for improving the usability of the texts they are translating and designed a set of usability instructions for translators. The results of her study indicated that the usability traits that translators were best able to influence were the comprehensibility, learnability and accuracy of a translation. However, translators' chances of influencing the contents of a text or the text's efficiency and compliance with safety standards (see point 3 below) were very small. In addition, translators' chances to affect the typography of the text were felt to be nearly nonexistent. The translators' opportunities for following usability instructions were highly dependent on the client's wishes, and the interviewed translators expressed a desire to work more closely with the client and the reader of the text. In all, usability instructions were considered a useful way of rethinking automatized translation routines. Therefore, during the research process, Harju first designed a set of usability instructions based on different existing heuristics and then had her informants test them. Based on the informants' comments, she then revised the list, the aim of which is to support the translators of user instructions:

1   *Presenting information*:

- Know the reader. If necessary, consult the client or someone who is a member of the target group.
- Describe tasks in the order in which they should be performed.
- Explain how something should be done rather than how a machine works.
- Use short, active sentences and only present one topic in a single sentence.
- Use positive constructs rather than negatives to present information.
- Use informative headlines.
- If two or more sentences or other textual components mean the same thing but are structurally different, translate them by using the same target-language sentence or structure.

2   *Terminology*:

- Consult the client or end user in questions of terminology.
- Pay attention to the client's/manufacturer's terminological conventions.
- Make sure that terms are correct, understandable and consistent throughout the text.
- Avoid foreign terms, if they are not familiar to the reader.
- When translating user instructions for consumer products, motivate the reader by using nontechnical vocabulary, if possible.
- Avoid nominalization and needlessly complicated language. Try to find a way to express some of the source text's noun strings as verbs or adjectives.

3   *Safety*:

- Check the source text and translation for errors, omissions and inconsistencies.
- Check that the source text is safe[3] (see Securedoc (2004) guidelines) and that the translation contains everything necessary for the reading context. Notify the client of any shortcomings.

Juho Suokas has also designed and tested a set of heuristics for the translation of an instructive text. Suokas built his project on our Finnish book (Suojanen *et al.* 2012), and designed a combination of heuristic expert evaluation and usability tests with end users. For the expert evaluation he devised a case-specific heuristics list, based on a combination of Purho (2000) and Daniel Gouadec's ideas (see Chapter 9). The list compiled by Suokas (2014: 43) is as follows:

- *Matching the real world*:

  – The text is compliant with the translation's physical limitations and the target community's rules, regulations as well as linguistic and cultural standards.

- *Accessibility*:
    - The text is well written, its overall language is familiar to the user.
    - The words, phrases and concepts used in the material are familiar and they are used consistently.

- *Accuracy*:
    - The text is as factual and as free of technical and semantic errors as possible.

- *Purposeful and ergonomic*:
    - The function/use of the text is clear to the user.
    - The information is focused on the task at hand.
    - An appropriate medium is used.

- *User support*:
    - The information is suitable for users with different levels of experience.
    - The text provides support for possible problems that might arise while using it.

- *Information design*:
    - The information is easily found and understood.
    - It is presented in a logical and natural way.
    - The paragraph sizes and use of graphics are used effective (*sic.*).

Both Harju's and Suokas's heuristics are intended primarily for the translation of instructive texts, but many of the individual suggestions can be applied either fully or with slight modifications to the translation of many other genres. These kinds of guidelines are a good starting point, and their usefulness and applicability to different situations and commissions should be examined further. One detail to be examined, for example, is the format of the heuristics. Susan Smith (2008: 55) notes that attention should be paid to the heuristics themselves: they should contain only key phrases and be well structured to be useful. As we stated above, heuristics often need to be modified to fit the current project and its aims. Thus, translators can also tailor different kinds of heuristics to serve their own purposes and to support user-centered translation in different situations.

6.2.2 Subtitling

In subtitling, projects are typically concentrated on a number of large, global actors who process massive translation volumes and whose production is carried out through long subcontracting chains. Another characteristic of subtitling is that the translation is constrained by strict technical restrictions. Due to these two fundamental aspects, subtitling requires a great deal of systematization, and one systematization tool is the use of various lists of rules and guidelines. Even though the term *usability* might not be explicitly used in connection with subtitling, the idea of usability is very relevant. Subtitles are not an independent work of art, or even an independent text. They are a part of a larger, multimodal textual entity, and they are the viewer's aid in watching a foreign-language program. Thus, the role of a translation in the viewing process is clearly subordinate and instrumental. In other words, the translation is *used* as support in the viewing. Therefore, usability is a significant characteristic of subtitling, and subtitling can be evaluated and developed with the help of guidelines based on research and experience.

Many subtitling agencies use an internal style guide to harmonize the work of their subtitlers and to comply with the expectations of both viewers and clients. As we pointed out above, style guides are one example of heuristics, and we could therefore say that many subtitling processes contain an element of heuristics, even though their foremost guiding principle tends to be quality control rather than usability. To be sure, in some companies the instructions are most likely minimal or dependent on translators' voluntary initiative, but the general tendency towards controlling the subtitling process through such guidelines is nevertheless worth discussing in the context of heuristics.

In addition to the internal style guides, some researchers have produced practical instruction lists for wider use. The criteria for good subtitles have been defined from the perspective of both the technical requirements of the audio-visual medium and the special linguistic and expressive characteristics of subtitles. Henrik Gottlieb's (1994) article "Subtitling: Diagonal Translation" provides one early example of subtitling guidelines. Gottlieb is a pioneer of subtitling research, and this article is quite widely known as an introductory text on the special characteristics of subtitles. In the article, Gottlieb (ibid.: 106–116) lists the subtitler's nine pedagogical pillars:

1   What am I going to subtitle?
2   Am I hearing what is actually said?
3   Do I know the exact meaning of the words in this context?
4   A congenial segmentation of dialog.
5   A loyal, yet idiomatic translation.
6   A minimized loss of information.
7   A "user-friendly" text composition.
8   Elegant and precise cueing.
9   Meticulous proofreading and listening.

This list is something of a precursor to more detailed subtitling guidelines. The list is considerably shorter and less detailed than some later lists. In fact, the purpose of Gottlieb's list appears to be to outline the main elements of subtitling and the most significant criteria for subtitle quality.

From a user-centered perspective, what is particularly relevant is pillar 7, which talks of user-friendliness. Gottlieb (1994: 113) lists two elements under this heading: line breaks, and text volume and syntax. According to Gottlieb, the subtitler should make the viewer's task easier because time constraints make subtitle reading quite challenging. Gottlieb points out that viewers should be able to both read the subtitles and enjoy the program. It is, however, surprising that Gottlieb would associate only these two elements with user-friendliness, without mentioning other subtitling challenges, such as timecueing and text segmentation or textual coherence, in this context. Although only one of Gottlieb's nine pillars is explicitly founded on user-centered thinking, this list is nonetheless a suitable first example of user-centered inclinations in subtitling. Gottlieb's list is a good checklist for a subtitler, because it offers a concrete framework of requirements for a high-quality end result.

Another fairly often cited list of subtitling guidelines, which is more viewer-centered, is the "Code of Good Subtitling Practice", initiated by Jan Ivarsson and Mary Carroll. The European Association for Studies in Screen Translation (ESIST) endorsed this list in 1998 as a European general standard of good subtitling practices. The purpose of the list has been to foster and improve subtitle quality, but it is not a binding set of regulations, and following the guidelines is entirely voluntary (Díaz Cintas and Remael 2007: 80).

The list is divided into two parts: the first part deals with questions related to translation and timecueing/spotting, and the second part with the technical aspects of subtitling. The translation and timecueing guidelines consist of 25 entries, and the technical guidelines of seven entries. Some of the translation and timecueing guidelines deal with subtitlers' rights, responsibilities and working conditions (e.g. availability of video material, subtitler credit at the end of the subtitles), while others are more directly related to the quality requirements of subtitles and timecueing (e.g. fluent and idiomatic text, synchronization of timecueing with the speech rhythm, the minimum and maximum durations of subtitles). The technical guidelines define, for example, line length, the position of subtitles on screen and the characteristics of the fonts used in subtitles.

As the above description demonstrates, the code is a rather general overview of different aspects of subtitling, but the guidelines also clearly reflect the users' perspective. Users are explicitly mentioned when the duration of subtitles is justified by a normal viewer's reading speed, when the subtitling of so-called "superfluous" information is justified by the large number of hearing-impaired viewers, and when the optimal position of line breaks is determined by the minimization of unnecessary eye movements. In addition, the technical solutions are supported by arguments for clarity, legibility and adherence to reading speed. In other words, the fundamental presupposition is that a high quality of the translation process and of the translation will guarantee the usability of the final product.

Another, even more comprehensive, subtitling checklist is presented by Fotios Karamitroglou (1998) in his article "A Proposed Set of Subtitling Standards in Europe". In comparison to Ivarsson and Carroll's "Code of Good Subtitling Practice", this list is even more strongly focused on user-centered thinking, because in this list, a successful and enjoyable reception experience is emphasized repeatedly, whereas Ivarsson and Carroll discuss, first and foremost, the high quality of the subtitling process itself. Karamitroglou explains the need for such guidelines, on one hand, by arguing that subtitling conventions should be harmonized throughout Europe, and, on the other hand, by advocating for the necessity of considering viewers' needs. Karamitroglou (1998: n.p.) defines the purpose of his presentation as follows:

> The general practice of the production and layout of TV subtitles should be guided by the aim to provide maximum appreciation and comprehension of the target film as a whole by maximising the legibility and readability of the inserted subtitled text.

As this quotation indicates, the fundamental rationale in Karamitroglou's guidelines is the watchability, comprehensibility and enjoyability of the subtitled program. Thus, Karamitroglou emphasizes user experience (see Section 2.5) and the effects of individual subtitling solutions on the overall experience. He divides his list into four different areas:

1   spatial parameter/layout;
2   temporal parameter/duration;
3   punctuation and letter case;
4   target text editing.

Under each heading, Karamitroglou lists a number of detailed and concrete subtitling guidelines, and the readability and easy watchability of subtitles is often repeated as a rationale for the guidelines.

Both the "Code of Good Subtitling Practice" and Karamitroglou's list seek to harmonize subtitling practices and conventions throughout Europe. That is a logical aim that would support viewers' interests, as it is certainly easier to follow subtitles that use familiar and understandable conventions than to attempt to understand heterogeneous conventions which vary from one context to another. Harmonization can, however, also cause problems. Each country has formed its own subtitling conventions, something of a subtitling culture, which serves the needs of a particular linguistic and cultural region. Viewers are used to their own local culture, and it can be difficult to change such cultures towards common European or international practices. From the viewers' point of view, harmonization might not feel like an improvement if it requires them to change their own viewing habits. This is why the two lists cannot automatically be thought of as useful checklists under all circumstances. The usability criteria of subtitles are, in part, localized and culture- and language-bound, just as usability criteria in other types of texts and products. In addition, clients' internal style guides might sometimes be in conflict with researchers' recommendations. However, style guides are not usually made public, and it is therefore impossible to compare them with Ivarsson and Carroll's or Karamitroglou's lists in any detail.

Despite their conflicts with each other, all of these lists are drawn up with the purpose of systematizing and improving subtitling and informing subtitlers of what "viewers want" or what kind of a product would presumably be comfortable to watch. However, the implicit tendency in the guidelines' viewer orientation is to see "the viewers" as a monolithic entity with homogeneous interests, as the compilers of the various lists expect a single set of guidelines to serve all audience segments and viewing contexts. From a user-centered perspective, these subtitling checklists could be improved and refined by targeting them to particular audiences. Some conventions, such as recommendations on reading speed and language register, might not be uniform for all audiences. For example, different genres attract different kinds of viewers, and some guidelines could therefore be genre-specific. On the other hand, some aspects of subtitling heuristics might indeed be more universal than many other heuristics: the technical constraints of the screen, for example, are quite similar in different countries, and the requirement of synchronizing subtitles with both picture and speech is universal. Consequently, subtitling heuristics can be both extremely context-bound and nearly universal.

In addition to general subtitling guidelines, we can find many examples of guidelines for intralingual subtitling, or subtitling that is primarily meant for the hard of hearing. The purpose of these guidelines is to assure the accessibility of the subtitled program (see Section 4.4) and quite explicitly to take the users into account. In contrast to the general instruction lists we discussed above, these guidelines are oriented to a more specific audience segment. Of course, intralingual subtitles are also used by other audience segments besides those viewers who are hard of hearing, such as language learners or those who watch television in noisy places (e.g. bars), but the primary target audience is specific. One example of a rather detailed and practical set of guidelines is the "Guidance on Standards for Subtitling" published by Ofcom (n.d.: n.p.), the British regulating authority for the communication industries. Ofcom's document provides guidelines for both technological and linguistic aspects of intralingual subtitles. Its introduction contains the following summary of the most important elements of "effective subtitling" (ibid.):

1   Allow adequate reading time.
2   Reduce viewers' frustration by:

    a)   attempting to match what is actually said, reflecting the spoken word with the same meaning and complexity without censoring;

    b)   constructing subtitles which contain all obvious speech and relevant sound effects; and

    c)   placing subtitles sensibly in time and space.

3   Without making unnecessary changes to the spoken word, construct subtitles which contain easily read and commonly used English sentences in a tidy and sensible format.

4   In the case of subtitles for children, particular regard should be given to the reading age of the intended audience.

This concise list of subtitling priorities is obviously very viewer-oriented, and readability and the viewer's perspective are explicitly present. With the exception of item 2 b, the list could well be also used as a set of objectives for interlingual subtitles.

What, then, is the relationship of these various checklists with user-centered translation? Are they genuine usability heuristics? To be sure, the lists do not consist exclusively of instructions arising from subtitle use, and on some occasions the focus is more on the subtitling process than on the reception or use of subtitles. However, each list gives some attention to reception, and when discussing subtitle quality, the idea that high-quality subtitles ensure a successful reception experience is at least implicitly present. The technical constraints and other special characteristics of subtitling, such as presenting spoken text in a written form, require the use of specific conventions, and it is, therefore, often the purpose of subtitling guidelines to harmonize these conventions. This naturally serves the viewers' interests. Even though, as we mentioned above, these guidelines tend to treat the audience as a homogeneous whole, they resemble heuristics in their contents and purposes, and they can therefore be a useful element in user-centered translation. Like other heuristics, these lists are based on research and practical experiences. In addition, these lists can be used to make the subtitling process iterative by offering subtitlers opportunities for observing and assessing their own work or providing tangible criteria for other experts to assess subtitles during the subtitling process.

6.3 Usability heuristics for translation

In this section, we present our own suggestion for general usability heuristics for user-centered translation. In the context of translation, heuristics can be used either for analyzing translated texts or for generating text – in other words, for producing as many usable translations as possible with the help of heuristics. Smith (2008: 60–61) criticizes professional writing scholars for favoring heuristics for invention – i.e. text generation, rather than heuristics for analysis. Many of the ideas about heuristics and the lists we present in this section, we think, can be used for both purposes, as is the case with style guides, for example. This also applies to our own list. However, we wish to emphasize invention for the following reason: translation studies has many source-text analysis models, and traditionally a great deal of attention has been paid to the source text and its relationship to the target text. Functional translation theories, skopos theory included, have directed attention more to the purpose of the translation and thus the target text, but in our view, translators need more concrete tools to be able to produce a target text appropriate for its users. Thus, we maintain an emphasis on invention, which is facilitated by the use of various user-centered translation methods introduced in this book.

The following tentative heuristics are designed for the translator to be used as an iterative tool during the entire translation process, and as an evaluation tool for revising purposes. The list has been designed based on all the lists presented above, but especially on Nielsen's principles and Purho's list for assessing the

Table 6.2 Usability heuristics for user-centered translation

1	Match between translation and specification	Why is the translation needed and does it fulfil the requirements defined in the specification?
2	Match between translation and users	Who are the users of the translation and how do their characteristics affect translation solutions? Are there possibilities for supporting different kinds of users? Do the textual choices reflect the information needs of the users?
3	Match between translation and real world	Is the translation aligned with its cultural context? Is cultural adaptation required?
4	Match between translation and genre	Does the translation match the conventions of the genre in question? Are the visual, auditory and other multimodal elements appropriate for the new context?
5	Consistency	Is the translation consistent in terms of style, terminology, phraseology and register?
6	Legibility and readability	Do the visual elements of the translation correspond to the reader's physiological capabilities and relevant cultural guidelines? Is the user guided through the translation by using appropriate signposting for the genre in question? Are the user's efforts of interpretation sufficiently minimized?
7	Cognitive load and efficiency	Is the translation well crafted enough to be easy to memorize and learnable – that is, clear and comprehensible? Do the users need guidance for using the translation and, if so, in which format?
8	Satisfaction	Does the translation produce a pleasurable and/or rewarding user experience?
9	Match between source and target texts	Has all relevant source material been translated? Is there unwanted linguistic or structural interference?
10	Error prevention	Have the potential risks of misunderstanding been minimized?

usability of technical documentation, as well as Daniel Gouadec's (2010: 76) checklist for translators which we will discuss in Chapter 9. Our suggested translation usability heuristics for user-centered translation are presented in Table 6.2:

Although the principles and their formulations reflect the world of usability, the items in the above list are familiar and identifiable from earlier discussions of translation. Traditionally, the match between source and target text is primary in translation. However, this list has been specifically designed from the viewpoint of the user and thus of user-centered translation.[4] We proceed from macro perspectives to textual and more detailed aspects at the micro level. Intentionally, the match between source and target text and the question of errors have been placed low on the list. This list provides a generalized framework based on which translators can proceed in developing their own, contextualized versions.

In this chapter, we have described the main elements of heuristic evaluation and provided a number of examples of heuristics designed for different purposes. Our own general translation usability heuristics is intended as a concrete interface between usability and translation. We hope that usability experts will find it recognizable from their perspective and translators from theirs.

Assignments

1 Use one of the heuristics in Section 6.2.1 to evaluate translated user instructions.

2 Evaluate the subtitles of a film or television program by using one of the subtitling checklists introduced in this chapter. Are there any elements in the list that do not apply in your local subtitling culture?

3 Take a translation assignment you have completed and choose either of the following tasks:

   a) Use the usability heuristics described in Table 6.2 to evaluate your translation, then assess the usability of the heuristics themselves.

   b) Draw up your own list of heuristics for evaluating this particular translation based on the generalized list in Table 6.2. When putting together the list, remember to consider the particulars of the special area of translation, genre, translation context and the users of the translation. Explain how you arrived at the heuristics you chose for the list.

4 Find a translation style guide. Do you think this style guide would qualify as *usability* heuristics? Why/why not?

Notes

1 However, in the localization industry, there are some interesting examples of more specialized, linguistically oriented usability heuristics with affinities to translation. One example is Dinesh S. Katre's (2006: 4) study on the use of Hindi in bilingual (Hindi and English) mobile phones.
2 For example, the European Standard for Translation Services lists some features of style guides (see www.babelia.pt/media/norma_en_15038.pdf).
3 Securedoc (TCeurope 2004) covers different aspects of safety, such as the content and form of warnings, and that the documentation overall meets the required safety standards. (Harju refers to the Finnish version of the guidelines, but an English version also exists. We have included the English version in the References.)
4 For a similar endeavor, see also Otava 2013: 45.

7 Empirical usability methods

Key points in this chapter:

- Empirical study of **real users** and their preferences is the core of a truly user-centered translation process.

- Compared to the persona or implied reader, which are essentially simplified, homogeneous abstractions, the real users are a heterogeneous, ambiguous and unpredictable group.

- In usability engineering, a typical method for analyzing real users and user situations is **usability testing**, which is often accompanied by methods such as **thinking aloud** and **eyetracking**.

- Users' attitudes and preferences can be investigated dialogically by using methods such as **questionnaires** and **interviews.**

- Observing users' behavior in their natural environment through different **fieldwork** methods reveals a rich set of contextual data.

In Chapter 5 we discussed a number of methods for enhancing the user-orientedness of the translation process with the help of mental models, and in Chapter 6 we introduced heuristic evaluation for translations. Constructing mental images and analyzing texts to discern their implied readers is intuitive and agreeable to many translators and translation students alike, and heuristic evaluation shares similar features with quality assessment familiar in the translation industry. Thus, it is easy to promote the use of these methods in the classroom as well as among translators and in translation agencies. Mental models and heuristics are indeed useful for the translator, but they always entail a degree of uncertainty, and they work best when combined with empirical usability research.

In this chapter we focus on empirical methods for gathering information about real users. In many ways, this chapter represents the defining features of UCT, and illustrates what makes it stand apart from more traditional approaches to reader-orientedness in translation. Encounters with actual readers may initially appear challenging to many translators, and stepping outside the textual framework may at first seem foreign. However, as will become clear in this chapter, many methods employed in usability research are actually familiar to translators from their theoretical courses, as many of these same methods have been employed in translation and interpreting research. The step from translator to translation usability expert is thus not as huge as it may first appear.

7.1 Usability testing

From among the wealth of usability research methods, Nielsen (1993: 165) advocates for one empirical method – namely, **usability testing**. According to him, it is the most fundamental usability method, as it gives direct information about the way in which people use computers and the problems they encounter. Usability testing can be defined as "a process that employs people as testing participants who are representative of the target audience to evaluate the degree to which a product meets specific usability criteria" (Rubin and Chisnell 2008: 21). So people belonging to the product's real target group and their behavior are observed while they perform predefined tasks in order to obtain information about effectiveness, efficiency and user satisfaction, for example (Koskinen, J. 2005: 188; Kuutti, W. 2003: 68). A wide range of tests is available: the sample size can be large and the test design complex, or one can conduct an informal qualitative study with only one participant. The selection of the approach depends on the objectives as well as time and available resources (Rubin and Chisnell 2008: 21). Usually one user is participating in a test at a time and there are 1–3 test observers, some of whom the user cannot see. One of the observers is the moderator, who monitors and runs the test situation (Koskinen, J. 2005: 188).

In practice, the target group participants are asked to perform different kinds of tasks, which correspond to real use situations as much as possible. The usability of the product is analyzed based on the collected data, which can comprise notes, video recordings of the use environment, screen recordings and log data that includes the user's think-aloud protocol and everything that has taken place during the test. In addition, the user's subjective impressions can be collected after the test with a written questionnaire or an oral interview (Koskinen, J. 2005: 188, 196–197).

The roots of usability testing are in the classical approach for conducting a controlled experiment, the aim of which is either to confirm or reject a predefined hypothesis. However, this classical approach is not appropriate for usability testing in a fast-paced development environment where the aim is not to obtain quantitative proof that one design is better than another. Instead of exact scientific proof, the goals are to fix usability problems and to redesign products (Rubin and Chisnell 2008: 23–25).

A usability test requires detailed advance planning. The plan varies according to the type of test and requirements of the organization, but typically a test plan comprises the following sections, which are explained by Rubin and Chisnell (2008).

Purpose and goals of the test

It needs to be clear why the test is being arranged and whether usability testing is, in fact, the right choice for that particular situation. The testing needs to be tied to the organization's business goals (Rubin and Chisnell 2008: 67–68).

Research questions

According to Rubin and Chisnell (2008: 69), designing research questions is the single most important element in the test plan. The research questions describe the issues to be resolved, and the questions focus the research and all the rest of the activities during the testing.

Participant characteristics

Choosing the right number of participants is important, but as Rubin and Chisnell (2008: 67) note, you can never have too many participants. If you need a true experimental design, there should be a minimum of 10–12 participants, but very often fewer is enough. Four to five users representing one audience segment, or audience cell, is enough to reveal about 80 percent of the usability problems observed by that audience, and the same 80 percent represent the majority of the most significant general usability problems (ibid.: 67). It is also crucial to acquire participants who are representative of the product's intended user. For that purpose, you need to build a user profile with a description of the behaviors, levels of expertise, knowledge, demographic information, etc., of future users (ibid.: 115–116). Users can be profiled in many ways: you can, for example, take advantage of mental models introduced in Chapter 5. As for recruiting participants for the test, there are a number of possible sources, which require a varied amount of work and expense. You can recruit participants internally from your organization, you can use friends and family, or you can have a website sign-up, just to mention a few options (ibid.: 131–132).

Method

The method section of the test plan describes in detail how the test will be carried out with the participants and how the session will unfold. Unlike one might expect, Rubin and Chisnell (2008: 73–79) do not bring up methods such as thinking aloud or interviewing here, but rather seem to use "method" to refer to the overall test design from the time participants arrive until the time they leave.

Task list

During the usability test, the participants will perform a set of tasks, which must be described in the test plan. The main components of each task are explained: overall description of the task, required materials and machine states, a description of a successful completion of the task, and finally, timing, error rates or other benchmarks to be used (Rubin and Chisnell 2008: 79). Designing the tasks is not a straightforward activity – for example, the tasks must be short and unambiguous, the language of instructions should be fluent and clear, and you should not use terms that are directly mentioned in the product (Koskinen, J. 2005: 191).

Test environment, equipment and logistics

The test environment should simulate actual conditions as far as possible: if a product is used in an office, for example, it is a good idea to try to create an office-like environment (Rubin and Chisnell 2008: 87). The best equipment for testing is provided by usability laboratories, which are usually divided into two sections: on one side, the user performs the test, and the other side is the observation and control room. The test personnel are in the control room, observing the test through a one-way mirror. The moderator and the participant communicate through an intercom and speaker. Other equipment may include video cameras, audio recorders and data loggers. Sometimes the test moderator may also be in the same room with the participant (Rubin and Chisnell 2008: 108–109). Figure 7.1 shows the usability laboratory at the University of Tampere, Finland. The photograph shows the test person's workstation, and the control room is located behind the one-way mirror.

Figure 7.1 The usability laboratory at the University of Tampere © Reijo Kalvas

Test moderator role

This section of the test plan explains the actions of the moderator. It is especially important to make it clear if the moderator will do any unconventional intervening, so that the observers who might not be familiar with the testing process will not be confused (Rubin and Chisnell 2008: 87–88).

Data to be collected and evaluation measures

Before the test, it is important to specify what kind of data is being collected: quantitatively measurable elements include error rates and time spent on tasks, for example. On the other hand, not all data collected with thinking aloud, questionnaires and interviews can be measured quantitatively, but qualitative measurements such as the user's satisfaction with the interface can be captured. The collected data should correspond to the research questions (Rubin and Chisnell 2008: 88).

Report contents and presentation

Finally, the test plan presents a summary of the main sections of the test report and ways in which the results will be communicated to the development team (Rubin and Chisnell 2008: 90), or in the context of translation, to the content management team.

To sum up, a usability test has three major stages: preparation, the test itself and the transformation of the collected information into observations that can be used in product design (Kuutti, W. 2003: 70). These stages include a number of small, both theoretical and in particular practical details, which should be thought through before testing.

When conducted with care, usability testing is a good indicator of potential problems in the product and provides means to solve them (Rubin and Chisnell 2008: 26). The observers try to detect instances where, for example, participants understand tasks but cannot complete them in a reasonable time; they give up, they experience frustration or they blame themselves for not being able to complete the task (Martin and Hanington 2012: 194). Compared to heuristic evaluation (see Chapter 6), the method gives more information about usability specifically from the real user's viewpoint. Thus, it is a relatively objective method. In addition, usability testing can be used in different stages of the product development cycle, and it can be used for prototypes as well as for finished products or product elements (Koskinen, J. 2005: 203).

However, usability testing also has its limitations. Whether the test is conducted in the laboratory or in the field, it is always an artificial situation, and even if the test renders statistically significant results, all usability issues may not be uncovered. Furthermore, the limited number of participants rarely represents the entire target population (Rubin and Chisnell 2008: 25–26; Kuutti, W. 2003: 69). Overall, usability testing is a heavy method, and to get the best results, several professionals need to be involved in the design, implementation and reporting of the tests. Recruiting participants, implementing the test and analyzing the results also take a lot of time (Koskinen, J. 2005: 204).

It is always important to pay attention to the choice of method, but this is particularly true for usability testing. As a term, *usability testing* is somewhat general and sometimes used in a slightly misleading way in that it might refer to methods which actually do not have the features of usability testing, such as heuristic evaluation (Koskinen, J. 2005: 188) – for example, an experiment where users surf a website explaining what they like and what they do not like cannot be called usability testing.

Within the UCT model, usability testing represents an area that offers the greatest potential for innovation in the research and practice of translation. Although some individual pioneers have applied usability testing into translation, the idea of bringing the end users into a laboratory context is fairly uncommon. Therefore, we urge our readers to experiment with this method creatively, trying out different approaches. A wealth of general usability testing literature exists, and it is important to familiarize oneself with the details of the method before embarking on a usability testing project. However, the existing literature does not provide ready-made models for translation-specific testing. This is where new input is needed from the field of translation. In fact, the most productive combination might be found in a team of translation experts and usability testing professionals.

Based on the above description of usability testing, we can see that it is an approach that combines several methods. Those that have a clear point of contact with translation studies and will be considered in this book include thinking aloud, eyetracking, questionnaires and interviews. In translation process research, thinking aloud and interviews have been used for a long time, whereas eyetracking has recently become more popular. Real users can also be studied with methods that are not in the realm of usability *testing*. In later sections of this chapter, we bring forward focus groups and ethnography, for example, which have also been used in translation research, although they have most often been adapted to other research agendas rather than considering usability per se.

7.2 Thinking aloud

During a usability test, participants can be asked to think aloud while performing tasks: **Thinking Aloud (TAP)** is a popular data-collection method in the usability community (Boren and Ramey 2000; Martin and Hanington 2012: 180). It is also a widely used traditional method in translation process research (e.g. Jääskeläinen 1999). Thinking aloud reveals users' mental models and problems related to the product. A mental model is a representation of a user's conceptualization of a product (cf. Chapter 5). In our daily lives, we create images that help us explain a phenomenon and understand the structure and functioning of a product (Sinkkonen *et al.* 2009a: 177; Ilves 2005: 209).

The roots of thinking aloud are in psychological research and it is a development of the older **introspection method**. The basic idea is that "one can observe events that take place in consciousness, more or less as one can observe events in the outside world" (van Someren *et al.* 1994: 29). The method was first used at the beginning of the 20th century, but several theoretical and methodological problems linked to replicating empirical studies and settling scientific discussions about thought processes were discovered, and thus the method did not catch on. However, interest in internal cognitive processes grew by the 1960s and researchers became more interested in the thinking aloud technique. From the 1980s onwards the method gained wider acceptance, when computer scientists started to develop expert systems, and computer simulations of cognitive processes became possible (van Someren *et al.* 1994: 29–32; Ilves 2005: 210). In addition to usability engineering, thinking aloud has been used to study writing and reading processes, text comprehension and cognitive processes involved in decision-making (Nielsen *et al.* 2002: 103–104; Ilves 2005: 210). However, usability engineering lacks a detailed description of theoretically motivated rules of practice for thinking aloud, which is why it is often called a technique instead of a method (Boren and Ramey 2000: 261; Ilves 2005: 209).

Thinking aloud can be applied in many different ways. In the literature on thinking aloud, one often finds references to K. Anders Ericsson's and Herbert Simon's (1993) thinking aloud theory: their **protocol analysis** was developed for the needs of cognitive psychology and it is cited in many usability studies. It is an appropriate approach if one wants to find out about the user's cognition and mental models, but the aims of a usability test often differ from those of cognitive psychology. Instead of building a model of the user's psychological processes, the aim is rather to develop the product by identifying system deficiencies. Moreover, in addition to verbalizing, interaction with the system is important (see Chapter 3). Consequently, Ted Boren and Judith Ramey (2000), among others, have suggested that speech communication theories might offer a more solid theoretical base for the thinking aloud used in usability tests. Ericsson and Simon's theory focuses on participant–participant communication, whereas Boren and Ramey propose focusing on researcher–participant communication. Ericsson and Simon's position is that listeners are entirely passive and users can be requested to "think aloud as if you were alone in this room" (example by Boren and Ramey 2000: 267). However, even in a usability test situation, there is always a listener and a speaker, and considering their roles and the speech genres that are invoked during a test situation offers an alternative way of examining usability testing and conducting usability test sessions (Boren and Ramey 2000; Ilves 2005).

There are three stages in thinking aloud: instruction and practice, the test situation and the analysis. Creating a natural atmosphere in which the user can perform tasks is important, and special attention should be paid to the moderator's role and actions during the test. Analyzing the data is often time-consuming, because usually the data consists of video recordings that need to be transcribed (Ilves 2005: 211–215). A **simplified thinking aloud** protocol has also been suggested: it does not require a usability laboratory, and instead of video recordings, the data analysis is made based on the experimenter's notes. The aim in the simplified protocol is to find as many usability problems as possible with minimal resources. Thus, the protocol is not suited for the purposes of research where the reliability of results is the most important criterion (Nielsen 1993: 18–19; Ilves 2005: 216). Along with heuristic evaluation, simplified thinking aloud has also been described as "discount usability engineering" (Nielsen 1994b: n.p.).

Concurrent thinking aloud is used most commonly within usability engineering: participants work through tasks and at the same time they articulate what they are doing, thinking and feeling (Martin and Hanington 2012: 180). Adaptations of thinking aloud include **constructive interaction** and **retrospective verbalization.** In constructive interaction, two users discuss and test the product together. In retrospective verbalization, the user and the moderator together watch a video recording of the test and the user comments on the situations. When choosing the thinking aloud method and its format, it is relevant to consider the product to be tested, participant profiles and the data to be collected (Ilves 2005: 216–220). If it is important to know how much time users spend on performing tasks, or if the tasks are difficult, thinking aloud might not be the most appropriate method, because the participants have to slow down their normal process to synchronize it with verbalization (van Someren *et al.* 1994: 33). It is typical in usability engineering to first carry out a heuristic evaluation (see Chapter 6) to recognize the major problems and then carry out a usability test on a modified product using thinking aloud.

Thinking aloud is assumed to give access to the users' cognitive processes. It is cost-effective and easy to learn, and the technique usually produces useful comments about the user interface and the user's feelings related to it. On the other hand, it slows down cognitive processes and participants may find it difficult, because they think faster than they talk (Nielsen *et al.* 2002: 201; Ilves 2005: 219). Research into thinking aloud in the field of translation studies has also shown that thinking aloud will not only slow down translation but also the pausing behavior of the test participant (Sun 2011: 937; see also Krings 2001).

7.3 Eyetracking

Eyetracking is a method for observing the user's eye movements in order to analyze interfaces, to measure usability and find out about human performance. The user's eye movements are recorded and then analyzed (Jacob and Karn 2003).

Eyetracking is nowadays widely used by academic researchers, as well as marketing and usability experts. In translation studies it has been introduced as a "spearhead" method in translation process research (Alves and Hurtado Albir 2010). Eyetracking technology has a long history dating back to the 1800s. First, eyetracking was restricted to education research and especially to use by medical researchers because it was a very expensive technique. The first devices were quite intrusive, because they were mounted on the participant's head, but gradually more sophisticated and less constraining devices were developed. In the 1980s, marketing groups began using eyetracking to study the effectiveness of advertisements in magazines. Researchers began to acquire a better understanding of the way in which our eyes and minds cooperate when we read or try to solve problems. In the late 1980s and early 1990s, eyetracking began to reveal significant differences in reading patterns between printed text and text on screen. In the past decade, eyetracking technology has become very popular in developing effective advertising campaigns and usable websites (Legget 2010). Overall, however, we can say that the technique has been slow to develop: it has technical problems, the most significant of which is the need to constrain the physical relationship between the eyetracking equipment and the participant; extracting data can be labour-intensive; and interpreting data is difficult (Jacob and Karn 2003). The technology is also still quite costly and thus beyond the means of the average person (Legget 2010).

Eyetracking systems available for usability laboratories are based on video images of the eye. The trackers are mounted on the users' head or in front of them, the equipment is calibrated, and the trackers then "capture reflections of infrared light from both the cornea and the retina" (Jacob and Karn 2003). Typically, the eyetracking system provides a horizontal and a vertical coordinate for each sample, so one can gain a lot of data fairly quickly. Usually, the data analysis starts with distinguishing between fixations (the eye is relatively stationary) and saccades (rapid reorienting eye movements). The crucial part, however, is interpreting the data.

Eye and gazetracking yield large amounts of quantitative data on the user's conscious and – importantly – unconscious eye-movements. It can be used either as a stand-alone method or in conjunction with other usability measures. However, the causal links between eye movements and cognitive processes are not fully understood yet, and the method does not allow the researcher an insight into *why* the user behaves in a particular way, as it offers no direct input on comprehension, cognitive processing or attitudinal factors (Martin and Hanington 2012: 86). It is thus often complemented with qualitative methods such as questionnaires or interviews. The analysis of large quantities of data can also be difficult and very time-consuming (Lehtinen 2005: 229–233). However, commercial entities are increasingly offering quick and easy tools for the analysis and visualization of data. Color-coded fixation "heat maps" and other visual images of the gaze can be quite revealing, but the quantitative nature of eyetracking data also allows for a sophisticated statistical analysis.

Eyetracking has been used in testing the usability of web designs, on-line services and other digital interfaces, but it also has a long history of use in other fields such as the automotive industry. In translation research, eyetracking has, for example, been used in analyzing translators' cognitive processes and in studying the reception of subtitles (see Section 8.3). In the translation industry, eyetracking has application potential in areas such as testing the reception of localized documents and services, in observing how swiftly subjects are able to process translated texts (to diagnose and remedy sections that stall the process), or in analyzing which (and how many) language versions users resort to in situations where multilingual content is available (to make informed decisions on language and translation policy). Another area where usability issues have rarely been studied is the translator's "cockpit". Contemporary translators often manage a workstation that contains multiple screens and programs, and eyetracking can be used to investigate interaction with the workstation (see O'Brien 2006). Eyetracking can also be used to analyze the translator's cognitive workload. The results of this analysis could then be used to assess the optimal levels of mental effort and to avoid excessive load (see Section 4.3). Another recent area of interest is the usability of machine-translated texts, and eyetracking is one feasible method of generating empirical data on users' cognitive load, efficiency and satisfaction with MT documentation (see Doherty and O'Brien 2012). In MT research, eyetracking is being used in a framework that is directly relevant for UCT, as real users of machine-translated material participate in assessing the adequacy of the translation.

7.4 Dialogic methods

Above, we have discussed two central usability methods of a controlled nature. In them the participants are being observed while they perform artificially created tasks in a laboratory environment. We now turn to another set of methods, ones that are based on asking the users about their *opinions* and *experiences*. This category contains a great number of different methods, of which we will introduce questionnaires, interviews and some forms of narration and storytelling. These methods of soliciting information are familiar from all kinds of research, and they are also widely used in translation studies. There are methods of differing degrees of structuredness in this category. Questionnaires are the most structured and they are typically analyzed quantitatively. Interviews can be conducted in an entirely structured manner, by using semi-structured questions or a combination of closed and open questions, or in a free and open-ended manner. Finally, focus groups can be used to obtain group attitudes in a free-form manner. Storytelling and other narratives are even more open-ended and allow for participants' own interpretations of the relevance of their lived experiences.

7.4.1 Questionnaire, interview and narrative methods

User experience is a significant aspect of usability, and dialogic methods are also needed for researching it. **Questionnaires** and **interviews** are used in many disciplines and research traditions, and the pros and cons of these methods – which are also widely discussed in methods literature – also apply in usability research. Because interested readers can easily find guidebooks for designing questionnaires and interviews, we will not give detailed descriptions of these two methods here. It is, however, worth pointing out that specialized applications of these methods have been designed particularly for usability purposes. One can, for example, acquire both openly available and commercial ready-made questionnaire forms for measuring subjective conceptions of the quality of products or user interfaces (e.g. http://hcibib.org/perlman/question.html). Many of these forms have been adapted for on-line use, and they have been carefully designed to meet high psychometric reliability and validity requirements (see Lewis 1993).

Standardized questionnaires for assessing the usability of translations, or texts in general, are less commonly available, but one can adjust existing questionnaires to fit that purpose. For example, the classic *SUS System Usability Scale* designed by Digital Equipment Corporation in 1986 (www.usabilitynet.org/tools/r_questionnaire.htm) contains a set of statements that the respondents are asked to respond to using a five-point Likert scale ranging from "I strongly agree" to "I strongly disagree". On the basis of the responses, one can calculate a composite measure of the overall usability of the system in question. The statements are of the following kind:

1 I think that I would like to use this system frequently.
2 I found the system unnecessarily complex.
3 I thought the system was easy to use.
4 I think that I would need the support of a technical person to be able to use this system.
5 I found the various functions in this system were well integrated.
6 I thought there was too much inconsistency in this system.
7 I would imagine that most people would learn to use this system very quickly.
8 I found the system very cumbersome to use.
9 I felt very confident using the system.
10 I needed to learn a lot of things before I could get going with this system.

Now, if we wanted to study the usability of, say, a translated recipe, we could adjust this questionnaire slightly by simply replacing *system* with *recipe*. With only a few extra modifications the questionnaire would begin to make sense for this new use.

It would indeed be good to have a repository of questionnaires that are commonly available and that have already been piloted to study translation usability, so they could be refined and validated by other users. Then we would gradually have at our collective disposal a set of robust instruments specifically designed to measure translation-specific aspects (see also Alves and Hurtado Albir 2010).

Interview, then, is a method well suited for gathering information on end users' attitudes and experiences, their conceptual models, and their beliefs and values. Interviews can take place subsequent to completing tasks, but experiences can also be gathered by stand-alone, one-to-one interviews at any stage of the process. There are many ways of conducting interviews, varying from fully structured survey interviews to open-ended, in-depth discussions. For usability purposes it is often advisable to design an interview protocol that is followed in each interview. It is still good to have some flexibility and open-ended questions in the protocol as it may well turn out that the users have viewpoints that never occurred to the researcher in advance.

One can often gain a lot of insight into users' attitudes and experiences from narrated incidents or anecdotes. Asking them for a particularly bad case of translation failure, or a huge success, for example, can be revealing in terms of values and attitudes. In this **critical incident technique** the researcher collects a sample of experiences of a gap between anticipations and reality, in good or bad experiences, and these are then analyzed and classified. The goal is to explain the incident and to provide recommendations for the future (see www.usability net.org/tools/criticalincidents.htm; Martin and Hanington 2012: 50). The technique can also be used in prioritizing usability efforts into areas that are considered most vulnerable to usability problems and critical from the point of view of the user experience (see also Nielsen 2010).

An attempt at employing this methodology was recently made in translation studies (Havumetsä 2012). As a subpart of a questionnaire study, Nina Havumetsä asked clients of translators to submit a sample translation that they thought was either exceptionally good or bad. Although she did not fully follow the approach, this case, with its contradictions between what the researcher thought was a successful translation and what the clients classified as such, demonstrates the potential of this approach in studying the experiences of the users of translations. In some genres one might even contemplate using the method called **The Love Letter and the Breakup Letter** (Martin and Hanington 2012: 114), which could be seen as an extreme case of critical incident. The users of a particular product are asked to write a personal letter to express their sentiments about a particular product that has been crucially important to them at some time of their life, or, in the case of the breakup letter, that they have become so dissatisfied with that they want to part company. In the case of translation, this method might be well suited for literary and audiovisual translations, as users often engage with these genres in a highly affective manner (cf. the discussion of player experience in Section 2.5). For example, readers could be asked to write this letter to a translated book that changed their life, or to a song translation to which they connected. The letter method can be used to better understand the users' affective reactions and commitments, and to find ways of fine-tuning translation styles to enhance users' engagement with the translations (for example, using a vocabulary or vernacular style with which the users can identify).

7.4.2 Focus groups

The **focus group method** is based on the tradition of focused group interviews in the social sciences, as it has been refined and developed by marketing researchers from the 1960s onwards. It is a flexible method, and it is widely used both commercially and in academic research – for example, in media studies – and it has also been used in translation studies (Koskinen, K. 2008; Tuominen 2012). In usability research, it can be used to support concept design, and it can be applied to studying visual design, terminology or functionality at any stage of the design process, and to eliciting new improvements for existing products. Well-designed and skillfully moderated focus groups can "provide deep insight into themes, patterns and trends" (Martin and Hanington 2012: 92). In UCT, focus groups can be used, for example, for the following purposes:

- to understand the contexts of use and their (sub-)cultural norms and values as well as the social acceptability of the translation;
- to find out the existing vocabulary and phraseology used by the target users;
- to explore emotions and affects related to the translated texts and documents;
- to identify stylistic preferences between various draft versions.

Focus groups are semi-structured and informal sessions moderated by a group leader. A skillful moderator keeps the discussion both free-flowing and focused. It is also advisable to organize the discussions in a location that supports the aims of the project. As opposed to individual interviews where one can solicit personal views and gather information, focus groups allow the researcher to access the social roles of the participants. They are used to elicit qualitative data on group meanings, shared attitudes, beliefs and life experiences, as well as on group dynamics and group norms. They can be productive in revealing how the participants talk about the topic; what their shared views, beliefs and myths are; and what kinds of emotional engagement evolve (see Koskinen, K. 2008: Chapter 5). It is often advisable to complement focus groups with usability tests or some other methods of data gathering, as the group context and the situationality of the group affect the results one can obtain (Parviainen 2005: 54–55; see also Nielsen 1997).

Recruiting and grouping the participants is of decisive importance, as group discussions bring in group dynamics, and this needs to be managed in research design. Group profiles should be matched with the most significant subgroups and the overall profile of the entire population (other methods such as personas can be used to support focus group design). Groups that are homogeneous in terms of particular characteristics such as age, gender, class, race or cultural affiliation – or education, IT skills, profession or work history – may sometimes be desired for ease of analysis, but group cohesion (a sense of common purpose and closeness crucial for success in focus group research) can equally well be achieved in a motivated heterogeneous group (see Fern 2001: 14–15).

Advice on group sizes varies, and it is important to consider what one aims to achieve. Small groups of four may be optimal for in-depth discussions of sensitive topics, whereas groups of up to 20 may sometimes be used to elicit a breadth of opinions (see Fern 2001 for more advice on how to map research aims with group design). Typically, advice given by authors falls somewhere between these two. According to James Conklin and George Hayhoe (2010: 273–274), for example, the optimal group size is between 6 and 12, allowing for different voices without creating a group that is too big to handle. The number of individual groups also varies: sometimes organizing just one group session may well suffice to determine the functionality of simple texts, whereas a complex comparative design (such as cross-cultural attitudes to a product) may require up to 50 or more groups of different characteristics (Fern 2001: 11). The number of groups has no bearing on how discussions are conducted, but the number of participants per group affects both group interaction and the role of the moderator. The bigger and the more diverse the groups, the more demanding the moderator task gets (on moderating focus groups, see Fern 2001: 74–95).

Focus groups can be video- or audio-recorded, or there can be an observer taking notes, and sometimes focus groups may also produce drafts, drawings or other materials. Methods for analysis need to be mapped to the aims of the project (Conklin and Hayhoe 2010: 273–274; Tuominen 2012: 116–120). Focus groups are a fairly agile method for eliciting rich qualitative data without getting lost in complex sampling systems. On the other hand, moderator skills are crucial, group-think may affect the results, the data cannot be quantified, and the results cannot be subjected to statistical analysis and are not generalizable.

7.5 Fieldwork methods

Interviews and group discussions are researcher-dominated forms of inquiry similar to experiments. As opposed to usability testing or eyetracking, where tests designed by researchers are performed in a laboratory setting, it may sometimes be advantageous to conduct extensive observations of users while they carry out their regular activities in their normal environment (Dray and Siegel 2006: 295). The researcher can then resort to various fieldwork methods that have an ethnographic orientation. Similar to focus groups, **ethnography** is a method used across the social sciences. Ethnography aims at understanding human action and its social meanings as they are manifested in a particular environment. One can, for example, study a particular group and the interaction that takes place among its members, or its cultural norms and internal ways of acting. Ethnography may be used in describing the working methods and norms of a particular workplace to support the design of a new system (Vuorinen 2005: 63–65).

Ethnography is a method for researching human action in everyday situations. Data is collected from numerous sources and by different methods, such as various forms of observation, discussions and interviews. Data gathering is not structured in advance, and its analysis is not based on pre-existing categorizations. Rather, the course of research is dictated by the conscious and nonconscious presumptions of the researcher. However, as David Fetterman puts it, "The ethnographer enters the field with an open mind, not with an empty head" (Fetterman 1998, cited in Martin and Hanington 2012: 60) – that is, the research project always begins with a specific problem or research question, and methodological decisions are made accordingly. Often the aim is to fully describe and understand a single event or the action of one group. The analysis aims to uncover meanings and goals of behavior. Reporting usually takes the form of written texts or explanations (Eskola and Suoranta 1998: 107).

As the most typical ethnographic methods include participant observation and interviews, immersive fieldwork is a crucial aspect of this approach. Rather than aiming for a maximally extensive group of informants, ethnographers often aim for a careful and deep understanding of a small group of users. Analysis is conducted simultaneously with data gathering, and the researchers' personalities and their interpretations are centrally important. Ethnography thus requires a careful consideration of any potential ethical conflicts (Koskinen, K. 2008: 55–57).

In usability research, ethnographic methods have been used in researching human–computer interaction and computer-assisted cooperation (Vuorinen 2005: 64). Ethnography works well during those phases where system requirements are only just being planned and defined, and when the design team needs to gain a better understanding of the target environment and the target group. It is particularly suited for narrowly defined milieus. Ethnography provides access to situated and contextual knowledge of the potential users' or customers' real needs, so that design decisions need not be based on intuition only (Vuorinen 2005: 70–71).

Susan Dray and David A. Siegel (2006: 300–302) report on their experiences in using naturalistic usability evaluations. This is a method that combines elements of usability testing with or alongside ethnography: the researcher observes the frustrations and successes of the user in completing particular tasks, but the tasks are *not* designed by the researcher and the event takes place in the user's normal environment. While ethnography aims at a cultural understanding, naturalistic usability evaluations focus on evaluating particular product designs, and their higher-level motivation is thus quite different.

Ethnography, as Dray and Siegel (2006: 296) point out, is particularly valuable in designing a product for international use. This is tantamount to saying that ethnography is particularly valuable in cases that involve translation and localization. An in-depth analysis of users' real environments in different linguistic and cultural contexts can have particular significance at the early stages of the process, when there is still flexibility in design. The difficulty is in pushing linguistic and cultural aspects upstream in the design process. A common problem for translation and localization projects is that experts in these fields are only invited to engage in the projects at later stages when many decisions have already been taken (see Section 2.4). This is a fundamental shortcoming that we aim at solving with the concept of UCT. If the design team is planning on using ethnography at an early stage for their own UCD purposes, it might offer an opportunity also to include intercultural and translational aspects into the design process early on, as localization experts could be included in ethnographic research and design teams.

In the translation industry, one existing element could easily be expanded to support UCT: the **In-Country Review (ICR)**, where local reviewers are employed to ensure that the translated version is linguistically, terminologically, technically and legally acceptable, and correct for the target locale. However, one of the review's challenges is the commonplace tension between translators and reviewers, caused by chain-of-command and work-flow problems, hiccups in feedback loops and issues of expertise (Fleischmann 2013: n.p.). Another disadvantage, from the point of view of UCT, is that reviewers tend to be local employees of the subsidiary, such as engineers or sales personnel conducting reviews on top of their other tasks (ibid.). In other words, they lack linguistic expertise and they do not represent the end users either. The review process could be significantly improved by integrating it with fieldwork methods that engage the actual users in the assessment process.

Within translation studies, fieldwork methods are gaining more popularity (see, e.g. Flynn 2010). However, they have so far been more commonly employed in researching translators' professional contexts and have not yet been widely used in unraveling how translations are being used in real contexts of use. There is a lot of untapped potential, and digitalization has opened up new avenues for nonobtrusive and participatory forms of fieldwork – for example, one can use spontaneously evolved discussions on translation quality for analyzing attitudes and trends (such discussions can be found on Internet discussion forums or other forms of social media).

Another interesting emerging area of research is **crowdsourcing**. It is more familiar in translation studies as a method of producing translations via micro-tasking and teamwork, but it can also be harnessed for eliciting a large quantity of user evaluations or other related data in an efficient and decentralized manner, at least as long as the tasks people are asked to complete are not too complex and time-consuming (Martin and Hanington 2012: 52).

Spontaneously occurring materials have already been used in a few studies investigating the reception of translations. One example of this is Ritva Leppihalme's (2000) study on translating elements of dialect from Finnish into English in a literary context. In addition to her own textual analysis, Leppihalme analyzes feedback letters sent voluntarily by readers to the translator, and finds that these letters offer a significantly different impression of the translator's strategies than what Leppihalme concludes in her analysis. The elements of dialect which were present in the Finnish source text have been largely eliminated in the translation, resulting in a translation which does not fulfill all the same functions as the source text, but the reader comments suggest that the translator's strategy was successful, as the readers who sent in comments considered the translation to be very good (Leppihalme 2000: 266). Thus, looking at reader comments provided an interesting opposing perspective to balance the researcher's analysis. This balancing act is indeed also what UCT aims to achieve. Translators have tended to act as target readers' advocates in a rather intuitive manner, assuming rather than exploring what the actual readers' preferences really are. Users' attitudes and expectations may often depart from expert evaluations in unexpected ways.

7.6 Case studies

Next we will give some examples of research in translation studies and technical communication where usability testing and related methods have been applied. We place them in this separate section rather than discussing them in the context of individual methods to emphasize a feature common to usability research; in practice, it is advantageous to combine different methods, and these case studies demonstrate the wealth of options.

In her Ph.D. thesis "Documents multilingues pour logiciels et utilisabilité" (2003), Leena Salmi investigated problems that users had in using English, Finnish and French software documentation of a word-processing program. The research material consisted of videotape data of use situations where Finnish and French users were performing different types of tasks. The participants were allowed to consult both the online help of the program as well as the printed manual. The users first completed a questionnaire on their previous experience of using the program, and some of the tasks were conducted in pairs, which also produced thinking aloud data. The research arrangement therefore took advantage of usability testing methods in many ways. The results revealed that using a word- processing program in one's mother tongue takes less time than using the software in English. However, many problems connected with the documentation overall could be explained by the differing background knowledge of the participants rather than language issues. A particular problem was that the writer had not been able to anticipate the variety of the users' needs.

The second example is a Master's thesis by Ville Karinen (2006), who compared the use of text and pictures in technical documentation with the aim of examining what types of tasks benefit from only text, only pictures or a combination of both. Karinen conducted a usability test with three different sets of instructions for a small logic puzzle. The puzzle in question consisted of two identical metal sticks ("pigtails") that have loops at both ends. The sticks can only be detached from each other in one way. One of the instruction sets consisted of only text, one had only pictures and the third combined the two. There were 24 test participants, each of whom used one type of instruction. The test measured the speed of their performance and whether the test participant had to return to the beginning of the test. Participants were also asked to evaluate their typical way of learning. Karinen's approach can be considered a simplified usability test. The instructions with only pictures proved to be the quickest to use, but the instructions with both text and pictures caused the participants to make the fewest errors, so they were somewhat more reliable. The instructions with text only were the poorest in every respect.

Our final example is Maria Överlund's Master's thesis (2008), which aimed to examine how the usability of user guides can be improved through considering different user groups and the ways in which they approach usability problems when encountering them. There were three methods: first, the material consisting of user guides was examined with Purho's (2000) set of documentation heuristics (see Section 6.2.1), after which a usability test was conducted. The test participants performed a set of tasks and could think aloud if they so wished. In addition, they filled in a questionnaire about their use of computers and user guides. The hypothesis was that novice users try to solve usability problems more diligently than expert users, who do not pay so much attention to solving the problem but rather rely on their previous knowledge or experience. However, the test revealed that expert users were more willing to get to the bottom of the problem, whereas the novice users were quicker to give up when they were faced with a usability problem. Based on the results of the usability test, a list of ways in which to improve the user guide was drawn up. Thus, Överlund's work follows the typical two-phase usability engineering procedure where a usability test is conducted based on a heuristic evaluation.

This chapter has concentrated on actual users and contexts of use. The methods and approaches introduced here can be used to produce rich data for the purposes of a user-centered translation process. Such data can be helpful for both research and the practice of translation in profiling and categorizing a group of individuals who together form the target audience of a translation. Information about real readers and realistic contexts of use can help translators to select suitable translation strategies for each situation and locate potential stumbling blocks in the reception process.

Assignments

1   Find a translated text (e.g. official document/guideline, advertisement, tourism website, instruction manual) and design a plan for investigating its usability. Use the source literature in the References as reference material, or you can find your own sources about the method you have chosen. For example, if you choose to design a usability test, draw up a testing plan which includes all the necessary elements (for further details on usability testing, see, e.g. Rubin and Chisnell 2008).

2   Write either a love letter or a break-up letter to a translation or a translation provider (television channel, book publisher, the government, etc.) that has been significant in your life.

3   In Section 7.4.1, we presented a list of questions used to analyze the usability of various systems. We suggested that, with some modifications, a similar list could be used to test the usability of translations. How would you modify the list to test the usability of, for example:

   a)   a multilingual user guide for a washing machine;

   b)   a translated EU document;

   c)   television subtitles or a dubbing translation;

   d)   a translated poem?

8 Reception research in translation studies

Key points in this chapter:

- Although usability research has not been prevalent in translation studies, similar methods, including questionnaires and interviews, have been frequently used in academically oriented **reception research** to analyze real users.

- Humor, culture-specific contexts, and linguistic and stylistic issues are among the most frequently investigated individual themes in reception research.

- Physiological aspects of reception have been studied with eyetracking, while recipients' attitudes and opinions have been charted in interviews, questionnaires and focus groups.

- In addition to empirical studies with real users, reception has also been studied by analyzing statistics and public or institutional accounts relating to reception.

In the previous chapter, we introduced studies and research methods dealing with actual users mainly from the perspective of usability research. Even though usability testing has not previously been a widely discussed topic within translation studies, translation studies has for quite some time been interested in actual readers and recipients. The approach it has taken has been largely one of **reception research**. The field of translation-related reception research is constantly expanding through interesting new studies and research frameworks. However, this research has been mostly conducted from the perspective of academic inquiry rather than for the purpose of creating practical tools for translators. Therefore, this chapter will offer an overview of academic studies on actual readers of translations (see also Section 3).[1]

As this chapter will show, we can easily find links between reception studies and usability research. User experience, which was introduced in Chapter 2, is an especially valuable concept to consider in connection with reception studies. After all, user experience includes all users' emotions, beliefs, preferences, perceptions, physical and psychological responses, behaviors and accomplishments that occur before, during or after use. Audiovisual translation provides a particularly illustrative example of the relevance of user experience to reception studies: the variety of multimodal elements involved in the viewing experience makes user experience a crucial consideration in attempts to fully understand the reception of audiovisual translations.

In the following sections we will introduce empirical reception studies conducted within translation studies. These studies provide examples of reception research approaches that can be used in user-centered translation and that approach translation-related user experience from a variety of perspectives. Many of them contain a combination of different methods. The studies have therefore not been divided into strict categories; the purpose of the categorization below is first and foremost to distinguish the different themes within translation-related reception research and to offer examples of studies that have employed particular approaches. A significant difference between these reception studies and UCT is that UCT emphasizes the eliciting of user feedback iteratively and during the translation process, whereas reception studies typically test completed translations. As we are dealing with academic research, there are also rarely any direct feedback loops back to the original translator or client.

8.1 Thematic studies: culture, humor, language

Many reception studies investigate how readers respond to some individual, micro-level element of a translation. In this section, we will introduce a number of studies that have investigated the reception of 1) culture-bound references; 2) humor; and 3) linguistic and stylistic factors. The purpose of such studies is to find out how readers understand translated texts or what kinds of translation strategies are most useful and acceptable from the readers' perspective. In some ways, such research questions share their objectives with usability engineering, as the purpose here, too, is to find out how well the readers of translations can perform the task of reading and interpreting a translation that contains certain specific features. On the other hand, the acceptability and comprehensibility of translations are certainly also connected to the concept of user experience. In addition, reception studies concentrating on concrete, practical details of texts can offer useful information for constructing mental models of the readers and thus provide support for user-centered translation practices.

In recent years, many empirical reception studies have concentrated on audiovisual translation. In fact, as subtitles and dubbing translations are primarily an instrumental text, a means to understanding the program as a whole, audiovisual translation is well suited for a usability perspective, even though the existing reception studies do not explicitly mention usability. The Italian university of Forlí has been a particularly active center of research on the reception of audiovisual translations, most often dubbing. The reception of **culture-bound references** has emerged as one popular research theme (see, e.g. Antonini 2008). The studies have revealed that references that are related to a foreign source culture, such as allusions to local popular culture, politics, educational institutions, food traditions or other culture-bound concepts, are difficult to understand and interpret; even though a large proportion of respondents might state that they have understood the references, their stated interpretations show that, in reality, only a small number of respondents truly have understood them (Antonini 2008: 146–147). Flavia Cavaliere has obtained similar results in her study, which investigates the understandability of cultural references in a subtitled Italian soap opera. Her findings indicate that it can be difficult to understand culture-bound elements and that any individual elements that are not understood can have an effect on understanding and enjoying the program as a whole (Cavaliere 2008: 179). Thus, the viewers' user experience is connected to their successful use of the translations.

In addition to the above studies on audiovisual translations, Leppihalme (1997) has studied the understanding of culture-bound allusions in literary and journalistic texts. We already mentioned Leppihalme's concept of culture bump in Chapter 2; Leppihalme uses this term to refer to a disturbance in intercultural communication that is less severe than a culture shock. In other words, it describes a situation where the different cultural backgrounds of the participants in a communicative situation hinder the understanding of the message (Leppihalme 1997: viii). Leppihalme conducted an empirical study where average readers read a number of short, translated text extracts and were then asked to provide their interpretations for allusions contained in these passages (Leppihalme 1997: 140). Leppihalme's study (ibid.: 196–197), much like the Italian studies above, suggests that allusions that originate in a foreign culture can be very difficult to interpret for readers of translations. Leppihalme found that particularly those translation strategies where the allusions are translated word-for-word and not modified or explained in any way are often problematic for the recipients, because the source of such references is often unfamiliar, or at least less familiar than to source-language readers. Leppihalme (ibid.: 197) concludes that

> translating the words of the allusions but ignoring their connotative and pragmatic meaning often leads to culture bumps, in other words, renderings that are puzzling or impenetrable from the target-text reader's point of view. This conclusion can be read as a recommendation for translators to take the needs of receivers into account when choosing translation strategies for allusions [. . .]. Clearly, target-text readers are entitled to translations which work – successful translations are those that give readers the materials needed for participation in the communicative process.

Thus, Leppihalme's empirical study reinforces the idea that the translator's solutions affect user experience and that user experience can be enhanced by incorporating information about actual reception experiences into the translator's decision-making.

The above studies demonstrate how existing reception research can benefit UCT; the findings of these studies offer concrete suggestions of how culture-bound elements are processed by the recipients of translations. The studies offer translators of similar materials indications of the readers' level of expertise, and thus they allow the construction of more accurate mental models than what would be possible without these studies.

Returning to the reception studies conducted at the University of Forlí, another theme that has been studied there is **humor**. The experience of humor is an integral part of affective experiences connected with consuming texts and, as such, research on the reception of humor constitutes another link with user experience. Humor has been a rather popular reception research theme, and, again, a significant number of studies have concentrated on audiovisual translations. Delia Chiaro has been a leading humor researcher in Forlí. Chiaro (2007) has studied, for example, the differences between a source-text audience's and target-text audience's reactions to humorous elements in films. In addition to the Forlí studies, the reception of humor has been investigated by Adrián Fuentes Luque (2000), whose Ph.D. thesis compares the reception of humor in the Marx brothers' film *Duck Soup* in its original English-language version and its Spanish dubbed and subtitled versions. Fuentes's (2003: 296–297) study combines a number of methods (observation, questionnaire, interview) through which he has compared the film's humorous effects on the viewers who speak English as their mother tongue and on Spanish-language viewers. In addition, Fuentes compared how well humor comes across in the dubbed and the subtitled versions of the film. The results of these studies reinforce the supposition that humor is a great challenge for a translator: a typical finding has been that translated humor has caused less amusement in its recipients than source-language humor in its recipients (Chiaro 2007: 145; Fuentes 2003: 298; Antonini 2005: 222). Thus, empirical reception studies distinguish humor as another area of translation where user experience is easily affected by the translator's solutions.

The final research theme to be introduced in this section is **language** itself, with its various structural and stylistic factors. Investigating the reception of linguistic elements can benefit user-centered translation in concrete ways, because knowing the target audience's preferences can help the translator determine what linguistic and stylistic choices are credible and fluent from the readers' point of view and thus improve the text's readability and comprehensibility. In Forlí, researchers have investigated audience opinions concerning **dubbese**, which is the Italian, somewhat artificial-sounding language variant typical of dubbed materials (see, e.g. Bucaria 2008; Antonini and Chiaro 2009). The studies have indicated that viewers do indeed consider the language of dubbing stylistically unnatural, but the results have suggested differences in views between different groups of respondents (ordinary viewers; television, cinema, journalism and trans-lation professionals; dubbing and subtitling professionals; Bucaria 2008: 163). These findings show how some segmentation of the intended audience in the research design can result in a better understanding of the audience's preferences. The logical follow-up question is whether such unnatural language affects the different audience segments' experience negatively or whether it simply shows that the language of dubbing is different from natural language and does not even attempt to imitate other types of language use (ibid.: 163).

In the area of literary translation, Tiina Puurtinen has investigated the acceptability and readability of some linguistic structures in children's literature. Puurtinen's empirical study compares the acceptability of different Finnish translations of *The Wizard of Oz* with both child readers and adults who read aloud to children. The comparison pays particular attention to the static or dynamic quality of the linguistic structures in the two translations and the possible effects of static and dynamic structures on reception (Puurtinen 1995: 25–26). Puurtinen studied readability through a cloze test and a read-aloud experiment, and, in addition, the adult respondents were allowed to express their subjective views in a questionnaire. Puurtinen's research design has a fairly close resemblance to the usability tests introduced in Chapter 7 and is, as such, a viable model for user-centered testing of translations.

In addition to the studies of literary and audiovisual translation, some studies have investigated the reception of linguistic elements in translated nonfiction. One example of this is Inkeri Vehmas-Lehto's (1989: 1–3) study, in which she evaluates the quality of journalistic texts translated from Russian into Finnish. The study includes a number of empirical tests which compare the translated texts to original Finnish texts. Vehmas-Lehto's study investigates readers' attitudes towards the texts in general and the feelings the texts evoke, which means that the study looks at the texts as a whole rather than their individual elements, and takes the readers' affective stance into consideration. The study is thus an example of how the overall user experience connected with the language of translations can be studied.

Vehmas-Lehto's study contains four different empirical tests: in the first test, the participants attempted to recognize which of the given texts were translations and which were the original Finnish texts (Vehmas-Lehto 1989: 69–70); in the second test, the participants evaluated texts through a number of scales reflecting positive and negative attitudes (ibid.: 79–80); in the third test, the participants evaluated whether individual words were positive or negative (ibid.: 97–98); and in the fourth test, the readability of the texts was tested through questions on their content (ibid.: 127). The tests showed that the participants were able to recognize translated texts fairly often (ibid.: 78), and their attitude towards translations on the level of both an entire text and individual words was often negative (ibid.: 82, 104). In addition, the readability of the translated texts was weaker than the readability of equivalent, original Finnish texts (ibid.: 129). Vehmas-Lehto's results show that the user experience connected to translations is well worth investigating, as negative feelings are certainly an obstacle in the communicative process. Vehmas-Lehto's approach is able to locate some sources for those negative feelings (e.g. stylistic and lexical choices that are not compatible with normal target-language usage), and is therefore another example of a reception study that can offer useful information for user-centered translation.

In addition to producing a variety of interesting data, studying readers' opinions and interpretations on various themes is valuable from the perspective of user-centered translation, because the results of such studies can be quite surprising. For example, Leppihalme's (1997) study and a number of studies conducted at the University of Forlí have suggested that recipients are surprisingly unaware of source culture-bound allusions. Translators might unwittingly assume that their target audience is as aware of allusions as they are themselves and therefore choose a translation strategy that is not optimal for the recipients' pre-existing knowledge levels. For example, a translator might recognize a reference to a television program, celebrity or historical event that is specific to the source culture, and assume that the readers of the translation would understand the reference equally well. The translator would therefore leave the reference unchanged in the translation, without, for example, adding explanations about its meaning. This strategy can then result in many target-culture readers missing or misunderstanding the reference. Thus, translators' mental models of their readers are not always a realistic reflection of actual readers, and empirical research results can help translators in refining these models, as well as provide new quality criteria for the evaluation of translations.

8.2 Researching experiences and attitudes

In addition to thematic studies, readers' opinions and approaches to reading translations can be gauged through questionnaires, interviews or focus groups (e.g. Widler 2004; Alves Veiga 2006; Tuominen 2012), which can also be seen as a way of investigating the overall user experience. Above, we have already mentioned some studies that have employed questionnaires or interviews as one research method. Indeed, it is quite common to complement other reception research methods with focused questionnaires or interviews, just as it is in usability testing, as we saw in Chapter 7. On the other hand, more general questionnaires and interviews can play a central role in a study, when the objective is to investigate attitudes, habits and opinions rather than capture the details of the reading experience, as is also the case with usability research.

Two examples of such studies – one questionnaire and one interview – again involve audiovisual translation: using a questionnaire, Maria José Alves Veiga (2006: 164–165) has investigated Portuguese high-school students' reading habits, and the reading of subtitles in particular, which revealed that Portuguese teenagers prefer subtitled to dubbed programs and that their evaluations of subtitle quality are positive. Brigitte Widler (2004: 98), on the other hand, describes an Austrian study, where cinema-goers were interviewed in order to accumulate data on the viewing of subtitled films, such as the viewers' demographic characteristics, reasons for choosing a subtitled rather than dubbed film, and opinions on subtitle quality. Widler's study also found that viewers were fairly satisfied with the quality of subtitles and enjoyed viewing subtitled programs (ibid.: 99–100). These two examples suggest that user experiences connected with subtitles are quite positive, but we would need to amass much more data before we could say anything reliable about viewers' general attitudes. In fact, such questionnaires and interviews can often be thought of as something of a preliminary survey and they can be complemented through other methods.

It is also possible to look at questions of attitude and experience in a particular reception situation. This is the case in Tiina Tuominen's Ph.D. thesis (2012), which employs focus group discussions to study the reception of a subtitled film. In Tuominen's study, three groups of informants viewed the film *Bridget Jones: The Edge of Reason* and then discussed their viewing experience and the film's subtitles. The purpose of the study was to construct a general impression of the role subtitles play as a part of viewers' reception experience and of the attitudes towards subtitles that can be detected. In other words, Tuominen's study does not investigate how viewers interpret individual textual elements; rather, its purpose is to analyze the viewing event as a whole. The study is therefore strongly focused on articulating user experiences related to viewing subtitled materials. Such a study can complement detail-oriented studies and introduce another perspective into reception research. For example, if a study finds that translated allusions are difficult to understand, a more holistic study can be a means of evaluating what effects this lack of understanding might have on user experience. From the point of view of user-centered translation, such an approach is useful for attempting to understand how audiences operate, what they expect of translations, and what aspects of translations should be prioritized to best serve different segments of the target audience.

Another example of a macro-level study where the focus is particularly strongly on user experience is Minako O'Hagan's study investigating a single user's experience of playing a localized video game. O'Hagan (2009: 212–213) points out that even though game development usually involves a number of different ways of receiving input from players, the same is seldom true of localization. She then presents an empirical study design in which a player plays through a localized video game, and the play trajectory as well as the player's hand movements and utterances are recorded. In addition, the player fills in a game log and answers interview questions. The purpose of the study was to analyze how the player's cultural background might influence the playing experience. Although this was a small pilot study with only one informant, O'Hagan (ibid.: 227–228) was able to detect some potential effects of cultural differences, such as in the player's opinions on the ending of the game, which appeared to be different from the opinions of players from the game's source culture, Japan. O'Hagan's conclusions (ibid.: 228–230) suggest that further research on experiences connected to localized games would be valuable and again demonstrate that studies evaluating user experience could make significant contributions to user-centered translation.

In the area of literary translation, Andrea Kenesei (2010) has employed a cognitive approach to "investigate the personal responses of readers to poems and their translations" (Kenesei 2010: xvii). She studies "[r]eaders' interpretation of poems in terms of mental conceptual units which are evoked during the reading of the poems", and compares the reactions of source-text and target-text readers (ibid.: xxi). Some of Kenesei's results suggest that the connotations evoked by translated poems can be both similar to and different from the original text, and different translated versions can evoke different reactions, even if the overall interpretation is similar (Kenesei 2004). This cognitive approach is another possible method of analyzing how readers use and experience texts and what the sources of potential differences are.

One further example of a study concentrating on the overall reception experience again comes from audiovisual translation. The study in question was conducted by Henrik Gottlieb (1995), and it is one of the earliest empirical reception studies concerning audiovisual translations. In Gottlieb's study, a questionnaire was used to find out how viewers understand and interpret subtitled program fragments, and what kinds of attitudes they express towards subtitled programs. The purpose of the study was to analyze the significance of subtitles in the understanding of the program as a whole rather than concentrate on evaluating the understanding of an individual element of the program fragments. In addition, the study investigated what kinds of factors cause viewers to protest against subtitles: the study participants were asked to press a button every time they saw something objectionable in the subtitles (Gottlieb 1995: 389–390). The study revealed that visual information is easier to remember than the verbal information contained in subtitles, and that viewers were surprisingly reluctant to protest against subtitles. The matters evoking protests were often the usual characteristics of subtitles, such as condensation of the text, or matters on which the translator had no influence, whereas intentionally poor subtitles did not cause notable reactions (ibid.: 409). Thus, the results again suggest that user experiences concerning subtitles are fairly positive, and Gottlieb's methodology offers another approach to investigating user experience and the factors which can affect it negatively.

This textbook is concerned with user-centered approaches to *translation*. However, it is also worth noting that interpreting researchers became interested in users rather early on – which is understandable, as interpreting differs from translating in that the users and the usability of interpreted texts are very concretely present in the interpreting situation. Ingrid Kurz's (1993/2002) article "Conference Interpretation: Expectations of Different User Groups" is an early example of a questionnaire survey investigating what kinds of expectations the users of interpreting express. Kurz concludes that expectations vary between different user groups, and contextual factors, such as the institutional setting, professional field or modes of delivery (for example, whether the auditive message is supported by written documentation or visualizations), play a significant role. Kurz emphasizes that the listener must be seen as a central factor in the communicative process and that the process does not end in the interpreter's booth.

Another example of research concerning the recipients and reception of interpreting is a study by Anna-Riitta Vuorikoski (1995). Vuorikoski used questionnaires and interviews to investigate how satisfied listeners are with simultaneous interpreting. Vuorikoski's study is another example of looking at user experience in the context of translation studies. In addition, Vuorikoski asked whether recipients' characteristics might have an effect on their attitudes towards simultaneous interpreting. In earlier research, listeners were thought of as a given, unchanging group, whereas Vuorikoski argues that we must collect information on the interpreting situation and on its users before we can draw any conclusions on user needs and expectations. Vuorikoski found in her study that user expectations concerning simultaneous interpreting are not tied to a specific conference or group and that users' needs do not remain unchanged throughout the entire interpreted seminar program. The study detected three different recipient categories: the first category does not need simultaneous interpreting; the second one uses interpreting as a support so that the users, for example, listen to both the source text and the interpreting; and the third one is entirely dependent on interpreting, because the users do not understand the source language or do not want to spend energy on trying to understand both the language and the substance of the talk.

These examples of interpreting research further show how texts – in this case spoken texts – are used, and how surveys can help us in understanding their users' needs and experiences. A user-centered translation approach could usefully adopt such research perspectives in order to further integrate readers' opinions and use habits into the translation process. It is, for example, instructive to consider Vuorikoski's finding of different user categories and remember that in some contexts readers can use a translation simultaneously with the source text, or alternate between different language versions. Information on the use of different language versions, as much as data on how readers interpret and understand translations, can be used to formulate translations that are best suited into the contexts in which the texts are used, and to profile and categorize users (see Chapters 3 and 5).

8.3 Studies on perception and on the reading process

Reception can also be investigated by studying the kinds of reactions of which readers themselves may not be aware. One example of this is O'Hagan's study (2009), introduced above, where the hand movements and utterances of a video-game player were recorded and analyzed. Another method for investigating unconscious reactions is eyetracking (introduced in Section 7.3) from the perspective of usability engineering. Eyetracking can be used to study how a reader follows the text and where the reader's attention is focused. The use of eyetracking has not been as widespread in translation-related reception research as it has been in usability engineering, but subtitle reading in particular has been investigated in a number of eyetracking studies, which bear some resemblance to usability tests. The psychologist Géry d'Ydewalle and his research group have conducted some of the best-known pioneering eyetracking studies on subtitle-reading. They have looked at, for example, the effects of the viewing context on how closely subtitles are read (d'Ydewalle *et al.* 1991). Following d'Ydewalle's studies, several other researchers have also studied subtitle reading through eyetracking from a variety of perspectives. Eyetracking has been used, for example, to study the effect of cohesion and word frequency on reading subtitles (Moran 2012) and the effect of line breaks on the readability of subtitles (Perego and del Missier 2008; Perego *et al.* 2010). In addition, eyetracking methods have been used to investigate the cognitive processing of subtitles (e.g. Perego *et al.* 2010; see ibid.: 245–247 for an overview of other studies in this area). Eyetracking can also be complemented by other methods, such as questionnaire surveys, which are used to discover the test subjects' conscious opinions and user experiences.

Colm Caffrey's Ph.D. thesis from 2009 is an ambitious example of a study that investigates subtitle reading by using both a questionnaire and eyetracking. More specifically, Caffrey's study looks at viewers' cognitive load by measuring the reaction (dilation or constriction) of their pupils (pupillometry). Caffrey's study concentrates on the question of how viewers process the pop-up glosses occasionally seen on DVD releases of anime. These textual additions offer English-language viewers background information on some of the film's elements connected to the Japanese culture. Caffrey's objective was to discover how taxing it is for viewers to process these additional fragments of text, and also how much positive additional value they provide for the viewing experience. The processing effort was studied through pupillometry, and the positive effects through a questionnaire. The study demonstrated that pupillometry is a promising method for researching the processing of subtitles. This measurement method further expands the potential uses of eyetracking and the areas of information to be gained through such research. Eyetracking will certainly continue to produce more and more varied data on how translations are read and how a viewer's attention is focused.

8.4 Public reception and reception statistics

Public reception is the type of reception analysis that does not consist of an investigation of "ordinary" readers but of more influential recipients, who often possess a gatekeeper status, such as literary critics or institutions responsible for publishing and disseminating translations. The reactions of such institutional actors can be seen as a useful indication of how a translation has generally been received and, for example, whether it has been considered successful. **Reception statistics**, on the other hand, include data such as ratings of translated television programs or sales figures of translated literature. Such data can be helpful in constructing general impressions of the consumers of translated materials. Statistical data can be used, for example, to draw conclusions on the overall acceptability and popularity of translations. Statistical analysis alone does not produce accurate information on reader opinions or interpretations, but statistical data can be helpful in creating an overview of the role translations play in their readers' lives. As such, statistical information can be a beneficial component of user-centered translation.

One example of analysis that is based on both public reception and statistical data is Anne Jäckel's study about the reception of the French film *La Haine*. Jäckel (2001: 231–232) analyzes the film's English subtitles and compares the film's reception in the UK and United States. The popularity of the film and the positivity or negativity of its reception is analyzed through reviews in the press and audience figures. The comparison suggests that the film was better received in the UK than in the United States, and that the differences in reception might be related to the significant cultural differences between France and the United States (ibid.: 234). In other words, Jäckel uses the analysis of the subtitles and the overall institutional and statistical picture of the film's reception to draw conclusions on the audience's interpretations and the effects of cultural differences on these interpretations.

One reason for analyzing public reception rather than actual readers' receptions could be that actual readers would be impossible to reach individually. This is the case, for example, when investigating the reception of historical material, such as in Friederike Von Schwerin-High's (2004) study, which analyzes the reception of Shakespeare's work, especially *The Tempest*, in Germany and Japan in different eras. The study combines textual and contextual analysis of Shakespeare's German and Japanese translations with an analysis of their public reception and reception statistics (Von Schwerin-High 2004: 9). Because the reception contexts being analyzed are in the past, the actual recipients cannot be accessed, and the only possible way of collecting data on reception is to study public accounts of the translation. In this way, looking at public discussions enables us to analyze how translations have been accepted into their target cultures even if actual recipients cannot be accessed.

Another method of investigating the reading of translations statistically is to measure people's reading habits. One example of such research is a set of Finnish studies which surveyed how much Finnish students read, and particularly how much translated material they read (Mäkisalo 2006; Vihonen and Salmi 2007). In the studies, the participants kept either a reading journal where they entered all the texts they read during one week (Mäkisalo 2006: 250–251), or a text journal where the participants entered all those texts they recognized as translations on a single day (Vihonen and Salmi 2007: 2). The position of translated texts in the participants' reading experience was then analyzed on the basis of the journal data. Although both studies were fairly small pilot studies, the data allowed the researchers to suggest that translated texts appear to play a central role in the everyday experiences of Finnish readers, and that the proportion of translations out of all texts read is quite significant (Mäkisalo 2006: 257; Vihonen and Salmi 2007: 6). Naturally, such preliminary conclusions should be complemented with a larger, more representative study which could provide a more solid basis for conclusions on general reading habits.

Bella Martin and Bruce Hanington (2012: 66–67) also suggest diary studies as a possible method for investigating user experiences as a part of a design process. However, in their description, diaries are a decidedly qualitative research method, where the informants are allowed to express themselves quite freely. The Finnish reading studies, on the other hand, consist of largely numerical data, as the study participants have not been asked to express their feelings but only to list the texts they have read. In other words, similar methods can be used to collect very different types of data, but all methods can produce useful information. It is easy to see possible applications for Martin and Hanington's diary method within user-centered translation where readers could be asked, for example, to describe how they use translations in their everyday lives.

Information on public reception is not available until translations already exist and have been published, which means that the information gained through this kind of research arrives too late for an individual translation project. However, analyses of statistics and public reception can be used for future projects just like any other empirical data – for example, statistical data can provide indications of which texts are worth translating. In addition, long-term translation projects, such as translation within the EU, can use data on public reception and reception statistics even within a single project and, if necessary, change the course of the project in accordance with the results of the research.

In this chapter, we have introduced a number of different approaches to reception research in translation studies and described many studies that serve as examples of those approaches. These studies represent an academic reception research tradition, which means that they have not been conducted with immediate practical applications in mind. However, as we have seen, these studies do have many possible links with usability thinking and, as such, these studies and others like them could be used to support user-centered translation. Any method which produces information on actual users and contexts of use can be relevant for user-centered translation. A further step would be to design similar studies as part of a UCT process and link reception research even more closely to translation practices.

Assignments

1   Find a translated text. Choose one of the reception research methods discussed in this chapter, and plan and describe a study that investigates the reception of this text.

2   Keep a text journal for one day. Enter all texts you encounter during that day and try to figure out which of those texts are translations. What percentage of the texts you read during the day are translations?

3   Select one of the studies or approaches introduced in this chapter. Describe a scenario where it could be integrated into a UCT process and explain what kind of information it could produce for the process.

4   Watch a translated film or television program. Describe your viewing experience. Did you enjoy watching the program? What was the role of the translation in your viewing experience? Did the visual and auditive elements of the program affect your understanding of the program or your opinion of the translation? How did working on the assignment affect your viewing experience?

Note

1   The studies introduced in this chapter are concerned with the reception of texts that cross linguistic and cultural barriers. However, a growing body of recent research focuses on situations where the transfer does not occur from one language to another but from one mode of communication to another. Studies about the reading of intralingual subtitles (e.g. de Linde and Kay 1999) are one early example of this kind of intermodal translation reception research. Other intermodal practices, such as audio description and print interpreting, have also become an area of research interest. Many intermodal practices are directly linked to issues of accessibility (see also Section 4.4).

9 User-centered translation and the translation industry

Key points in this chapter:

- Traditional translation processes tend to suffer from end-of-the-line problems. Applying the UCT methods increases **iterativity**, and the focus is shifted from the client's wishes to the end user's needs.

- The translation industry puts considerable resources into **quality assessment.** A shift from quality to usability offers an alternative basis for evaluation.

- Quality assessment can feel intimidating for translators due to its judgmental nature and potential negative repercussions. Usability focuses on improving the interaction between user and product, not on assessing its producers or its users.

- Various elements of UCT have been tested in practical case studies. The case studies show that UCT tools can be easily and productively applied.

Previous chapters have introduced various aspects of user-centered translation. We have looked at mental models, heuristic evaluation, usability testing and reception research. In this chapter, we place the UCT model in professional practice. Our aim is twofold: first, we look at the current translation industry to identify both differences in emphasis and points of contact with user-centered translation. Here we rely heavily on Daniel Gouadec's book, *Translation as a Profession* (2010), which we take to represent current professional practice as it offers a detailed discussion of contemporary industrial translation practices. Second, we describe case studies that test how the UCT model functions in practice.

9.1 Translation industry practices from a user-centered perspective

Since the publication of the Finnish book on user-centered translation in 2012, we have received quite a lot of feedback from the field. Many, if not most, individual translators we have heard from express their delight in the model, but also seriously doubt its applicability in the translation industry. "The industry is driven by time and money only", runs the argument. We are convinced that there are some players in the field interested in widening the palette of the services they provide, and clients willing to extend the usability approach they already otherwise employ to also cover the translations they purchase. This faith lies at the heart of this book. This final section is dedicated to showing that it can be done, and that it is meaningful to do so.

The translators' ambivalence also reveals their position in the contemporary translation industry: they do not have much decision-making power. Most translators run their own small businesses and work as subcontractors for big agencies. They are, somewhat ironically, outsiders in the translation process, and they are typically not involved in negotiations with clients – the most logical phase for discussing the steps to be taken to ensure the usability of the future translations. In this, translators differ from technical communicators, who are often either directly employed by the client or physically placed in the design teams even if they are hired by a service provider. We have, however, also come to realize that the scene in Finland, a fringe market serving global players through agency networks and subsidiaries, may be quite dramatically different from the hubs and headquarters in cities like London or Berlin where both openness and room for maneuver for new ideas and different models may be much greater (see, e.g. Drugan 2013).

9.1.1 Usability versus quality control in the translation industry

In the software industry, usability evaluation is a large-scale business, but in the translation industry usability evaluation procedures are not established practice yet. In translation studies, methods similar to usability evaluation, such as eyetracking or focus groups, have been predominantly used by researchers rather than practitioners. Where the software industry employs different usability engineering methods, the translation industry focuses on **quality control** and **quality assessment.** Quality assessment and quality control are, of course, nothing new in translation (see also Drugan 2013). Throughout the centuries, countless researchers have attempted to define a good, effective translation and the best methods of translation. Most traditional quality assessment models highlight the close analysis of the source text and its specific features, and they measure the quality of a translation by evaluating how closely it succeeds in achieving equivalence with various features of the source text (e.g. House 1997).[1] In contrast, some analysis models within the translation studies tradition also emphasize the functionality of a translation. The best known of these is probably Christiane

Nord's model of text analysis. In Nord's (1991) conception of translation, the skopos of a translation is defined by functionality and the relationship between the source and the target text: the translator must synthesize the content gained from the source text, on one hand, and the material needed for the target text, on the other hand. The fundamental concept is loyalty: the translator is responsible both to the sender of the source text and to the recipient of the target text. The function of the text arises out of the communicative situation, which means that each recipient and each situation creates its own function.

To see how prominently quality figures in current translation industry, one only needs to glance through the table of contents in Gouadec's book, *Translation as a Profession* (2010). Gouadec's (2010: 312) focus is on the modern language industry, where large-scale translation and localization projects with their detailed specifications, translation memories and style guides also contain highly developed elements of quality control. The word *usability* does not appear in the book's index, but *quality* and its derivatives receive 12 different entries and hundreds of page references. In defining the goal of the translation process, however, Gouadec comes close to usability approaches. In Chapter 2 we mentioned that, according to Nielsen (1993: 26), the components of usability are easy learnability, efficiency, memorability from one instance of use to the next, low error rate during use, and the user's subjective satisfaction. According to Gouadec's (2010: 6–8) similar list, a successful translation is:

- *Accurate*: the unattainable goal is "zero-defect", a perfect translation (cf. low error rate).
- *Meaningful*: the translation should be meaningful in the target language and culture (cf. memorability).
- *Accessible*: i.e. easy to understand (cf. easy learnability).
- *Effective and ergonomic* (cf. efficiency).
- *Compliant with any applicable constraint* (linguistic and cultural standards, rules and regulations, official standards, physical limitations and functional constraints).
- *Compatible with the client's interests* (missing from Nielsen's list, which is user-oriented).
- *Economically viable* (missing from Nielsen's list).[2]

Without mentioning the word *usability* at all, Gouadec thus defines a successful translation using criteria that are rather similar to Nielsen's definition of usability. In Chapter 2, we offered a fairly practical definition for usability. According to this definition, a product or service is usable when users can employ it for their chosen purpose and in accordance with their expectations, without having to slow down, hesitate or ask questions (Rubin and Chisnell 2008: 4). Gouadec (2010: 5) defines a successful translation similarly: a translation is successful when users can get whatever they were supposed to get out of it, i.e. the translation is "fit for purpose". The fundamental aim of usability approaches and translation quality assessment is identical: to make sure that the product is as fit for its purpose as it can be. There are also a number of ideological differences that deserve to be pointed out.

First, whereas usability methods are used iteratively and corrective measures are taken as needed, translation quality assessment focuses on measuring the end product, and any changes can be costly both financially and in terms of missed deadlines. In other words, traditional **Translation Quality Assessment (TQA)** practices are a prime example of the end-of-the-line problem we have discussed before. For example, Byrne (2010: 177–178), who has surveyed the connections between usability and (technical) translation quite comprehensively, approaches the use of heuristics in a translation process only from a summative perspective of assessing the finished translation. But why not also assess the usability of translations formatively, i.e. during the development process? The practice of translation would greatly benefit from innovations for testing, feedback and usability evaluation in all stages of the translation process, from planning (e.g. evaluation of the appropriateness of terminological and stylistic choices) and implementation (e.g. visual features, cultural adaptations) to investigating the use of the finished product in its actual use contexts.

The second significant difference concerns the target of evaluation: usability is always a quality of the interaction between the product and the user; TQA is used to assess either the end product or the process of translation, to decide, for example, whether the same subcontractor will be used again in the future. The changes that are currently taking place in the translation market (such as the constant increase in volume, globalization, outsourcing and long subcontracting chains – see, e.g. Abdallah and Koskinen K. 2007) have resulted in increasing control needs within a field that has traditionally relied on direct contacts and trust. Therefore, quantitative and mechanistic quality assessment have increased (Konttinen and Veivo 2008). Iterativity inherent in the evaluation of usability is more positive by its ethos than quality assessment, because it does not contain similar implied elements of value judgment. Translators often feel that quality assessment is intended as negative criticism of their work – and that is, in fact, how it is often used (see, e.g. Williams 2009: 8). In UCT, usability efforts are directed at achieving an optimal match between the translation and its users, not at judging the translators.

Third, it has proved extremely difficult to reach a consensus on definitions of quality, and views of error-free, total quality tend to be subjective. Usability metrics, defined well in advance in the specifications, would offer an alternative basis for evaluation. Rather than listing criteria for a successful translation, user-centered translation concentrates on imagining what kind of a process will produce a variety of successful translations to serve the needs of different commissions. Understandably, companies and professionals are concerned with return on investment (ROI), but as Chauncey Wilson (2005: 8) notes, it might be more important to understand how usability evaluation affects internal development processes than to focus on how it makes products better. For example, sound and solid processes can reduce problems that might require rework later. In other words, improving the process will eventually improve the product as well, and the UCT model aims to cater to both.

Joanna Drugan's (2013) extensive survey of quality assessment practices in UK-based translation agencies offers an excellent window to contemporary efforts in safeguarding translation quality. Drugan's findings show that as translation has become more and more controlled and industrialized, and as supply chains for translations have grown longer and longer, the industry has been forced to dedicate extensive amounts of time and resources into various translation quality measurements. From the point of view of UCT, this indicates that deadlines and profit shares are not too tight to accommodate UCT processes either, as UCT can be seen to support aims very similar to quality assessment methods. TQA and UCT emphasize different things, but both aim at guaranteeing the best possible outcome. To summarize the differences, one could argue that TQA measures tend to have the following features:

- *End focus*: quality assessments and quality control mainly conducted once the translation has been completed, not during the translation process.
- *Error focus*: searching for translation errors and untranslated segments.
- *Source text focus*: the point of comparison is the source text rather than the skopos.
- *Client focus*: rather than focusing on the end user, project decisions are based on the client's wishes.
- *Expert execution*: rather than involving actual users.
- *Lack of feedback, limited learning cycles*: the translator does not always get feedback at all, and it rarely arrives in time to change course of action in the translation in question.
- *Judgmental ethos*: translators' performance assessment rather than support; focus on random segments rather than crucial parts.
- *Automation*: measuring the easily measurable, often resulting in false alarms.

In comparison, UCT is an iterative process, and usability assessments are completed incrementally, to verify translation strategies and textual choices before the text is finalized. Errors, especially translation mistakes in comparison to the source text, are evaluated according to their relevance in terms of functionality and usability, and rather than searching for mistakes made by the translator, the usability team aims to eliminate problems that the end users might encounter. Indeed, the focus is on the end users and their preferences, not (only) on the client's wishes, and if the two collide, the end users are given priority (in agreement with the client who has requested a user-centered translation). The UCT model is a learning system with structured feedback loops back to the translation team, but also optimally further upstream in the design process: usability problems detected in the translation phase are reported back to the source text design, and since usability evaluation is conducted throughout the process, the source text design can also benefit from the findings. For this learning system to work, open communication and the flow of information throughout the entire process are crucial.

9.1.2 Revision and heuristic evaluation

Even though the word *heuristics* itself is rarely used in the field of translation, most translation projects contain and have always contained implicit heuristic quality control. Habitually it goes by the name of **revision**.[3] The central role of revision in translation quality models underlines the linear nature of the exercise: translation is seen as a cascade that runs from one phase to the next, and revision is decisively a post-translation phase. There is, however, one iterative element in most translation processes – namely, **self-revision** or **checking** by the translator: most translators quite automatically reflect on their process and product at different phases of translating.

In most translation processes, the translator's own heuristic quality assessment is followed by the revision of the translation, which is, essentially, an expert evaluation of the translation's usability, conducted by a subject matter expert, native speaker or a fellow translator, depending on the priorities and the context. As we mentioned in Chapter 6, in usability heuristics, the evaluators can be usability experts, novices or so-called dual experts, who are experts in both usability and the product that is being evaluated. In the revision process of translations, another translator (or a copy-editor in the case of literary texts) can act as an expert reader. Another alternative is to use a subject matter expert for issues such as the accuracy and appropriateness of terminology. For example, translations of nonfiction books often have two evaluators: the copy-editor and a subject matter expert. One fundamental decision is whether the revision contains comparisons with the source text or only evaluations of the translation. If the aim is to control the output quality of an outsourced translation provider, the quality assessment might consist of random spot checks, which clearly have little to do with usability assessments.

Gouadec (2010: 78) states that it is the translator's sole responsibility to make sure, for example, that all required parts of the text are translated and that there are no unintentional omissions. The reviser, on the other hand, assesses style and fluency, quality of transfer, and correctness of factual information and meaning. Gouadec puts particular emphasis on the overall functionality of the translation. However, Gouadec's book does not give any additional advice on what kinds of assessment criteria could be used for measuring functionality. In other words, it does not provide the reviser with an actual heuristic tool, and the reviser is not expected to take on responsibility for specifically confirming the text's usability.

The commissioners or clients of translation projects can also introduce changes to translations on the basis of their internal quality control or usability assessment measures. Gouadec lists cultural adaptations or functional changes among such potential revisions. The final version will be produced by either the translator, reviser or the client, and then the translation proceeds to a stage that Gouadec calls **qualification.** Gouadec (2010: 81) also refers to this final stage with the term **qualification** *test*, where the aim is to ensure that the translation is both functionally and ergonomically compliant with the commission. Ergonomics should, in this context, be understood in a wide sense. It is not only concerned with adjustments of office chairs or other concrete actions related to the physiology of work; it also means, among other things, the cognitive load demanded for the reading of a text (as we noted in Section 4.3).

Even though the term is different, qualification is, in fact, a usability assessment, which is executed either virtually or *in situ* (Gouadec 2010: 82). Virtual qualification is a heuristic expert evaluation, where the evaluator is "in the end user's shoes". Gouadec recommends that the virtual test should be performed by an expert whose characteristics are as close as possible to those of the real users. Another alternative is to test the translation with real end users (*in situ*); Gouadec gives a practical example of a translated user guide with which a real user attempts to perform the given tasks. According to him, some sort of functionality testing is a necessity in the case of, for example, localization and multimedia products, because their technical performance must be checked with all the different language versions.

The section concerning qualification in Gouadec's book is short and cursory – only approximately half a page – and, as we already mentioned, it or the rest of the book does not use the word *usability*. However, it obviously describes a process where the usability and usefulness of the finished product are being evaluated. Gouadec's model differs from the usability testing models introduced in Chapter 7 in two ways: first, it does not offer detailed descriptions of qualification methods, and second, in Gouadec's model testing is performed at the end of the process. In modern-day usability research, design and various usability methods alternate with each other and become intertwined in the course of the design process. Such iterative processes are, however, still quite rare in the translation industry. For example, the *Programme for Quality Management in Translation*, published by the Directorate-General for Translation of the European Commission (2009b), only mentions feedback as part of the final product's assessment (in Action 14 and 21). The publication does describe a proposal for a project-based translation practice (Action 9), which could have easily contained the idea of iterative feedback during the translation process. However, this was an initiative which, according to the publication, was abandoned and not developed further.

9.1.3 Error elimination versus usability

Revision aims at producing a translation without errors, with zero-defect, and any other improvement is considered "an added bonus" (Martin 2007: 58). Defining and evaluating errors has been a perennial topic in translation. Because of the reliability issues linked with subjective assessment, attempts have been made to build quantitative translation assessment tools. For example, Malcolm Williams, who has long worked for the Canadian Translation Bureau, has responded to the lack of evaluation tools by introducing the quantitative *Sical* system (Williams 2009: 7–8). The system is in use in Canada, and it is based on calculating the number of errors and determining their level of severity (minor/major), but Williams also emphasizes the problems inherent in such a mechanistic approach.

Through a skopos theoretical and functionalist approach, he concludes that the quality assessment of translations should primarily focus on the preservation of the text's macro-level argumentative structure (ibid.: 11). The evaluator or reviser's central role is to analyze what the argumentative objectives of a text are and how well these objectives have been achieved. Williams states that if the text's core logic has been damaged it puts the *usability* of the translation into question (ibid.: 13). In the contemporary translation industry where texts are more and more often based on machine-translated raw material and fragmented text segments, this aspect becomes even more critical: the reviser or post-editor is responsible for making sure that the fragments make sense when put together.

In Jakob Nielsen's (1995c) classification, which we mentioned in Section 6.1, usability problems are placed on a five-point severity rating scale:

0 = I don't agree that this is a usability problem at all.
1 = Cosmetic problem only: need not be fixed unless extra time is available on project.
2 = Minor usability problem: fixing this should be given low priority.
3 = Major usability problem: important to fix, so should be given high priority.
4 = Usability catastrophe: imperative to fix this before product can be released.

In Williams's four-degree scale, an equivalent severity scale for translation errors might look something like this:

0 = This is a matter of taste, not a quality problem.
1 = Small/cosmetic error (e.g. typo); correct if extra time is available.
2 = Error which does not break the argumentative structure; equivalent to item 1 on this list, i.e. small/cosmetic error.
3 = Critical error; translation cannot be published.

Similar error classification models are included in most quantitative models of quality assessment, where errors are often given numerical values on the basis of their severity level. For example, LISA, the now defunct Localization Industry Standards Association, defined a critical error as the kind of error which causes the translation product to be rejected and returned to the translator. The characteristics of a **critical error** have been defined by Eeva Niinimäki (2009: 64) on the basis of the LISA model in the following way:

• An error which changes the meaning of the entire text or some part of it.
• An error which occurs in the most visible part of the text (such as the front page or main headline).
• A **major error** which is repeated three or more times.

A major error, then, is an error which is significant but does not by itself lead to the rejection of a translation product. A major error can be one of the following:

- An error which makes one individual statement misleading.
- An error which occurs in a particularly visible part of the text (such as headline or picture).
- An error which results in a phrase that might be considered offensive in the target culture.
- A **minor error** which is repeated three or more times.

(Niinimäki 2009: 64)

Williams's evaluation criteria differ from other criteria such as the LISA model in that they focus on a single criterion: whether the text is misleading in its argumentation. It is therefore reminiscent of Ernst August Gutt's relevance theory (1991: 101–102), which has received a great deal of attention in translation studies. According to Gutt, the translation should be equivalent to the source text in those aspects and in those ways that make the translation relevant for the *recipients* and contextualize it in accordance with the reader's view of the world. Even though Williams starts from the source text's central argumentation structure and Gutt emphasizes the recipients, they both offer a system of classification for evaluating a translation: what is at the heart of evaluation and of potential corrective procedures are those weaknesses that are critical or significant to relevance, and not just any differences in equivalence between the source text and the translation. One could argue that UCT is an application of Gutt's principle of relevance: what is considered most relevant for the future users is the translation's usability.

9.1.4 Specification

Above, we have discussed errors in terms of the textual composition of the translation only. Gouadec's approach to errors or revision is more holistic. He lists five key elements (2010: 76) to be checked during the revision stages:

a) *Material quality checks*: checking that everything that had to be translated has, in fact, been translated and that the translation complies with all applicable specifications.
b) *Language, style and register quality checks*: checking that anything related to language, style and register is 1) correct, 2) homogeneous, and 3) in compliance with all applicable specifications.
c) *Technical–factual–semantic quality checks*: checking that all the factual information, data, or logical or chronological sequences are adequate and comply with all applicable specifications.
d) *Transfer quality checks*: checking that all the relevant and significant elements in the source document are present in the translation (with allowance for the necessary adaptations), and that the translation complies with 1) professional standards, 2) the work provider's specifications, and 3) any specific constraints related to end user needs and requirements.
e) *Homogeneity and consistency checks*: checking that the style, terminology, phraseology and register are perfectly homogeneous. This is particularly essential when dealing with batch translations (material translated by several different translators).

On Gouadec's list a central role is given to **specification**.[4] Whereas many academic quality assessment models concentrate on a textual analysis of the translation and the source text, the translation industry has developed a wider perspective on process-related issues affecting quality, and the better these various issues are specified at the outset of the project, the likelier it is that they are also dealt with during it (see Drugan 2013). Specification, a regular element of development projects, is still a relatively new concept in discourses about translation (a translation brief is a more traditional idea, and the difficulty of extracting any information from clients is a problem regularly discussed by translators). In line with Alan Melby's pioneering work on translation specifications since the 1990s (see Melby 2012), in Gouadec's model the client's specification is the central criterion for evaluation, and ideally it defines the target audience, terminological solutions as well as matters related to style and register, and the expected quality level. Gouadec's heuristics also contain an explicit usability element under d), where the final product is evaluated with respect to the end users' needs, but the specification mainly determines what kind of a translation is useful to the *client*. This is where we see a significant difference between Gouadec's approach and UCT, where the recognition and fulfillment of the actual end user's needs is key. In Gouadec's approach, by contrast, the end users' will is at the hands of the client: if the client's specification emphasizes the end user's role, the translation process will be focused accordingly, but if the client's interests or understanding are different, the translation process is also fine-tuned differently. This is a crucial issue in UCT: it is not about completing clients' wishes but about making sure, together with the client, that the end users' needs are fulfilled.

Gouadec's list is also noteworthy in the sense that the concept of translation error, or an explicit drive to eliminate errors, is not visibly emphasized. This is a fresh departure from traditional approaches, even though the idea of error elimination is built into both factual correctness and professional standards. Additionally, aesthetic considerations, which, for example, have their own section in Nielsen's usability attributes introduced in Chapter 2, are omitted from the list entirely. In this aspect, Gouadec's list departs from the translation studies tradition, which has a strong element of aesthetic evaluations, and it also differs from user-centered translation. In UCT, aesthetic assessment is linked to user experience and user satisfaction, and in the specification this aspect can be emphasized if the translation project involves a strong aesthetic element.

In this section we have concentrated on the assessment of translations. As the quality of a translation is always tied to the quality of the source text, it would be equally important to subject the source text to usability and quality evaluation. Unfortunately, this is not very common. Many of the elements of UCT presented in this book can be employed to improve the usability of original texts.

9.2 Experimenting with UCT in the translation industry

In this section, we will introduce case studies in which the user-centered translation model or some element of it is tested in practice. As we have described in this book, UCT need not be a burdensome, time-intensive and expensive process, and it is not only reserved for large companies. It can be applied differently in different circumstances. While it is possible for a translation company or perhaps even an individual translator to implement the entire UCT model, it is equally possible to adopt such individual elements of the model that are particularly suited for a specific context. To exemplify the possibility of using both the full model and individual parts of it, we present the following case studies, in which UCT has been applied in different ways.

We start with three case studies where three different mental models – personas, audience design and the implied reader – are applied in different translation contexts and by different translators. In addition, the implied reader case study also makes use of heuristics (see Chapter 6). Then, we present a case where some usability testing methods were used to investigate the translation of an online course. Finally, we discuss the findings from an interview study where a coordinator at a translation agency expressed her opinions on whether the full UCT model could be implemented in practice.

9.2.1 Personas in magazine translation and in translator training

As we mentioned in Section 5.3, personas are a tool that fits easily within a translator's intuitive work process. Many translators consider, at least on some level, at whom or at what kind of a reader they target their translation. We can also find real-life examples of personas being used in translation work. One such example is from a Finnish translation agency, which has used the persona Aripekkajuhani[5] as a fictive reader model for popular, translated scientific magazines for over a decade. Aripekkajuhani is described as a teenage boy who is interested in science and technology. Consequently, when a translator is translating an article for this magazine and has to decide, for example, whether some detail should be explained or not, the criterion is not whether a vague notion of "Finnish readers" would require an explanation; rather, the question is "Does Aripekkajuhani know this?" Even though Aripekkajuhani, or other reader personas used by the same translation agency (such as Mr Mähönen, an elderly gentleman who is knowledgable about and interested in military matters, and an avid reader of the same publisher's translated history magazine), have not been consciously constructed through the methods of usability engineering, the fundamental purpose is clearly the same. The personas have been created through cooperative brainstorming, and in addition to their usefulness in translation, they also demonstrate that developing personas can be a creative and rewarding project for a translation team.

We have also found personas to be an engaging and enlightening way of teaching target audience analysis to translation students, and personas have been successfully used on several translation courses by ourselves and our colleagues. In translation courses, from first-year introductory courses all the way to Master's level seminar workshops, students have been asked to create personas either for a predetermined source text or for a text of their own choosing. The text might then be translated with the persona in mind, or the creation of the persona can be an independent exercise demonstrating target audience analysis. In either case, the exercise typically arouses active discussion, and students are often quite creative in constructing their personas. Most importantly, the resulting personas present an opportunity to discuss translation strategies, the information structure of a text, typography and many other features of translations from the perspective of this persona's needs and preferences. The practical questions involved in the translator's decision-making come to life when being presented in the context of a fictional but realistic persona. The persona can thus be a very constructive tool in translation class when discussing the translator's solutions, which can sometimes be reduced to generalities or platitudes if discussed without a specific target user in mind. Based on our experience, once students have been introduced to the idea of personas and they have experimented with using a persona, it also easily becomes a tool that they can then transfer to other assignments or classes on their own accord.

9.2.2 Audience design in subtitling

Anni Otava (2013) has conducted several case studies on the use of UCT in the translation industry. Otava's first UCT test case involved a professional subtitler, who applied the concept of audience design to a subtitling task where an extract of the American reality program *Celebrity Apprentice* was subtitled into Finnish. According to Otava (2013: 31–32), the subtitler stated that "audience design appealed to him because he considered it to be an extension of how he already viewed the audience, albeit less polarized". In other words, audience design was a rather intuitive method of characterizing the audience for this subtitler, but it presented more fine-grained distinctions than his habitual way of analyzing the audience. His analysis of the audience for the subtitling task used in this case was as follows (ibid.: 34; our formulations):

- *addressees*: television viewers in general;
- *auditors*: viewers who happen to be watching, although they are not keen followers of that particular series but may watch the entire program if the circumstances are opportune;
- *overhearers*: anybody who just happens to surf into the channel;
- *referees*: American TV reality show aficionados.

In this scenario, the subtitler did not find any eavesdroppers, which is the fifth recipient type in Bell's classification (see Section 5.2). Otava (2013: 34–35) aptly argues that the subtitler's categorization is somewhat surprising, as it positions the primary target audience of the program in the referee category, rather than as addressees. Thus, the subtitler appears to have a slightly different understanding of audience design than might have been intended, even though his reasoning is certainly within the logic of the model.

Otava (2013: 35–36) then analyzed the resulting subtitles to see whether audience design had any discernible effects on the translation. However, she decided to focus her analysis on whether the translation served the referee group, as that was the group that the subtitler named as the main target audience. Secondarily, she investigated whether the other audience categories were taken into account in the subtitles in any visible way. Otava concluded that the subtitler had indeed translated the extract in a way that serves the program's primary audience (ibid.: 38–39). However, she found it difficult to determine whether the other audience categories had been taken into account in the translation (ibid.: 61–62). She argued that it would have been difficult for the subtitler to translate for the auditors or overhearers: their level of knowledge cannot be known, and the medium of subtitles does not allow for additional information or explanation to be provided for less knowledgable audience groups. Otava (ibid.: 62) thus concludes that

> [a]udience design works fairly well in audiovisual translation in the sense that once the target audience is defined, the audience can quite easily be taken into account in the translation process. [. . .] However, other audience groups besides addressees and referees are difficult to take into account due to technical restrictions and the nature of the translation. This would suggest that while user-centered translation and mental models are an excellent approach to audiovisual translation, audience design might not be the best possible tool for it.

Otava's analysis suggests that, while the experiment was not entirely successful, it did demonstrate the potential of UCT in audiovisual translation. However, the case was also a useful reminder of the fact that not all methods are ideal for all contexts, and the UCT model must be implemented slightly differently in different situations. The case also indicated that translators using the tools of UCT could benefit from systematic guidance as to how the tools can be applied in practice in order to optimize the usefulness of the methods.

9.2.3 The implied reader in nonfiction translation

In Otava's second case study, a translator of nonfiction documents translated a sample document from Finnish into English after analyzing the source text in terms of its implied reader positions and determining the implied reader of the translation. Once the translation was complete, Otava used heuristics to evaluate the resulting translation (see Section 6.3). The text to be translated was an annual action plan of the Youth Forum of the Finnish town Tampere (2013: 41). In the analysis, the translator first considered the source text and its implied reader, but then primarily focused on the translated text and described the implied reader of the translation in the following way (ibid.: 43):

- is an adolescent or an adult;
- does not know any Finnish or feels more comfortable reading the text in English;

- lives in Finland (possibly even Tampere) and is familiar with the local culture, at least on a general level;
- is fairly familiar with the basic structure of an action plan and the general flow of operations in an organization;
- is looking for background information on the forum and its operations;
- is or considers becoming involved in the forum's operations or granting funding for its operations.

The above list is rather target-oriented, and indicates that translators may be inclined to bend towards their future readers even when using a model that starts from a source text analysis. The resulting implied reader actually resembles a persona, and the list contains several characteristics that arise from the context rather than the text itself. Had the translator opted for a more thorough analysis of the implied reader in the source text, she might have come up with a different kind of list.

Otava (2013: 42) considers the implied reader a suitable mental model for this particular context, because the translator did not receive any information about the target audience and was thus forced to formulate a reader construct largely based on text analysis. The translator's analysis of the implied reader presents a credible and easily applicable list of reader characteristics, and it demonstrates an ability and a willingness to approach the translation task from a user-centered perspective. The implied reader is a somewhat flexible concept, and it can be quite plausibly applied in the way it has been applied in this case, so that characteristics of the source text are used and modified to construct an image of the implied reader of the prospective target text.

In all, Otava (2013: 63) found the implied reader case quite successful, concluding that

> [the] implied reader is a cost-effective and relatively easy way of considering the target audience of the text while translating in order to make the translation as usable as possible. All the translator needs for creating an implied reader model is the knowledge and understanding of how to construct it as well as a little time. Granted, time is often of the essence when translating, but once the translator is familiar with the process of creating an implied reader, I would attest that it will become routine and the time constraints will level over time. Moreover, the translation process itself will also become easier as all possible translation problems can be reflected through the implied reader and the model's level of language and knowledge.

Thus, the implied reader can be a useful tool even for individual freelance translators in small projects. It can be particularly helpful in situations where the translation brief does not specify the target audience and the translator must find the means to determine the target audience in some other way.

9.2.4 Usability of a translated online course

The University of Eastern Finland decided to set up a new Master's degree program in linguistic sciences, with a subprogram in translation studies and translation technology (operational since 2013). The basics of translation technology have, for quite some time, been taught to the Finnish translation students of the university on an online learning platform. This course now needed to be translated into English for the purposes of the new international program. To achieve this aim, an independent team of translators was recruited from among advanced translation students in spring 2013. The translation was to meet the needs of the target audience of nonnative English-speaking students, and culture-specific Finnish elements were to be avoided. In other words, the focus was on delocalizing the locally produced course material. The team was asked to read on UCT (Suojanen *et al.* 2012) and to select some ideas to be implemented in their translation process. From among the UCT tools, the team found usability tests the most appealing method for their purposes, and they decided to attempt to apply usability testing methodology.

The translator team recruited a test group of 14 visiting international language students (i.e. a group very similar to the targeted audience of international students), and conducted two separate test sessions. The first session aimed at gathering the users' subjective comments on the material and finding usability issues on a textual level. An introductory text extract was selected for this purpose, and the participants were first asked to go through the text individually, positioning themselves as a student in a course where the test material was used, and to write down comments and notes about any parts of the text that somehow stood out and hampered their reading. Following refreshments, the text and their comments were discussed in group. Among the issues that came up, some were of direct relevance to user-centeredness. The team found out, for example, that their projection of the English skills of the target audience had been too high, and sentence structures and formulations needed to be simplified. Another interesting finding was that the students preferred a more formal register in the translation.

The second usability test concerned the usability of instructions in completing a task (creating a new project by using translation memory software), and was also divided into two sections: moderators observed the participants' success in completing the task, and it was then followed by a group discussion. The results were positive in the sense that the test group considered the user instructions clear and useful, but since no major usability problems arose, the usefulness of the test was less obvious than for the first one. All in all, these two small experiments represent a new application of usability testing designed to examine the usability of *texts*, and they indicate promising new avenues for further development (see also Suokas 2014, discussed in Section 6.2.1).

9.2.5 Towards a complete UCT process

As her third case, Otava also interviewed a translation coordinator working in a translation agency. The purpose of the interview was to find out whether any of the tools introduced in the UCT model were already in use, or whether the coordinator thought some of them might be introduced into the translation projects carried out at that agency. The interview revealed (Otava 2013: 56–60) that, even though the coordinator stated that user-centered translation was not used by the agency, some of the procedures and policies in this translation agency resembled some stages of user-centered translation. For example, the translation process in this agency contains systematic quality controls and a degree of iterativity, as the coordinator checks the translations and sends them back to individual translators if revision is needed. Iterativity in itself, however, is no guarantee of a user-centered approach. The coordinator also uses a checklist reminiscent of heuristics in checking the translations, and individual translators tend to use some methods of audience analysis in determining their translation strategies. What distinguishes the policies of this agency from a genuine user-centered translation model is that its user-orientation is not systematic or conscious, and the translators are not specifically advised to use user-centered tools in their work (ibid.: 66). This lack of conscious attention to user-centeredness is perhaps one reason why the coordinator expressed reluctance to implement UCT at this translation agency. According to Otava (ibid.: 60), the coordinator stated that

> [p]erforming usability tests or [additional] quality assessments within the agency is not possible at the moment. The reason for this is that the agency simply does not get paid for them, and the time constraints related to each translation commission prevent any extensive testing. Even though the timeframe[s] for translation commissions in the agency are generally good, they do not accommodate both the translation and testing that is already done as well as additional usability assessment.

However, as Otava (2013: 60–61) points out, usability testing as such is not a necessary requirement of the UCT model, and it is possible to adopt a user-centered approach to translation even without heavy investments of time and money, particularly if the implementation of the model is performed in stages and planned carefully in advance. It is true that, as Otava (ibid.: 61) suggests, the potential costs of implementing UCT might make the concept unattractive to small translation agencies. However, as the previous cases have demonstrated, in the case of small agencies and individual translators, it is entirely plausible to use some tools of UCT – and to adopt a systematic, explicit ethos of user-centeredness – without causing extensive strains on resources. In fact, implementing even the full UCT model could be possible in smaller as well as larger agencies, as long as it is not seen as a cumbersome, large-scale addition to existing practices but a way of streamlining processes to include a user-centered perspective and slightly redefining the translator's role. Once the new model has been implemented, the new tools will most likely replace and systematize some previous practices, such as quality assessment procedures, guidance for translators, processing feedback and the translation work itself. For example, usability heuristics can be used in place of more traditional quality assessment practices, and translators will be able to select translation strategies more decisively if they have first constructed a mental model. In this way, investments in UCT can create benefits by improving the overall process.

Skepticism and financial concerns are not foreign in the usability engineering field either: Nielsen (1994b: n.p.) notes that very often even basic usability engineering techniques such as early focus on users or iterative design are not used in real-life software development projects. One of the reasons is the perceived cost, although many techniques are quite cheap. To tackle the obstacles to employing usability engineering methods, Nielsen (ibid.) has suggested "guerrilla methods" and the previously mentioned "discount usability engineering" approach, which includes heuristic evaluation, simplified thinking aloud and scenarios.[6]

Otava (2013: 66–67) concludes that user-centered translation can be adopted by individual translators and translation agencies alike: all that is needed is to become aware of the model and the tools it contains, and to decide to use them in practice. In fact, she points out that "both the translators in case studies 1 and 2 stated that the knowledge of user-centered translation methods has made them more aware of the recipient's role in the translation process", which suggests that becoming familiar with UCT has already affected their translation practices. Otava (ibid.: 68) feels that the case studies have confirmed the usefulness and applicability of UCT, even though all elements of it might not be ideally suited for each translation context. User-centered translation appears to have potential as a way of thinking which allows translators and translation agencies to pay more systematic attention to the users. What is required is knowledge of the model, understanding of how it can be implemented and willingness to spend some time on the initial stages of becoming accustomed to the new system.

In this chapter, we have looked at the translation industry, finding parallels and differences between existing practices and UCT. We are convinced that the UCT model can be productively implemented in various contexts. The case studies discussed above indicate promising avenues for further innovation on the interface of usability and translation.

Assignments

1   Williams (see Section 9.1.3) classifies translation errors into four categories, of which "critical error" is the most serious. Give some examples of critical translation errors and explain why they are so.

2   One well-known academic approach to quality assessment is Christiane Nord's classic model that focuses on text analysis. Find out what this model is (see e.g. Nord 1991), and discuss its similarities and differences with UCT.

3   Interview a translator. Find out what type of quality assessment procedures he or she currently uses. Based on the interview, consider how UCT could be implemented in the translator's practice.

Notes

1   In translation studies, quality has been an ongoing theme since the 1990s. For an overview, see Drugan 2013.
2   Gouadec's book is aimed at private translator-entrepreneurs, and this final section suggests that translators' work must be a profitable business for them.
3   Revising, editing and proofreading constitute a complex and ill-defined terminological web. Revision has been defined and understood in various different ways, and agreement as to what a revision process should entail are manifold – for example, should the reviser check the translation against the source text or not?; Is self-revision a form of revision or not?; What is the optimal level of revision? (see Martin 2007; Mossop 2010). In our usage, revision is an umbrella term for all kinds of text-amendment activities.
4   **Specification** is also used in the American translation industry standard (ASTM F2575 2006), and it is in all likelihood becoming more generally used in the translation business. In fact, the term **Produktspezifikation** (product specification) was already in use in Justa Holz-Mänttäri's (1984) classic treatise, where the translator's expert role is approached in the framework of translational action. The modern translation industry has brought renewed significance to Holz-Mänttäri's thoughts concerning cooperation and the roles of the different participants in translational action.
5   "Aripekkajuhani" is a rather unusual amalgamation of three common Finnish male first names: Ari, Pekka and Juhani.
6   Scenarios are another usability research method, which we have not discussed in this book. It is an affordable way of prototyping system functionalities.

10 Conclusion

In this book, we have investigated selected interfaces between usability (research) and translation (studies) in order to formulate a user-centered model for translation. We first looked at these interfaces from a theoretical viewpoint, contemplating key usability research concepts and their meanings and applicability in practical translation and in translation studies. We also looked at usability from the perspective of texts, reading and readability, and reviewed some long-standing ideas within translation studies from the viewpoint of usability. In Chapters 5–9 we offered practical methods for involving end users and assessing usability in different phases of the user-centered translation process, and discussed how the translation industry can benefit from UCT. In this final chapter, we recapitulate the main points of the model and reflect on its future potential. In the spirit of user-centered translation, we encourage readers to use and develop the model for their own purposes.

10.1 UCT and the future of the translation industry

One of the main target groups of this book are future translators. The translation profession is, once again, going through dramatic changes and the translation industry is becoming reorganized. Translation is a growing business, but the changes have also created new demands for increasingly sophisticated technological tools, and for agility in terms of fast delivery, iterative updates, rolling deadlines, teamwork and multiple-language service provision (Drugan 2013). Translation technologies are developing rapidly, and it is evident that in the near future many of the translation tasks presently performed by human translators are gradually being reassigned to machine translation, with humans in support and development roles.

A recent report summarizes its main findings in its title: *Can't Read, Won't Buy* (DePalma *et al.* 2014). The report is based on a survey of more than 3,000 respondents in 10 non-English speaking countries, and the results clearly indicate that translation to a local language is a significant boost for sales as consumers are "unlikely to purchase what they don't understand" (ibid.: 2). This is a significant selling point for translation, but it is relevant to note that non-user-centered translation, especially a machine translation, can easily be considered equally strange or even stranger than a foreign language, and relying on machine translation, especially when the output is not post-edited, can also be costly. The speed of fully automated translation obviously vastly exceeds any human capability, but human translation activity contains a number of tacit elements that computers are – at least to date – not very good at dealing with. To avoid strangeness, it may be necessary to depart from the source text style and content, and such decision-making that human translators often tacitly employ is not presently achievable for artificial intelligence.

User-centered translation is about making this tacit knowledge of reader-orientedness explicit. The idea of focusing on the readers is by no means a novelty in translation studies. However, translators often complain that the hectic pace and low prices in the contemporary translation industry do not allow them to take their readers sufficiently into account. Still, we believe usability measures can be incorporated into the present industry setting and, what is more, we are convinced that there is sufficient demand for projects where usability is more valued than low price and fast delivery. In fact, we may be witnessing a new development in the translation sector that is emerging in many others as well – namely, that the homogenizing mass-production market is increasingly splitting into two: the high end of tailor-made luxury products and the low end of cheaper and cheaper low-quality production where even the low-paid workers are being replaced by robots. As the translation industry is based on offering services to operators in other fields, a dualistic division of markets would have (and is, we argue, already having) repercussions: the high end will want premium translations to support elite branding, and price will not be a dominant factor; the low end will increasingly rely on automated translation wherever suitable MT products exist, and quality issues related to machine translation are not perhaps considered relevant (cf. Drugan 2013: 23). At the higher end of the translation market, UCT can cater for the needs of those companies who have chosen a user-centered approach in their core business as well. The need for diversification in the translation sector has been increasingly recognized (Adams 2013). We agree that innovative thinking is needed in this rapidly changing field, and there is plenty of room for new kinds of services. UCT is one direction this diversification can take.

UCT offers a chance for translation agencies to diversify their services, and it can even be developed into a distinctive translation business profile, but its methodology also includes quick and easy solutions that do not require extensive resources or big research teams. Personas and usability heuristics, for example, can be fairly easily taken up by self-employed translators, whereas recruiting participants for usability tests or using eyetracking devices require earmarked resources in terms of time, money and new expertise. What remains constant across the palette of methods, both those described in this book and in the many others that one can find in usability research and adapt to translation, is that UCT offers translators and translation agencies new tools and new ways of thinking with which they might be able to bring a more user-centered approach to their work. The case studies discussed in Chapter 9 show that sometimes methods can be fruitfully employed in ways that diverge from the original intent, and the methods need not even be explicitly used; the mere knowledge of UCT can support the translator in making more usable translations, as Otava (2013: 72–73) observed:

> User-centered translation theory does indeed help translators to better cater for the needs of the translation's intended recipient and thus produce a translation that is more user-friendly. However, it should be noted that the various methods for implementing the theory [. . .] are not all ideal or even applicable to all translation tasks. Therefore, the methods should be carefully chosen so that the result will be a translation that is usable and user-friendly. However, this thesis shows that even the translators' knowledge of user-centered translation methods brings the target audience to focus and thus enables the translators to produce translations that are more usable.

10.2 User-centered translation practice

In the Introduction, with Figure 1.1, we visualized user-centered translation as a cyclical process. A translation need initiates an iterative translation process that contains a number of named methods for ensuring that the resulting translation is oriented towards its future users. The specification builds a common ground between the translator and the client, also offering a point of comparison for future usability evaluation. At the beginning of the translation process, the translator can use mental models to build a picture of the user and to select appropriate translation strategies that enable meeting the user's needs. During the process, usability evaluation methods such as heuristic evaluation and usability testing are used to provide support for translation. The new information produced during these phases may compel the translator to change strategies. Once the final translation has been submitted, a post-mortem analysis ensures feedback that is important for future projects. In addition, various reception research methods provide more information on the successfulness of the translation and the results also feed into the subsequent process cycles.

All of these methods, used consistently and strategically during the actual translation process, allow the translation team to acquire accumulative information about the users of the translation and to gain an advanced understanding of their usability needs and preferences, and this knowledge is taken to inform the translation as it evolves. Within the UCT model, the leap that is left for the translator to make is interpreting the results from the usability evaluation and matching them with the strategies that are used while translating. As the UCT model is tested in practical settings and more experience with its implementation is gained, researchers and translators will learn how to best make this leap in different contexts.

As with any model, the practical application of UCT may take various forms. For example, it is important to test the applicability of the usability heuristics we developed for user-centered translation, but it is equally important to modify the list to suit different genres and purposes. From a theoretical viewpoint, usability has in this book been reviewed through some selected ideas from translation studies, allowing for many more discussions about the interfaces between usability and translation theory. The model in its entirety is also open for adaptation for different translation and academic contexts.

10.3 Two-way street between usability research and translation studies

Usability (research) has been at the forefront in this book, and selected usability approaches have then been examined through the lenses of translation (studies). Our main argument is that the practice of translation can benefit greatly from a close engagement with usability research. We are interested in hearing the views of usability experts concerning our adaption of user-centered design and various usability research methods. Perhaps more importantly, however, we also think that the flow of influence need not be one way only. It is also worth considering what translation (studies) has to offer to usability (research). Cultural usability is an obvious area of overlap. For example, acceptability, satisfaction and other norms and conventions inherent in usability are largely culture-bound, and usability research often takes place in a multilingual and multicultural context. Multilingual textual products and their cultural usability is an element that is most obviously within the translator's competencies. As intercultural communication has a central role in the translation process, trained translators are well equipped to recognize and deal with culture-bound elements related to usability.

Cultural usability is not an easy target for analysis. *Culture* in itself has become a problematic notion. It connotes coherence, continuity and uniformity of a given social unit, and pushes us to focus on differences between groups as well as on homogeneity within them. We need to be aware of the risks of essentialization and stay tuned to the multiplicity of viewpoints and power play within groups. We also need to accept the artificial nature of any fixed and absolute boundaries between groups. However, in spite of all the conceptual and social problems linked to culture, we still feel that an awareness of cultural differences and the competence to deal with them are significant both for successful translation and usable design. Cultural usability is an area where translation studies and usability research can support one another, both in terms of finding pragmatic solutions for particular cultural contexts and in terms of designing research programs to enhance our knowledge on cultural differences and their effects.

In Chapter 2 we explained how usability research has developed in three waves, which indicates that as society and technology change, more and more challenges are also placed on usability research to find new angles on design. In addition to translation studies offering support to cultural usability, translation research can also be a valuable area in the emerging third wave, in which more participatory technologies are being integrated with the more designer-led approaches. The field of translation studies has a long history of looking at transcultural interaction, and this has recently been combined with an increasing focus on crowdsourcing and volunteer translation as well as reception research. Translation studies thus combines elements central for both the second and the third wave, and UCT takes this combination even further. We hope our model of user-centered translation demonstrates that translation is just as involved in producing a usable product and a good user experience as the initial design processes are.

10.4 Empowerment through users

Translation is and will be a thriving business. In an era of globalization, multilingualism is the default, and thus is its corollary, translation. Multiple languages and multiple cultural backgrounds place more and more demands on usability methods, and different user groups need to be taken into consideration with cultural usability in mind. In today's digital world, these users are increasingly active, and they expect to play participatory roles during the entire product life-cycle. User-centered translation responds to these recent developments and offers practical tools for taking the end users into account in multilingual projects. Translators always think about the users; user-centered translation allows translators to advocate for them.

According to Drugan (2013: 179), the current professional paradigm is "active translation agents and passive or unknowable translation recipients". With her, we wish to argue against this view. UCT propagates for engaging in active inter-action with the end users, and making them not only knowable but also known and ratified. Drugan (2013: 192) ends her book on translation quality with enthus-iasm as follows: "Observing real translators in real action is becoming increasingly possible, and increasingly rewarding." We add: UCT makes observing real users of translations in real action increasingly possible and increasingly rewarding.

Assignments

1   Apply one of the tools described in this book to analyze the usability of this book or one of its chapters. Produce an assessment and suggestions for improvement.

2   Interview a translator, a representative of a translation agency or a client. Introduce the UCT model to the interviewee and ask what they think about it and its applicability to their own context. Write a report.

3   Search for usability research methods that have not been introduced in this book. You can, for example, browse Martin and Hanington's book (2012), or find ideas from the website usability.gov. Introduce one method and discuss how it could be applied in translation or used within the UCT model.

4   Write a business proposal for a UCT-oriented translation agency in the form of an elevator pitch and then present it in class (for more about elevator pitches, see, e.g. http://sbinformation.about.com/od/marketingsales/a/How-To-Write-An-Elevator-Pitch.htm).

References

Abdallah, Kristiina and Kaisa Koskinen (2007) "Managing Trust: Translating and the Network Economy", *Meta*, 52(4): 673–687.

Adams, Nicole Y. (2013) *Diversification in the Language Industry: Success Beyond Translation*, Brisbane: NYA Communications.

Agboka, Godwin Y. (2013) "Participatory Localization: A Social Justice Approach to Navigating Unenfranchised/Disenfranchised Cultural Sites", *Technical Communication Quarterly*, 22: 28–49.

Akrich, Madeleine (2000) "The De-Scription of Technical Objects", in Wiebe E. Bijker and John Law (eds) *Shaping Technology/Building Society: Studies in Sociotechnical Change*, Cambridge, MA: The MIT Press, 205–224.

Alanen, Anukaisa (2008) *Sairaalan käyttöohje: Potilasohjeet autistisille käyttäjille – mitä, miksi, kuinka? (The User Guide of a Hospital: Patient Guidelines for Autistic Users – What, Why, How?)*, Master's thesis, Tampere: University of Tampere. Available at: http://urn.fi/urn:nbn:fi:uta-1-18489 (last accessed 12 June 2014).

Al-Khalifa, Hend S. and Amani A. Al-Ajlan (2010) "Automatic Readability Measurements of the Arabic Text: An Exploratory Study", *The Arabian Journal for Science and Engineering* 35(2C): 103–124. Available at: http://ajse.kfupm.edu.sa/articles/352C_P.07.pdf (last accessed 15 April 2013).

Alves, Fabio and Amparo Hurtaro Albir (2010) "Cognitive Approaches", in Yves Gambier and Luc van Doorslaer (eds) *Handbook of Translation Studies*, Vol. 1, Amsterdam and Philadelphia, PA: John Benjamins, 28–35.

Alves Veiga, Maria José (2006) "Subtitling Reading Practices", in João Ferreira Duarte, Alexandra Assis Rosa and Teresa Seruya (eds) *Translation Studies at the Interface of Disciplines*, Amsterdam and Philadelphia, PA: John Benjamins, 161–168.

Anderson, Richard (2011) "User (Experience) Research, Design Research, Usability Research, Market Research: A Changing Interconnected World", *UX Magazine* 648, 2 April 2011. Available at: http://uxmag.com/articles/user-experience-research-design-research-usability-research-market-research (last accessed 6 June 2014).

Antonini, Rachele (2005) "The Perception of Subtitled Humor in Italy", *Humor: International Journal of Humor Research*, 18(2): 209–225.

—— (2008) "The Perception of Dubbese: An Italian Study", in Delia Chiaro, Christine Heiss and Chiara Bucaria (eds) *Between Text and Image: Updating Research in Screen Translation*, Amsterdam and Philadelphia, PA: John Benjamins, 135–147.

Antonini, Rachele and Delia Chiaro (2009) "The Perception of Dubbing by Italian Audiences", in Jorge Díaz Cintas and Gunilla Anderman (eds) *Audiovisual Translation: Language Transfer on Screen*, Basingstoke and New York: Palgrave Macmillan, 97–114.

Appiah, Kwame Anthony (1993/2000) "Thick Translation", in Lawrence Venuti (ed.) *The Translation Studies Reader*, London and New York: Routledge, 417–429.

ASTM F2575 (2006) *Standard Guide for Quality Assurance in Translation*, West Conshohocken, PA: ASTM International.

Bannon, Liam J. (1991) "From Human Factors to Human Actors: The Role of Psychology and Human–Computer Interaction Studies in Systems Design", in Joan Greenbaum and Morten Kyng (eds) *Design at Work: Cooperative Design of Computer Systems*, Hillsdale, NJ: Lawrence Erlbaum Associates, 25–44.

Barber, Wendy and Albert Badre (1998) "Culturability: The Merging of Culture and Usability", in *Conference Proceedings: 4th Conference on Human Factors and the Web*. Available at: http://research.microsoft.com/en-us/um/people/marycz/hfweb98/barber/ (last accessed 6 June 2014).

Battarbee, Katja and Ilpo Koskinen (2005) "Co-Experience: User Experience as Interaction", *CoDesign*, 1(1): 5–18.

Becher, Viktor (2010) "Abandoning the Notion of 'Translation-Inherent' Explicitation: Against a Dogma of Translation Studies", *Across Languages and Cultures*, 11(1): 1–28.

Beckett, Sandra L. (ed.) (1999) *Transcending Boundaries: Writing for a Dual Audience of Children and Adults*, New York: Garland.

Bell, Allan (1984) "Language Style as Audience Design", *Language in Society*, 13(2): 145–204.

—— (2001) "Back in Style: Reworking Audience Design", in Penelope Eckert and John R. Rickford (eds) *Style and Sociolinguistic Variation*, Cambridge: Cambridge University Press, 139–169.

Bennett, Karen (2013) "English as a Lingua Franca in Academia: Combating Epistemicide through Translator Training", *The Interpreter and Translator Trainer*, 7(2): 169–193.

Bergvall-Kåreborn, Birgitta and Anna Ståhlbröst (2010) "User Expressions Translated into Requirements", *Human Technology*, 6(2): 212–229.

Beu, Andreas, Pia Honold and Xiaowei Yuan (2000) "How to Build Up an Infrastructure for Intercultural Usability Engineering", *International Journal of Human–Computer Interaction*, 12(3&4): 347–358.

Boren, Ted M. and Judith Ramey (2000) "Thinking Aloud: Reconciling Theory and Practice", *IEEE Transactions on Professional Communication*, 43(3): 261–278.

Bringhurst, Robert (2002) *The Elements of Typographic Style*, Point Roberts, WA: Hartley & Marks, 2nd edn.

Bucaria, Chiara (2008) "Acceptance of the Norm or Suspension of Disbelief? The Case of Formulaic Language in Dubbese", in Delia Chiaro, Christine Heiss and Chiara Bucaria (eds) *Between Text and Image: Updating Research in Screen Translation*, Amsterdam and Philadelphia, PA: John Benjamins, 149–163.

Burke, Kenneth (1969) *A Rhetoric of Motives*, Berkeley, CA: University of California Press.

Byrne, Jody (2010) *Technical Translation: Usability Strategies for Translating Technical Documentation*, Dordrecht: Springer.

Caffrey, Colm (2009) *Relevant Abuse? Investigating the Effects of an Abusive Subtitling Procedure on the Perception of TV Anime Using Eye Tracker and Questionnaire*, Ph.D. thesis, Dublin: Dublin City University.

Calabria, Tina (2004) "An Introduction to Personas and How to Create Them". Available at: www.steptwo.com.au/papers/kmc_personas/index.html (last accessed 6 June 2014).

Cavaliere, Flavia (2008) "Measuring the Perception of the Screen Translation of Un Posto al Sole: A Cross-Cultural Study", in Delia Chiaro, Christine Heiss and Chiara Bucaria (eds) *Between Text and Image: Updating Research in Screen Translation*, Amsterdam and Philadelphia, PA: John Benjamins, 165–180.

Chandler, Daniel and Rod Munday (2011) *A Dictionary of Media and Communication*, Oxford: Oxford University Press.

Chiaro, Delia (2007) "The Effect of Translation on Humour Response: The Case of Dubbed Comedy in Italy", in Yves Gambier (ed.) *Doubts and Directions in Translation Studies: Selected Contributions from the EST Congress*, Amsterdam: John Benjamins, 137–152.

Choi, Boreum, Inseong Lee and Jinwoo Kim (2006) "Culturability in Mobile Data Services: A Qualitative Study of the Relationship Between Cultural Characteristics and User-Experience Attributes", *International Journal of Human–Computer Interaction*, 20(3): 171–206.

Clarity (n.d.) "Clarity Advocating Clear Legal Language". Available at: www.clarity-international.net/ (last accessed 6 June 2014).

Clemmensen, Torkil (2011) "Templates for Cross-Cultural and Culturally Specific Usability Testing: Results from Field Studies and Ethnographic Interviewing in Three Countries", *International Journal of Human–Computer Interaction*, 27(7): 634–669.

Clemmensen, Torkil, Morten Hertzum, Kasper Hornbæk, Qingxin Shi and Pradeep Yammiyavar (2009) "Cultural Cognition in Usability Evaluation", *Interacting with Computers*, 21: 212–220.

Coney, Mary B. (1992) "Technical Readers and their Rhetorical Roles", *IEEE Transactions on Professional Communication*, 35(2): 58–63.

Conklin, James and George Hayhoe (2010) "Focus Group Workshop: Communication in a Self-Service Society", in *IEEE International Professional Communication Conference Proceedings (IPCC 2010)*: 273–274.

Cook, Guy (1995) "Principles for Research into Text Accessibility", in Heikki Nyyssönen and Leena Kuure (eds) *Principles of Accessibility and Design in English Text – Research in Progress*, publications of the Department of English, University of Oulu, *Text and Discourse Studies*, 12, 9–18.

Couture, Barbara (1992) "Categorizing Professional Discourse: Engineering, Administrative, and Technical/Professional Writing", *Journal of Business and Technical Communication*, 6(1): 5–37.

Cummings, Michael (2010) "UX Design Defined". Available at: http://uxdesign.com/ux-defined (last accessed 6 June 2014).

Danska, Anna, Sakari Herranen and Markku Reunanen (1996) "Euroopan integraatio: Koneiden, laitteiden ja tuotteiden käyttöohjeet" ("European Integration: User Guides for Machines, Appliances and Products"), *Integraatiotiedote 22*, Helsinki: Metalliteollisuuden keskusliitto MET.

Day, Daniel L. (1998) "Shared Values and Shared Interfaces: The Role of Culture in the Globalisation of Human–Computer Systems", *Interacting with Computers* 9: 269–274.

de Bortoli, Mario, Robert Gillham and Jesús Maroto (2003) "Cross-Cultural Interactive Marketing and Website Usability", *Global Propaganda*. Available at: www.globalpropaganda.com/articles/InternationalWebsiteUsability.pdf (last accessed 6 June 2014).

de Linde, Zoë and Neil Kay (1999) *The Semiotics of Subtitling*, Manchester: St. Jerome.

DePalma, Donald A., Vijayalaxmi Hedge and Robert G. Stewart (2014) *Can't Read, Won't Buy: How Translation Affects the Web Customer Experience and E-Commerce Growth*, Cambridge, MA: Common Sense Advisory.

Díaz Cintas, Jorge and Aline Remael (2007) *Audiovisual Translation: Subtitling*, Manchester: St. Jerome.

Directorate-General for Translation (2009a) *Web Translation as a Genre: Studies on Translation and Multilingualism*, Brussels: European Commission. Available at: http://bookshop.europa.eu/is-bin/INTERSHOP.enfinity/WFS/EU-Bookshop-Site/en_GB/-/EUR/ViewPublication-Start?PublicationKey=HC8009160 (last accessed 9 June 2014).

Directorate-General for Translation (2009b) *Programme for Quality Management in Translation*, Brussels: European Commission. Available at: http://ec.europa.eu/dgs/translation/publications/studies/quality_management_translation_en.pdf (last accessed 6 June 2014).

Dobrin, David N. (1983) "What's Technical about Technical Writing?", in Paul V. Anderson, John Brockmann and Carolyn R. Miller (eds) *New Essays in Technical and Scientific Communication: Research, Theory, Practice*, Farmingdale, NY: Baywood, 227–250.

Doherty, Stephen (2012) *Investigating the Effects of Controlled Language on the Reading and Comprehension of Machine Translated Texts: A Mixed-Methods Approach*, Ph.D. thesis, Dublin: Dublin City University. Available at: http://doras.dcu.ie/16805/1/Stephen Doherty.pdf (last accessed 6 June 2014).

Doherty, Stephen and Sharon O'Brien (2012) "A User-Based Usability Assessment of Raw Machine Translated Technical Instructions", Conference of the Association for Machine Translation in the Americas, Research Papers. Available at: www.mt-archive.info/AMTA-2012-Doherty-2.pdf (last accessed 6 June 2014).

Dray, Susan M. and David A. Siegel (2006) "Melding Paradigms: Meeting the Needs of International Customers through Localization and User-Centered Design", in Keiran J. Dunne (ed.) *Perspectives on Localization*, American Translators Association Scholarly Monograph Series, Vol. XIII, Amsterdam and Philadelphia, PA: John Benjamins, 281–308.

Drugan, Joanna (2013) *Quality in Professional Translation: Assessment and Improvement*, London: Bloomsbury.

d'Ydewalle, Géry, Caroline Praet, Karl Verfaillie and Johan Van Rensbergen (1991) "Watching Subtitled Television: Automatic Reading Behavior", *Communication Research*, 18: 650–666.

Ehn, Pelle and Jonas Löwgren (1997) "Design for Quality-in-Use: Human–Computer Interaction Meets Information Systems Development", in Martin G. Helander, Thomas K. Landauer and Prasad V. Prabhu (eds) *Handbook of Human–Computer Interaction*, The Netherlands: Elsevier Science, 299–313, 2nd edn.

Ericsson, K. Anders and Herbert A. Simon (1993) *Protocol Analysis: Verbal Reports as Data*, Cambridge, MA: MTT Press, revised edn.

Eskola, Jari and Juha Suoranta (1998) *Johdatus laadulliseen tutkimukseen* (*Introduction to Qualitative Research*), Tampere: Vastapaino, 2nd edn.

Fern, Edward F. (2001) *Advanced Focus Group Research*, Thousand Oaks, CA: Sage.

Fetterman, David M. (1998) *Ethnography Step by Step*, Thousand Oaks, CA: Sage, 2nd edn.

Fleischmann, Klaus (2013) "A Cornerstone of Translation Quality: Getting In-Country Review Right Part I", *Gala Blog*, 12 December. Available at: www.gala-global.org/blog/2013/a-cornerstone-of-translation-quality-getting-in-country-review-right-part-i/ (last accessed 6 June 2014).

Flynn, Peter (2010) "Ethnographic Approaches", in Yves Gambier and Luc van Doorslaer (eds) *Handbook of Translation Studies*, Vol. 1, Amsterdam and Philadelphia, PA: John Benjamins, 116–119.

Ford, Gabrielle and Paula Kotze (2005) "Designing Usable Interfaces with Cultural Dimensions", in Maria F. Costabile and Fabio Paternò (eds) *Interact '05: Proceedings of the 2005 IFIP TC13 International Conference on Human–Computer Interaction*, 713–726.

Frandsen-Thorlacius, Olaf, Kasper Hornbæk, Morten Hertzum and Torkil Clemmensen (2009) "Non-Universal Usability? A Survey of How Usability Is Understood by Chinese and Danish Users", in *Proceedings of the SIGCHI Conference on Human Factors in Computing Systems (CHI 1990)*, New York: ACM, 41–50.

Fuentes Luque, Adrián (2000) *La recepción del humor audiovisual traducido: studio comparative de fragmentos de las versions doblada y subtitulada al español de la pelicula Duck Soup, de los Hermanos Marx (The Reception of Translated Audiovisual Humor: A Comparative Study of Spanish Dubbed and Subtitled Versions of Marx Brothers' Duck Soup)*, Ph.D. thesis, Granada: University of Granada.

—— (2003) "An Empirical Approach to the Reception of AV Translated Humour: A Case Study of the Marx Brothers' 'Duck Soup'", *The Translator*, 9(2): 293–306.

Gabriel-Petit, Pabini (2013) "UXmatters: What is User Experience?" Available at: www.uxmatters.com/glossary/ (last accessed 6 June 2014).

Garrett, Jessie James (2002) *The Elements of User Experience: User-Centered Design for the Web*, Indianapolis, IN: New Riders, Chapter 2 and diagram also available at: www.jjg.net/elements/ (last accessed 6 June 2014).

Geertz, Clifford (1973) *Description: Toward and Interpretive Theory of Culture: The Interpretation of Culture*, New York: Basic Books.

Göpferich, Susanne (2009) "Comprehensibility Assessment Using the Karlsruhe Comprehensibility Concept", *Journal of Specialised Translation*, 11: 31–51. Available at: www.jostrans.org/issue11/art_goepferich.pdf (last accessed 6 June 2014).

Göpferich, Susanne, Arnt Lykke Jakobsen and Inger M. Mees (eds) (2008) *Looking at Eyes: Eye-Tracking Studies of Reading and Translation Processing*, Copenhagen Studies in Language 36, Copenhagen: Samfundslitteratur Press.

Gottlieb, Henrik (1994) "Subtitling: Diagonal Translation", *Perspectives: Studies in Translatology*, 2(1): 101–121.

—— (1995) "Establishing a Framework for a Typology of Subtitle Reading Strategies: Viewer Reactions to Deviations from Subtitling Standards", in Yves Gambier, Eija Salo, Erkki Satopää and René Haeseryn (eds) *Communication audiovisuelle et transferts linguistiques: Translatio – Nouvelles de la FIT*, 14(3–4): 388–409.

Gouadec, Daniel (2010) *Translation as a Profession*, Amsterdam and Philadelphia, PA: John Benjamins, 2nd, corrected edn.

Gulliksen, Jan, Susan Harker and Gregg Vanderheiden (2004) "Guidelines, Standards, Methods and Processes for Software Accessibility", *Universal Access in the Information Society* (UAIS), 3(1): 1–5.

Gutt, Ernst August (1991) *Translation and Relevance: Cognition and Context*, Oxford: Blackwell.

Hackos, JoAnn T. (2002) *Content Management for Dynamic Web Delivery*, New York: John Wiley & Sons.

Hall, Marinda, Menno de Jong and Michaël Steehouder (2004) "Cultural Differences and Usability Evaluation: Individualistic and Collectivist Participants Compared", *Technical Communication*, 51(4): 489–503.

Harju, Anna (2008) *Kääntäjä käyttöohjeiden käytettävyyden parantajana (How the Translator Can Improve the Usability of User Instructions)*, Master's thesis, Tampere: University of Tampere. Available at: http://urn.fi/urn:nbn:fi:uta-1-17853 (last accessed 6 June 2014).

Harkness, Janet (2013) "Cross-Cultural Survey Guidelines: VIII: Translation". Available at: http://ccsg.isr.umich.edu/translation.cfm (last accessed 6 June 2014).

Hart-Davidson, William (2001) "On Writing, Technical Communication, and Information Technology: The Core Competencies of Technical Communication", *Technical Communication*, 48(2): 145–155.

Hartley, Anthony, Midori Tatsumi, Hitoshi Isahara, Kyo Kageura and Rei Miyata (2012) "Readability and Translatability Judgments for 'Controlled Japanese'", in *Proceedings of the 16th EAMT Conference*, 28–30 May 2012, Trento, Italy, 237–244. Available at: http://hltshare.fbk.eu/EAMT2012/html/Papers/56.pdf (last accessed 6 June 2014).

Hartson, Rex and Pardha S. Pyla (2013) *The UX Book: Process and Guidelines for Ensuring a Quality User Experience*, Amsterdam: Elsevier.

Hatim, Basil and Ian Mason (1990) *Discourse and the Translator*, London: Longman.

—— (1997) *The Translator as Communicator*, London: Routledge.

Havumetsä, Nina (2012) *The Client Factor: A Study of Clients' Expectations Concerning Non-Literary Translators and the Quality of Non-Literary Translations*, Ph.D. thesis, Helsinki: University of Helsinki.

Herman, David, Manfred Jahn and Marie-Laure Ryan (eds) (2005) *Routledge Encyclopedia of Narrative Theory*, London and New York: Routledge.

Hermans, Theo (1996) "The Translator's Voice in Translated Narrative", *Target*, 8(1): 23–48.

Hertzum, Morten (2010) "Images of Usability", *International Journal of Human–Computer Interaction*, 26(6): 567–600.

Hertzum, Morten, Torkil Clemmensen, Kasper Hornbæk, Jyoti Kumar, Qingxin Shi and Pradeep Yammiyavar (2011) "Personal Usability Constructs: How People Construe Usability Across Nationalities and Stakeholder Groups", *International Journal of Human–Computer Interaction*, 27(8): 729–761.

Hofstede, Geert (1980) *Culture's Consequence: Comparing Values, Behaviours, Institutions and Organizations Across Nations*, London: Sage.

Holz-Mänttäri, Justa (1984) *Translatorisches Handeln: Theorie und Methode*, Annales Academiae Scientarum Fennicae, Ser. B 226, Helsinki: Suomalainen tiedeakatemia.

House, Juliane (1997) *Translation Quality Assessment: A Model Revisited*, Tübingen: Gunter Narr Verlag.

Huckin, Thomas N. and Leslie Olsen (1991) *Technical Writing and Professional Communication For Nonnative Speakers of English*, Singapore: McGraw-Hill, 2nd edn.

Hühn, Peter, John Pier and Wolf Schmid (2009) *Handbook of Narratology – Narratologia: Contributions to Narrative Theory*, 19, Berlin: De Gruyter.

Ilves, Mirja (2005) "Ääneenajattelu" ("Thinking Aloud"), in Saila Ovaska, Anne Aula and Päivi Majaranta (eds) *Käytettävyystutkimuksen menetelmät* (*Methods in Usability Engineering*), Tampere: Tietojenkäsittelytieteiden laitos, Tampereen yliopisto, raportti B-2005-1: 209–222. Available at: www.cs.uta.fi/usabsem/luvut/14-Ilves.pdf (last accessed 6 June 2014).

International Ergonomics Association (2014) "Definition and Domains of Ergonomics". Available at: www.iea.cc/whats/ (last accessed 10 June 2014).

ISO 9241-11 (1998) *Ergonomic Requirements for Office Work with Visual Display Terminals (VDTs), Part 11: Guidance on Usability*, Geneva: International Organization for Standardization.

ISO 9241-171 (2008) *Ergonomics of Human–System Interaction, Part 171: Guidance on Software Accessibility*, Geneva: International Organization for Standardization.

ISO 9241-210 (2010) *Ergonomics of Human–System Interaction, Part 210: Human-Centred Design for Interactive Systems*, Geneva: International Organization for Standardization.

ISO/IEC Guide 37 (1995) *Instructions for Use of Products of Consumer Interest*, Geneva: International Organization for Standardization, 2nd edn.

Ivarsson, Jan and Mary Carroll (1998) "Code of Good Subtitling Practice". Available at: www.transedit.se/code.htm (last accessed 21 March 2011).

Jäckel, Anne (2001) "The Subtitling of la Haine: A Case Study", in Yves Gambier and Henrik Gottlieb (eds) *(Multi) Media Translation: Concepts, Practices, and Research*, Amsterdam and Philadelphia, PA: John Benjamins, 223–235.

Jääskeläinen, Riitta (1999) *Tapping the Process: An Explorative Study of the Cognitive and Affective Factors Involved in Translating*, Joensuun yliopiston humanistisia julkaisuja 22, Joensuu: University of Joensuu.

Jacob, Robert J. K. and Keith S. Karn (2003) "Eye Tracking in Human–Computer Interaction and Usability Research: Ready to Deliver the Promises" (section commentary), in Jukka Hyönä, Ralph Radach and Heiner Deubel (eds) *The Mind's Eye: Cognitive and Applied Aspects of Eye Movement Research*, Amsterdam: Elsevier Science, 573–605. Available at: www.cs.tufts.edu/~jacob/papers/ecem.pdf (last accessed 6 June 2014).

Jakobson, Roman (1978) "Closing Statement: Linguistics and Poetics", in Thomas A. Sebeok (ed.) *Style in Language*, Cambridge, MA: MIT Press, 350–377.

Jiménez-Crespo, Miguel A. (2011) "To Adapt or Not to Adapt in Web Localization: A Contrastive Genre-Based Study of Original and Localised Legal Sections in Corporate Websites", *Journal of Specialised Translation*, 15: 2–27. Available at: www.jostrans. org/issue15/art_jimenez.php (last accessed 6 June 2014).

Johnson, Robert R., Michael J. Salvo and Meredith W. Zoeteway (2007) "User-Centered Technology in Participatory Culture: Two Decades 'Beyond a Narrow Conception of Usability Testing'", *IEEE Transactions on Professional Communication*, 50(4): 320–332.

Jokela, Timo (2010) *Navigoi oikein käytettävyyden vesillä: Opas käytettävyysohjattuun vuorovaikutussuunnitteluun* (*Navigate the Waters of Usability Correctly: A Guide for Usability-Led Interaction Design*), Rovaniemi: Väylä-Yhtiöt Oy.

Kamppuri, Minna (2011) *Theoretical and Methodological Challenges of Cross-Cultural Interaction Design*, Ph.D. thesis, Publications of the University of Eastern Finland, Dissertations in Forestry and Natural Sciences, 29. Available at: http://epublications. uef.fi/pub/urn_isbn_978–952–61–0407–2/urn_isbn_978-952-61-0407-2.pdf (last accessed 6 June 2014).

Karamitroglou, Fotios (1998) "A Proposed Set of Subtitling Standards in Europe", *Translation Journal*, 2(2), April 1998. Available at: www.bokorlang.com/journal/ 04stndrd.htm (last accessed 6 June 2014).

Karinen, Ville (2006) *Illustrated Text or Textual Illustration: Whether to Use Text or Pictures in Instructional Documents*, Master's thesis, Tampere: University of Tampere.

Katre, Dinesh S. (2006) "Position Paper On Cross-cultural Usability Issues of Bilingual (Hindi and English) Mobile Phones", in *Proceedings of Indo-Danish HCI Research Symposium*, 1–20. Available at: www.hceye.org/UsabilityInsights/?page_id=83 (last accessed 6 June 2014).

Kenesei, Andrea (2004) "Frame-Based Interpretation of Readers' Reception of the Parallel Translations of Ady Endre, On Elijah's Chariot (Az Illés szekerén)", *Translation Directory.com*. Available at: www.translationdirectory.com/article221.htm (last accessed 6 June 2014).

—— (2010) *Poetry Translation through Reception and Cognition: The Proof of Translation is in the Reading*, Newcastle upon Tyne: Cambridge Scholars.

Kim, W. Chan and Renée Mauborgne (2005) *Blue Ocean Strategy: How to Create Uncontested Market Space and Make Competition Irrelevant*, Boston, MA: Harvard Business School Press.

Konttinen, Kalle and Outi Veivo (2008) "Kääntämisen arviointi työelämässä ja koulutuksessa" ("Translation Assessment in Working Life and in Training"), in *MikaEl, Electronic Proceedings of the KäTu Symposium on Translation and Interpreting Studies*, 1. Available at: https://sktl-fi.directo.fi/@Bin/41023/Konttinen_Veivo.pdf (last accessed 6 June 2014).

Korvenranta, Heli (2005) "Asiantuntija-arvioinnit" ("Expert Evaluations"), in Saila Ovaska, Anne Aula and Päivi Majaranta (eds) *Käytettävyystutkimuksen menetelmät (Methods in Usability Engineering)*, Tampere: Tietojenkäsittelytieteiden laitos, Tampereen yliopisto, raportti B-2005-1: 111–124. Available at: www.cs.uta.fi/usabsem/luvut/8_Korvenranta. pdf (last accessed 6 June 2014).

Koskinen, Joni (2005) "Käytettävyystestaus" ("Usability Testing"), in Saila Ovaska, Anne Aula and Päivi Majaranta (eds) *Käytettävyystutkimuksen menetelmät (Methods in Usability Engineering)*, Tampere: Tietojenkäsittelytieteiden laitos, Tampereen yliopisto, raportti B-2005-1: 187–208. Available at: www.cs.uta.fi/usabsem/luvut/13-Koskinen.pdf (last accessed 6 June 2014).

Koskinen, Kaisa (2008) *Translating Institutions: An Ethnographic Study of EU Translation*, Manchester and Kinderhook, NY: St. Jerome.

—— (2012) "Domestication, Foreignization and the Modulation of Affect", in Hannu Kemppanen, Marja Jänis and Alexandra Belikova (eds) *Domestication and Foreignization in Translation Studies*, Berlin: Frank & Timme.

Kotro, Tanja (2006) "Käyttäjät tuotekehityksessä: lihaa, verta ja mielikuvia" ("Users in Product Development: Flesh, Blood and Images"), in Petteri Repo, Ilpo Koskinen and Heidi Grönman (eds) *Innovaatioiden kotiutuminen (The Domestication of Innovations)*, Kuluttajatutkimuskeskuksen vuosikirja 2006, Helsinki: Kuluttajatutkimuskeskus, 159–168.

Krings, Hans P. (2001) *Repairing Texts: Empirical Investigations of Machine Translation Post-Editing Processes*, Kent, OH: Kent State University Press.

Kunelius, Risto (2003) *Viestinnän vallassa: Johdatus joukkoviestinnän kysymyksiin (Controlled by Communication: An Introduction to Questions of Mass Communication)*, Helsinki: WSOY.

Kurz, Ingrid (1993/2002) "Conference Interpreting: Expectations of Different User Groups", in Franz Pöchacker and Miriam Schlesinger (eds) *The Interpreting Studies Reader*, London and New York: Routledge, 313–324.

Kuutti, Kari (2001) "Hunting for the Lost User: From Sources of Errors to Active Actors – and Beyond", in the seminar Cultural Usability, 24 April 2001, Helsinki, Finland. Available at: http://mlab.uiah.fi/culturalusability/papers/Kuutti_paper.html (last accessed 6 June 2014).

Kuutti, Wille (2003) *Käytettävyys, suunnittelu ja arviointi (Usability, Design and Evaluation)*, Helsinki: Talentum.

Lefevere, André (1992) *Translation, Rewriting, and the Manipulation of Literary Fame*, London and New York: Routledge.

Legget, David (2010) "A Brief History of Eye-Tracking". Available at: www.uxbooth. com/articles/a-brief-history-of-eye-tracking/ (last accessed 6 June 2014).

Lehtinen, Merja (2005) "Katseenseuranta" ("Eyetracking") in Saila Ovaska, Anne Aula and Päivi Majaranta (eds) *Käytettävyystutkimuksen menetelmät (Methods in Usability Engineering)*, Tampere: Tietojenkäsittelytieteiden laitos, Tampereen yliopisto, raportti B-2005-1: 223–236. Available at: www.cs.uta.fi/usabsem/luvut/15-Lehtinen.pdf (last accessed 6 June 2014).

Lentz, Leo and Jacqueline Hulst (2000) "Babel in Document Design: The Evaluation of Multilingual Texts", *IEEE Transactions on Professional Communication*, 43(3): 313–322.

Leppihalme, Ritva (1997) *Culture Bumps: An Empirical Approach to the Translation of Allusions*, Clevedon: Multilingual Matters.

—— (2000) "The Two Faces of Standardization: On the Translation of Regionalisms in Literary Dialogue", *The Translator*, 6(2): 247–269.

Lewis, James R. (1993) "IBM Computer Usability Satisfaction Questionnaires: Psychometric Evaluation and Instructions for Use", *Technical Report 54.786*. Available at: http://drjim.0catch.com/usabqtr.pdf (last accessed 6 June 2014).

Livingstone, Sonia (2004) "The Challenge of Changing Audiences: Or, What is the Audience Researcher to do in the Age of the Internet?", *European Journal of Communication*, 19(1): 75–86.

"LIX räknare" (n.d.) Available at: www.lix.se (last accessed 6 June 2014).

Mäkisalo, Jukka (2006) "Kuinka paljon käännöksiä luetaan? Lukupäiväkirjan esitutkimus" ("How Much do People Read Translations? A Pilot Study of a Reading Diary"), *Virittäjä* 2/2006: 250–259.

Malhotra, Naresh K., James Agarwal and Mark Peterson (1996) "Methodological Issues in Cross-Cultural Marketing Research: A State of the Art Review", *International Marketing Review*, 13(5): 7–43.

Marcus, Aaron and Emilie West Gould (2000) "Crosscurrents: Cultural Dimensions and Global Web User-Interface Design", *Interactions*, 7(4): 32–46.

Martin, Bella and Bruce Hanington (2012) *Universal Methods of Design: 100 Ways to Research Complex Problems, Develop Innovative Ideas, and Design Effective Solutions*, Beverly, MA: Rockport.

Martin, Tim (2007) "Managing Risks and Resources: A Down-to-Earth View of Revision", *Journal of Specialised Translation*, 8: 57–63. Available at: www.jostrans.org/issue08/art_martin.pdf (last accessed 9 March 2014).

Mason, Ian (2000) "Audience Design in Translating", *The Translator*, 6(1): 1–22.

Melby, Alan K. (2012) "Structured Specifications and Translation Parameters (version 6.0)". Available at: www.ttt.org/specs/ (last accessed 27 May 2014).

Miquel-Iriarte, Marta, Anna Vilaró, Pilar Orero, Javier Serrano and Héctor Delgado (2012) "Entitling", in Elisa Perego (ed.) *Eye Tracking in Audiovisual Translation*, Rome: Aracne editrice S.r.l., 259–276.

Mitra, Ananda (2010) *Alien Technology: Coping with Modern Mysteries*, New Delhi, Thousand Oaks, CA and London: Sage.

Moran, Siobhan (2012) "The Effect of Linguistic Variation on Subtitle Reception", in Elisa Perego (ed.) *Eye Tracking in Audiovisual Translation*, Rome: Aracne editrice, 183–222.

Mosconi, Mauro and Marco Porta (2012) "Accessibility and Usability in the Context of Human–Computer Interaction", in Elisa Perego (ed.) *Eye Tracking in Audiovisual Translation*, Rome: Aracne editrice S.r.l., 105–133.

Mossop, Brian (2007) "Reader Reaction and Workplace Habits in the English Translation of French Proper Names in Canada", *Meta*, 52(2): 202–214.

—— (2010) *Editing and Revising for Translators*, Manchester: St. Jerome, 2nd edn.

Nida, Eugene A. (1964) *Toward a Science of Translating*, Leiden: E. J. Brill.

Nida, Eugene A. and Charles R. Taber (1974) *The Theory and Practice of Translation*, Leiden: United Bible Societies.

Nielsen, Jakob (1993) *Usability Engineering*, Boston, MA: Academic Press.

—— (1994a) "Enhancing the Explanatory Power of Usability Heuristics", in *Proceedings of Human Factors in Computing Systems (CHI 1994)*, New York: ACM, 152–158. Available at: http://portal.acm.org/citation.cfm?id=191666&CFID=7497679& CFTOKEN= 66272942 (last accessed 28 May 2014).

—— (1994b) "Guerrilla HCI: Using Discount Usability Engineering to Penetrate the Intimidation Barrier", *N N/g Nielsen Norman Group*. Available at: www.nngroup.com/ articles/guerrilla-hci/ (last accessed 28 May 2014).

—— (1995a) "10 Usability Heuristics for User Interface Design", *N N/g Nielsen Norman Group*. Available at: www.nngroup.com/articles/ten-usability-heuristics/ (last accessed 28 May 2014).

—— (1995b) "Characteristics of Usability Problems Found by Heuristic Evaluation", *N N/g Nielsen Norman Group*. Available at: www.nngroup.com/articles/usability-problems-found-by-heuristic-evaluation/ (last accessed 28 May 2014).

—— (1995c) "Severity Ratings for Usability Problems", *N N/g Nielsen Norman Group*. Available at: www.nngroup.com/articles/how-to-rate-the-severity-of-usability-problems/ (last accessed 28 May 2014).

—— (1997) "The Use and Misuse of Focus Groups", *N N/g Nielsen Norman Group*. Available at: www.useit.com/papers/focusgroups.html (last accessed 28 May 2014).

—— (2010) "Interviewing Users", *N N/g Nielsen Norman Group*. Available at: www.useit.com/alertbox/interviews.html (last accessed 28 May 2014).

Nielsen, Jakob and Rolf Molich (1990) "Heuristic Evaluation of User Interfaces", in *Proceedings of Human Factors in Computing Systems (CHI 1990)*, New York: ACM, 249–256. Available at: http://dl.acm.org/results.cfm?h=1&cfid=466900177&cftoken= 67970579 (last accessed 28 May 2014).

Nielsen, Jakob and Don Norman (n.d.) "The Definition of User Experience", *N N/g Nielsen Norman Group*. Available at: www.nngroup.com/articles/definition-user-experience/ (last accessed 28 May 2014).

Nielsen, Janni, Torkil Clemmensen and Carsten Yssing (2002) "Getting Access to What Goes on in People's Heads? – Reflections on the Think-Aloud Technique", in *Proceedings of the Nordic Conference on Human–Computer Interaction (NordiCHI 2002)*, ACM, 101–110.

Niinimäki, Eeva (2009) *Käännösprojektien laadun arviointi osana käännöstoimiston laadunhallintajärjestelmää* (*A Model for Translation Project Quality Assessment as a Part of a TSP's Quality Management System*), Master's thesis, Tampere: University of Tampere. Available at: http://urn.fi/urn:nbn:fi:uta-1–19888 (last accessed 10 June 2014).

Nikunen, Kaarina (2008) "Minne katosi sohvaperuna? Tylsyyden haaste televisio-tutkimukselle digitalisoitumisen aikakaudella" ("Where Did the Couch Potato Go? The Challenge of Boredom to Television Studies in the Era of Digitalization"), in Heidi Keinonen, Marko Ala-Fossi and Juha Herkman (eds) *Radio- ja televisiotutkimuksen metodologiaa: Näkökulmia sähköisen viestinnän tutkimiseen* (*Methodology for Radio and Television Studies: Perspectives on the Study of Electronic Communications*), Tampere: Tampere University Press, 235–252.

Nord, Christiane (1991) *Text Analysis in Translation: Theory, Methodology, and Didactic Application of a Model for Translation-Oriented Text Analysis*; trans. Christiane Nord and Penelope Sparrow, Amsterdam: Rodopi.

—— (2000) "What Do We Know About the Target-Text Receiver?" in Allison Beeby, Doris Ensinger and Marisa Presas (eds) *Investigating Translation: Selected Papers from the 4th International Congress on Translation, Barcelona 1998*, Amsterdam and Philadelphia, PA: John Benjamins, 195–212.

—— (2012) "Quo Vadis, Functional Translatology?", *Target*, 24(1): 26–42.

O'Brien, Sharon (2006) "Eye-Tracking and Translation Memory Matches", *Perspectives: Studies in Translatology*, 14(3): 185–205.

—— (2010) "Controlled Language and Readability", in Gregory M. Shreve and Erik Angelone (eds) *Translation and Cognition*, Amsterdam and Philadelphia, PA: John Benjamins, 143–165.

Ofcom (n.d.) "Guidance on Standards for Subtitling". Available at: www.ofcom.org.uk/static/archive/itc/itc_publications/codes_guidance/standards_for_subtitling/index.asp.html (last accessed 6 June 2014).

O'Hagan, Minako (2009) "Towards a Cross-Cultural Game Design: An Explorative Study in Understanding the Player Experience of a Localised Japanese Video Game", *Journal of Specialised Translation*, 11: 211–233. Available at: www.jostrans.org/issue11/art_ohagan.php (last accessed 6 June 2014).

O'Hagan, Minako and Carmen Mangiron (2013) *Game Localization: Translating for the Global Digital Entertainment Industry*, Amsterdam and Philadelphia, PA: John Benjamins.

Oittinen, Riitta (2000) *Translating for Children*, New York: Garland.

Olohan, Maeve and Mona Baker (2000) "Reporting that in Translated English: Evidence for Subconscious Processes of Explicitation?", *Across Languages and Cultures* 1(2): 141–158.

Otava, Anni (2013) *Focus on the Audience: Three Cases of User-Centered Translation*, Master's thesis, Tampere: University of Tampere. Available at: http://urn.fi/URN:NBN:fi:uta-201311151601 (last accessed 27 May 2014).

Oudshoorn, Nelly and Trevor Pinch (2005) *How Users Matter: The Co-construction of Users and Technology*, Cambridge, MA: MIT Press.

Ovaska, Saila, Anne Aula and Päivi Majaranta (2005) *Käytettävyystutkimuksen menetelmät* (*Methods in Usability Engineering*), Tampere: Tietojenkäsittelytieteiden laitos, Tampereen yliopisto, raportti B-2005–1. Available at: www.cs.uta.fi/usabsem/osallistujat.html (last accessed 6 June 2014).

Överlund, Maria (2008) *Meeting the Users: A Study of Different User Groups and Their Approach to Usability Problems*, Master's thesis, Tampere: University of Tampere. Available at: http://urn.fi/urn:nbn:fi:uta-1-18728 (last accessed 27 May 2014).

Padilla, Michael (2006) "Content Personalization: Planning and Implementation". Available at: www.oracle.com/technetwork/articles/entarch/personalization-086673.html (last accessed 6 June 2014).

Paloposki, Outi (2011) "Domestication and Foreignization", in Yves Gambier and Luc van Doorslaer (eds) *Handbook of Translation Studies*, Vol. 2, Amsterdam and Philadelphia, PA: John Benjamins, 40–42.

Parviainen, Leena (2005) "Fokusryhmät" ("Focus Groups"), in Saila Ovaska, Anne Aula and Päivi Majaranta (eds) *Käytettävyystutkimuksen menetelmät* (*Methods in Usability Engineering*), Tampere: Tietojenkäsittelytieteiden laitos, Tampereen yliopisto, raportti B-2005–1: 53–62. Available at: www.cs.uta.fi/usabsem/luvut/4-Parviainen.pdf (last accessed 6 June 2014).

Perego, Elisa (ed.) (2012) *Eye Tracking in Audiovisual Translation*, Rome: Aracne editrice S.r.l.

Perego, Elisa and Fabio del Missier (2008) "Is a Reading Situation Better than Another for Subtitled Film Viewers?", presentation at the conference Audiovisual Translation: Multidisciplinary Approaches Conference, Montpellier, France, 19–20 June 2008.

Perego, Elisa, Fabio del Missier, Marco Porta and Mauro Mosconi (2010) "The Cognitive Effectiveness of Subtitle Processing", *Media Psychology*, 13: 243–272.

Perelman, Chaïm and Lucie Olbrechts-Tyteca (1969) *The New Rhetoric: A Treatise on Argumentation*; trans. John Wilkinson and Purcell Weaver, West Bend, IN: University of Notre Dame Press.

Perrino, Saverio (2009) "User-Generated Translation: The Future of Translation in a Web 2.0 Environment", *Journal of Specialised Translation*, 12: 55–78. Available at: www.jostrans.org/issue12/art_perrino.pdf (last accessed 6 June 2014).

PICT (2013) "Promoting Intercultural Competence in Translators". Available at: www. pictllp.eu/ (last accessed 6 June 2014).

Piller, Ingrid (2011) *Intercultural Communication: A Critical Introduction*, Edinburgh: Edinburgh University Press.

Pilto, Risto and Tuija Rapakko (1995) "Testing Accessibility of Utility Texts: Work in Progress", in Heikki Nyyssönen and Leena Kuure (eds) *Principles of Accessibility and Design in English Text: Research in Progress*, Publications of the Department of English, University of Oulu, *Text and Discourse Studies*, 12: 9–18.

Preece, Jenny, Yvonne Rogers, Helen Sharp, David Benyon, Simon Holland and Tom Carey (1994) *Human–Computer Interaction*, Harlow: Addison Wesley.

Purho, Vesa (2000) "Heuristic Inspections for Documentation: 10 Recommended Documentation Heuristics", *Usability Interface, STC Usability SIG Newsletter*, 6(4). Available at: www.stcsig.org/usability/newsletter/0004-docsheuristics.html (last accessed 27 May 2014).

Puurtinen, Tiina (1995) *Linguistic Acceptability in Translated Children's Literature*, Ph.D. thesis, Joensuu: Joensuun yliopiston humanistisia julkaisuja, 15.

Pym, Anthony (2010) *Exploring Translation Theories*, London and New York: Routledge.

Rauterberg, Matthias (2006) "From Personal to Cultural Computing: How to Assess a Cultural Experience", in *Proceedings of the 4th Usability Day, Applied University Vorarlberg*, Dornbirn, Austria: Pabst Science.

Reiss, Katharina (1971) *Möglichkeiten und Grenzen der Übersetzungskritik*, Munich: Max Hueber Verlag.

Reiss, Katharina and Hans J. Vermeer (1986) *Mitä kääntäminen on (What is Translation?)*, trans. and abr. Pauli Roinila, Helsinki: Gaudeamus.

Risku, Hanna (2004) "Migrating from Translation to Technical Communication and Usability", in Gyde Hansen (ed.) *Claims, Changes and Challenges in Translation Studies: Selected Contributions from the EST Congress*, Copenhagen 2001, Amsterdam and Philadelphia, PA: John Benjamins, 181–195.

Robinson, Douglas (1997) *Translation and Empire: Postcolonial Theories Explained*, Manchester: St. Jerome.

Rodman, Lilita (2001) "You-Attitude: A Linguistic Perspective", *Business Communication*, 64 (4): 9–25.

Routio, Pentti (2007) "Tuotteen käytettävyys" ("The Usability of a Product"). Available at: www2.uiah.fi/projects/metodi/068.htm (last accessed 6 June 2014).

Rubin, Jeffrey and Dana Chisnell (2008) *Handbook of Usability Testing: How to Plan, Design, and Conduct Effective Tests*, Indianapolis, IN: Wiley, 2nd edn.

Saldanha, Gabriela (2008) "Explicitation Revisited: Bringing the Reader into the Picture", *Trans-kom*, 1(1): 20–35.

Salmi, Leena (2003) *Documents multilingues pour logiciels et utilisabilité (Multilingual Software Documentation and Usability)*, Ph.D. thesis, Turun yliopiston julkaisuja, Annales universitatis Turkuensis, Series B Part 269, Turku: University of Turku.

—— (2008) "Lokalisoinnin käsitteestä" ("On the Concept of Localization"), in Heli Katajamäki, Merja Koskela and Suvi Isohella (eds) *Lukija- ja käyttäjälähtöinen viestintä (Reader and User-Oriented Communication)*, Viestinnän tutkimuksen päivät 2007, Vaasa: Vaasan yliopiston julkaisuja, selvityksiä ja raportteja 152, 55–63. Available at: www.uwasa.fi/materiaali/pdf/isbn_978–952–476–233–5.pdf (last accessed 17 October 2011).

Salvo, Michael J. (2001) "Ethics of Engagement: User-Centered Design and Rhetorical Methodology", *Technical Communication Quarterly*, 10(3): 273–290.

Schiavi, Giulia (1996) "There is Always a Teller in a Tale", *Target*, 8(1): 1–21.

Schleiermacher, Friedrich (1813/1977) "On the Different Methods of Translating", in André Lefevere (ed. and trans.) (1977) *Translating Literature: The German Tradition from Luther to Rosenzweig*, Amsterdam: Rodopi, 67–90.

Schopp, Jürgen (2005) *Gut zum Druck? Typographie und Layout im Übersetzungsprozeß (Fit to Print? Typography and Layout in the Translation Process)*, Ph.D. thesis, Acta Universitatis Tamperensis 1117, Tampere: University of Tampere.

Schotter, Elizabeth R. and Keith Rayner (2012) "Eye Movements in Reading: Implications for Reading Subtitles", in Elisa Perego (ed.) *Eye Tracking in Audiovisual Translation*, Rome: Aracne editrice S.r.l., 83–104.

Schriver, Karen A. (1997) *Dynamics in Document Design: Creating Texts for Readers*, New York: John Wiley & Sons.

Shannon, Claude E. and Warren Weaver (1949) *The Mathematical Theory of Communication*, Urbana, IL: University of Illinois Press.

Si, Luo and Jamie Callan (2001) "A Statistical Model for Scientific Readability", in *CIKM '01 Proceedings of the Tenth International Conference on Information and Knowledge Management*, New York: ACM, 574–576.

Simon, Sherry (1999) *Gender in Translation: Cultural Identity and the Politics of Transmission*, London: Routledge.

Sinkkonen, Irmeli, Hannu Kuoppala, Jarmo Parkkinen and Raino Vastamäki (2009a) *Käytettävyyden psykologia (The Psychology of Usability)*, Helsinki: Adage, 3rd edn.

Sinkkonen, Irmeli, Esko Nuutila and Seppo Törmä (2009b) *Helppokäyttöisen verkkopalvelun suunnittelu (Designing an Easy-to-Use Web Service)*, Hämeenlinna: Tietosanoma.

Smith, Andy and Fahri Yetim (2004) "Global Human–Computer Systems: Cultural Determinants of Usability", *Interacting with Computers*, 16: 1–5.

Smith, Susan N. (2008) *Teaching Analysis to Professional Writing Students: Heuristics Based on Expert Theories*, Ph.D. thesis, Arizona, AZ: University of Arizona. Available at: http://arizona.openrepository.com/arizona/bitstream/10150/194794/1/azu_etd_2684_sip1_m.pdf (last accessed 6 June 2014).

Snow, Charles Percy (1993) *The Two Cultures and the Scientific Revolution*, New York: Cambridge University Press.

Sousa, Cristina (2002) "TL versus SL Implied Reader: Assessing Receptivity when Translating Children's Literature", *Meta*, 47(1): 16–29.

Spinuzzi, Clay (2001) "Grappling with Distributed Usability: A Cultural-Historical Examination of Documentation Genres Over four Decades", in *SIGDOC '99 Proceedings of the 17th Annual International Conference on Computer Documentation*, New York: ACM, 16–21.

Sullivan, Patricia (1989) "Beyond a Narrow Conception of Usability Testing", *IEEE Transactions on Professional Communication*, 32(4): 256–264.

Sun, Huatong (2006) "The Triumph of Users: Achieving Cultural Usability Goals with User Localization", *Technical Communication Quarterly*, 15(4): 457–481.

Sun, Sanjun (2011) "Think-Aloud-Based Translation Process Research: Some Method-ological Considerations", *Meta*, 56(4): 928–951.

Sun, Xianhong and Qingxin Shi (2007) "Language Issues in Cross Cultural Usability Testing: A Pilot Study in China", in *HCI International 2007*. Available at: www.sciweavers.org/publications/language-issues-cross-cultural-usability-testing-pilot-study-china (last accessed 6 June 2014).

Suojanen, Tytti (2010) "Comparing Translation and Technical Communication: A Holistic Approach", in Tuija Kinnunen and Kaisa Koskinen (eds) *Translators' Agency*, Tampere Studies in Language, Translation and Culture, B4, Tampere: Tampere University Press, 47–60. Available at: http://urn.fi/urn:isbn:978–951–44–8082–9 (last accessed 27 May 2014).

Suojanen, Tytti, Kaisa Koskinen and Tiina Tuominen (2012) *Käyttäjäkeskeinen kääntäminen (User-centered translation)*, Tampere Studies in Language, Translation and Literature, B1. Available at: http://urn.fi/URN:ISBN:978–951–44–8839–9 (last accessed 27 May 2014).

Suokas, Juho (2014) *Nothing Freeze-Dried: Usability Evaluation in Translation Quality Assessment*, Master's thesis, Joensuu: University of Eastern Finland.

Taras, Vas, Julie Rowney and Piers Steel (2009) "Half a Century of Measuring Culture: Approaches, Challenges, Limitations and Suggestions Based on the Analysis of 112 Instruments for Quantifying Culture", *Journal of International Management*, 15(4): 357–373.

TCeurope (2004) "SecureDoc: Usable and Safe Operating Manuals for Consumer Goods. A Guideline". Available at: www.tceurope.org/images/stories/downloads/projects/Secure Doc_EN.pdf (last accessed 8 June 2014).

Toury, Gideon (1995) *Descriptive Translation Studies and Beyond*, Amsterdam and Philadelphia, PA: John Benjamins.

Tuominen, Tiina (2012) *The Art of Accidental Reading and Incidental Listening: An Empirical Study on the Viewing of Subtitled Films*, Ph.D. thesis, Tampere: Tampere University Press. Available at http://urn.fi/URN:ISBN:978–951–44–9008–8 (last accessed 6 June 2014).

Tymoczko, Maria (1999) *Translation in a Postcolonial Context: Early Irish Literature in English Translation*, Manchester: St. Jerome.

"User Experience Definitions" (n.d.) *All About UX*. Available at: www.allaboutux.org/ux-definitions (last accessed 28 May 2014).

van Someren, Maarten W., Yvonne F. Barnard and Jacobijn A.C. Sandberg (1994) *The Think Aloud Method: A Practical Guide to Modelling Cognitive Processes*, London: Academic Press. Available at: http://staff.science.uva.nl/~maarten/Think-aloud-method.pdf (last accessed 6 June 2014).

Vehmas-Lehto, Inkeri (1989) *Quasi-Correctness: A Critical Study of Finnish Translations of Russian Journalistic Texts*, Helsinki: Neuvostoliittoinstituutti.

—— (1999) *Kopiointia vai kommunikointia? Johdatus käännösteoriaan (Copying or Communication? An Introduction to Translation Theory)*, Helsinki: Finn Lectura, 2nd, revised edn.

Venuti, Lawrence (1998) *The Scandals of Translation: Towards and Ethic of Difference*, London and New York: Routledge.

—— (2013) *Translation Changes Everything: Theory and Practice*, London and New York: Routledge.

Vermeer, Hans J. (1989) "Skopos and Commission in Translational Action", in Andrew Chesterman (ed.) *Readings in Translation Theory*, Helsinki: Finn Lectura, 173–187.

—— (1996) *A Skopos Theory of Translation (Some Arguments For and Against)*, *TEXTconTEXT Wissenschaft 1*, Heidelberg: TEXTconTEXT-Verlag.

Vihonen, Inkaliisa and Leena Salmi (2007) "Arjen käännöstekstien jäljillä: Käännökset ympärillämme -hankkeen jatkoa" ("Tracking Everyday Translations: A Continuation of the Translations Around Us Project"), in *MikaEl, Electronic Proceedings of the KäTu Symposium on Translation and Interpreting Studies*, 1. Available at: www.sktl.fi/@Bin/ 41152/Vihonen+Salmi.pdf (last accessed 6 June 2014).

von Schwerin-High, Friederike (2004) *Shakespeare, Reception and Translation: Germany and Japan*, London and New York: Continuum.

Vuorikoski, Anna-Riitta (1995) *Audience Response to Simultaneous Interpreting*, Licentiate thesis, Tampere: University of Tampere.

Vuorinen, Kimmo (2005) "Etnografia" ("Ethnography"), in Saila Ovaska, Anne Aula and Päivi Majaranta (eds) *Käytettävyystutkimuksen menetelmät* (*Methods in Usability Engineering*), Tampere: Tietojenkäsittelytieteiden laitos, Tampereen yliopisto, raportti B-2005–1: 63–78. Available at: www.cs.uta.fi/usabsem/luvut/5-Vuorinen.pdf (last accessed 6 June 2014).

W3C (2012) "About W3C". Available at: www.w3.org/Consortium/ (last accessed 6 June 2014).

—— (2013) "Accessibility". Available at: www.w3.org/standards/webdesign/accessibility (last accessed 6 June 2014).

Weiss, Edmond H. (1985) *How to Write a Usable User Manual*, Philadelphia, PA: ISI Press.

Widler, Brigitte (2004) "A Survey Among Audiences of Subtitled Films in Viennese Cinemas", *Meta* 49(1): 98–101.

Williams, Malcolm (2009) "Translation Quality Assessment", *Mutatis Mutandis*, 2(1): 3–23.

Wilson, Chancey E. (2005) "Usability and User Experience Design: The Next Decade", *intercom*, January: 6–9.

Yuste Frías, José (2012) "Paratextual Elements in Translation: Paratranslating Titles in Children's Literature", in Anna Gil-Bajardí, Pilar Orero and Sara Rovira-Esteva (eds) *Translation Peripheries: Paratextual Elements in Translation*, Frankfurt am Main, Berlin, Bern, Brussels, New York, Oxford, Vienna: Peter Lang, 117–134. Available at: www.joseyustefrias.com/docu/publicaciones/JoseYusteFrias2012_Para-Translation-Peripheries.pdf (last accessed 6 June 2014).

Zakaria, Norhayati, Jeffrey M. Stanton and Shreya T.M. Sarkar-Barney (2003) "Designing and Implementing Culturally-Sensitive IT Applications: The Interaction of Culture Values and Privacy Issues in the Middle East", *Information Technology & People*, 16(1): 49–75.

Index